Issues in Fetal Medicine

Proceedings of the Twenty-Ninth
Annual Symposium of the Galton
Institute, London 1992

Edited by

S. L. Barron
Emeritus Consultant Obstetrician and Gynaecologist
Princess Mary Maternity Hospital
and Royal Victorian Infirmary
Newcastle upon Tyne

and

D. F. Roberts
Emeritus Professor of Human Genetics
University of Newcastle upon Tyne

St. Martin's Press

in association with
Palgrave Macmillan

First published in Great Britain 1995 by
THE MACMILLAN PRESS LTD
Houndmills, Basingstoke, Hampshire RG21 2XS
and London
Companies and representatives
throughout the world

This book is published in Macmillan's *Studies in Biology, Economy
and Society* series
General Editor: Robert Chester

A catalogue record for this book is available
from the British Library.
ISBN 978-1-349-23814-9   ISBN 978-1-349-23812-5 (eBook)
DOI 10.1007/978-1-349-23812-5

First published in the United States of America 1995 by
Scholarly and Reference Division,
ST. MARTIN'S PRESS, INC.,
175 Fifth Avenue,
New York, N.Y. 10010

ISBN 978-0-312-12161-7

Library of Congress Cataloging-in-Publication Data
Galton Institute (London, England). Symposium (29th : 1992 : London,
England)
Issues in fetal medicine : proceedings of the twenty-ninth annual
Symposium of the Galton Institute, London 1992 / edited by S. L.
Barron and D. F. Roberts.
p.   cm.
Includes bibliographical references and index.
ISBN 978-0-312-12161-7
1. Parental diagnosis—Congresses.   2. Fetus—Abnormalities-
-Treatment—Congresses.   3. Fetus—Diseases—Treatment—Congresses.
4. Fetus—Legal status, laws, etc.—Congresses.   5. Fetus-
-Abnormalities—Treatment—Moral and ethical aspects—Congresses.
6. Prenatal diagnosis—Moral and ethical aspects—Congresses.
7. Fetus—Diseases—Treatment—Moral and ethical aspects-
-Congresses.   I. Barron, S. L.   II. Roberts, D. F. (Derek Frank)
III. Title.
RG627.G35   1995
618.3'2—dc20   94–233
                                                  CIP

ISSUES IN FETAL MEDICINE

Contents

PART III   ETHICAL AND LEGAL ISSUES

List of Plates, Figures and Tables

Plates

Figures

Tables

Preface

The past twenty years have seen astonishing advances in the control of human reproduction. The development of *in vitro* fertilisation of human eggs, which culminated in the birth of Louise Brown in 1978, signalled a series of new ethical problems concerned with the status of the human embryo. A Royal Commission headed by Mary (now Baroness) Warnock made a number of recommendations which gave rise to the Human Fertilisation and Embryology Act and to the formation of a statutory Authority. At the same time, genetics was advancing at an accelerating pace, increasing our understanding of human disease but also presenting additional conflicts for ethics, law and religion, discussed in the 1989 Galton Institute symposium 'Molecular Genetics and Medicine'.

Alongside the discoveries in human biology, there were the developments of techniques which provided high quality ultrasound images of the fetus, without the risks of ionising radiation. The ability to recognise developmental anomalies of the fetus *in utero* gave rise to some difficult decisions for parents and doctors involved in antenatal diagnosis. Inevitably, early diagnosis of genetic anomalies has led to attempts at treatment and the fetus has now become a patient in its own right. To explore some of these issues was the object of the 29th annual symposium of the Galton Institute 'Issues in Fetal Medicine', held 17–18 September 1992, the papers of which are published in this volume. It opens with the 1992 Galton Lecture, which reviews the ways in which perceptions of the fetus have changed in terms of religion, science, medicine and law, and points out some of the ethical dilemmas, which will grow as fetal medicine increases in importance. It thus provides the background to, and a brief synthesis of, the theme which the whole symposium explores.

Part I of the volume is devoted to the scientific basis for fetal diagnosis. Dr Ann Curtis describes the techniques which are now used for examining the structure of DNA in specimens obtained from embryonic and fetal tissues, which make it possible to identify some genetic disorders at a very early stage of embryonic development. The ability to amplify tiny fragments of DNA by polymerised chain reaction has proved to be a major technical advance for genetic diagnosis. Such advances will make it possible to introduce a normal genetic sequence into the abnormal cell for therapeutic purposes in due course.

High quality ultrasound images of the embryo enable us to see changes in anatomy which were previously only visible in laboratory specimens and textbooks, and thus to identify the early stages of development of anomalies and their timing. Interpretation of sonar images needs a more accurate account of embryonic anatomy and Dr Mary Seller has been able to provide pictures of outstanding quality using micro-dissection of the mouse embryo enhanced by the scanning electron microscope. Her chapter spans exquisite science and fine art.

In families where there is a high risk of a congenital anomaly, very early diagnosis may offer the possibility of selective implantation of a fertilised ovum. Professor Braude describes the technique of polar body biopsy which allows the examination of chromosomes and of DNA without directly interfering with the embryo.

Part I ends with a paper on the clinical aspects of fetal diagnosis. Walkinshaw discusses the methods and techniques of screening and of clinical diagnosis which can now be applied to the fetus *in utero*.

This clinical discussion leads naturally to Part II of the volume, on management and treatment. In the opening paper Professor Lind recounts his experience in managing a fetal medicine clinic and the practical problems that arise in managing a multi-disciplinary team. Above all he emphasises the choices, uncertainties and problems that are faced by the parents when a fetus is suspected to be abnormal.

The idea of performing surgery on the animal fetus is not new, but attempts to operate on the human fetus were unsuccessful until the work of the San Francisco group of which Dr Nakayama was formerly a member. Dr Nakayama discusses some of his experiences in surgical treatment of various conditions in the fetus. The technical problems of operating on the fetus are great, but it is the problems of the surviving newborn which have overshadowed progress in fetal surgery and which make it less attractive than was at first thought.

Improvements in ultrasound imaging have made it possible to carry out therapeutic procedures without having to open the uterus. Professor Whittle discusses his experience of treating fetal haemolytic anaemia and attempting to insert tubes of various kinds into the fetus. As with fetal surgery, attempts to relieve urinary obstruction in the fetus are rather disappointing, but a great deal of new knowledge is accumulating.

Molecular biology and the understanding of the chemistry of DNA are revolutionising our views about human disease. The idea of replacing a defective gene with a good one holds out the ultimate promise of treating disease before it is manifest. Professor Pembrey discusses the basis of gene therapy for autosomal and stem line cells and also describes the way in which the mitochondria play a part in the maternal transmission of defects.

Part III of the volume is devoted to ethical and legal issues. The theme of the anxiety produced by uncertainty, introduced earlier by Professor Lind, is continued by Professor Gordon Dunstan in his paper on the ethics of screening. Although screening for fetal anomaly is now commonplace, a positive result for such a test may come as a devastating blow to the parent. Screening tests, by their very nature, pick out those who are at high risk, but the tests also produce false negative and false positive results; how to deal with the worry engendered by the latter exercises all those responsible for the testing programmes. Such tests also have implications for society as a whole.

As a result of the recommendations of the Warnock Committee, there have been changes in the law relating to assisted reproduction and Derek Morgan discusses the Human Embryology and Fertilization Act and its effect on the legal status of the fetus. He also discusses other laws concerned with the protection of the stillborn and newborn infant.

The volume concludes with an article by Dr McCall Smith, who considers some of the ethical and legal issues raised when a fetus undergoes diagnostic tests or treatment. The legal status of the fetus is still uncertain and there is always a potential conflict of interest between the mother and fetus.

Previous symposia of the Galton Institute have discussed some of the scientific and ethical issues which have emerged from the advances in the treatment of human reproduction. We hope that by adding a clinical dimension to the emerging speciality of fetal medicine, this book will be of interest to all those engaged in this exciting new branch of medicine.

S. L. Barron
D. F. Roberts

Newcastle upon Tyne

Notes on the Contributors

S. L. Barron is Emeritus Consultant Obstetrician and Gynaecologist at Princess Mary Maternity Hospital and Royal Victoria Infirmary, Newcastle upon Tyne.

P. R. Braude holds the Chair of Obstetrics and Gynaecology of the United Medical and Dental School of Guy's and St Thomas's, and was formerly Consultant/Lecturer in Obstetrics and Gynaecology at the University of Cambridge.

Ann Curtis is a Scientific Officer at the Regional Genetics Advisory Service, Newcastle upon Tyne, dealing with large numbers of prenatal diagnoses using molecular methods.

G. R. Dunstan is Professor Emeritus of Moral and Social Theology in the University of London and Honorary Research Fellow in the University of Exeter.

Tom Lind is Consultant in Fetal Medicine at the Princess Mary Maternity Hospital, Newcastle upon Tyne; and was formerly Professor of Human Reproductive Physiology at the same institution.

Alexander McCall Smith is Associate Dean in the Faculty of Law at the University of Edinburgh.

Derek Morgan is Senior Fellow in Health Care Law at the Centre for Philosophy and Health Care, University College, Swansea.

Don K. Nakayama is Associate Professor at the University of Pittsburgh School of Medicine.

M. Pembrey is the Mothercare Professor of Clinical Genetics and Fetal Medicine at the Institute of Child Health, London, and is currently Consultant Adviser to the Chief Medical Officer, Department of Health.

Mary J. Seller is Reader in Developmental Genetics at the Paediatric Research Unit, Guy's Hospital Medical School, now the Division of Medical and Molecular Genetics, United Medical and Dental School of Guy's and St Thomas's.

Stephen A. Walkinshaw, now Consultant in Maternal–Fetal Medicine at Liverpool Maternity Hospital, was formerly Senior Research Associate in the Department of Obstetrics at the University of Newcastle upon Tyne.

Martin J. Whittle is Professor of Fetal Medicine at Birmingham Maternity Hospital, and was formerly Director of Fetal Medicine at the Queen Mother's Hospital, Glasgow.

1 The Galton Lecture for 1992: The Changing Status of the Fetus

S. L. Barron

INTRODUCTION

It is customary, in an eponymous lecture, to make a reference to the person in whose honour the lecture is given, often to show how the subject relates to his interests, but I do not know what Francis Galton would have made of the subject of Fetal Medicine. He started to study medicine in 1838 and by the age of sixteen had seen pre-anaesthetic surgery and some of the diseases allied to extreme poverty which were so common in the mid-nineteenth century. He was not, apparently, repelled by the experience but was more attracted to scientific observation and statistical method and he abandoned his medical studies after two years (Middleton, 1982).

During a professional career as an obstetrician, I have been privileged to witness changes in scientific medicine which were as profound as any of those of the previous three hundred years. In 1949, the year I qualified, obstetrics was preoccupied with the mechanics of delivery and saving the life of the mother. The fetus was vulnerable and remote but unassailable, and obstetric intervention for the sake of the fetus was uncommon. How different the situation is today this lecture will show.

HISTORICAL VIEWS OF THE FETUS

The account, in Genesis, of the creation of Adam and Eve takes no account of sexual reproduction, and the use of a large fig leaf in some of the early paintings of Adam were not just for modesty, but to avoid the theological controversy over whether or not Adam had an umbilicus.

Adam and Eve went on to have children by sexual reproduction. As Genesis puts it 'And Adam knew Eve his wife; and she conceived, and bare Cain, and said, I have gotten a man from the Lord' (*Genesis* 4, v 1). In the Apocrypha (Wisdom of Solomon) v 7 Apocrypha, *New English Bible*) there is an account of how the fetus was formed:

1

I too am a mortal man like the rest, descended from the first man, who was made of dust, and in my mother's womb I was wrought into flesh during a ten-months space, compacted in blood from the seed of her husband and the pleasure that is joined with sleep.

As long ago as the fourteenth century BC, Amenophis IV wrote a poem describing the germ in woman and the seed of man (Speert, 1973). Hippocrates (460–377 BC) in his treatise *On the Generation of Animals* recognised the stages of fetal growth and estimated that the limbs formed at about 40 days and that pregnancy lasted 210 to 300 days. In Europe, the idea that menstrual blood and semen mixed to form a coagulum from which the fetus unfolded, persisted until Harvey (1578–1657) disproved it (Seller, 1990). The Chinese had some idea that the fetus developed from an embryo as illustrated in Plate 1.1.

The Fetus in European Art

Contemporary art provides an insight into European perceptions of the fetus. Although there must have been opportunities to inspect the products of spontaneous miscarriage, the representations of the fetus were surprisingly inaccurate. Most of the early European paintings were ostensibly religious in nature. In the painting of Mary and Elizabeth *The Visitation* (Plate 1.2), oval windows in the robes of the pregnant cousins permit a view of fetal John in the womb of Elizabeth, and of the Christ-child within Mary. In the illustration of a seventeenth-century Spanish statuette of the virgin (Plate 1.3) her uterus is opened to show the Infant Jesus.

In all these representations, the fetus is seen as a little man, standing up, with no indication of the changes in form that are part of fetal growth and development. Albertus Magnus (c. 1200–1280), also known as St Albert the Great, was an important philosopher and early scientific thinker, who studied Aristotle and whose pupils included Thomas Aquinas (Huby, 1990). He demonstrated a better idea of fetal proportions than many that followed him and showed various malpresentations of the fetus inside the uterus (Plate 1.4). By comparison, the sixteenth-century drawings of Leonardo da Vinci, *Embryo in the Uterus*, which are in the Royal Collection at Windsor (Plate 1.5), are breathtaking in their accuracy and realism and even show the partial effacement of the cervix in pregnancy.

SCIENTIFIC BIOLOGY AND THE MICROSCOPE

The invention of the microscope in 1609, heralded a new phase in the understanding of biology. The new observations flooded in but were not always understood. De Graaf described the ovarian follicle in 1672, but did not realise its significance. In 1673 van Leeuwenhoek wrote a series of letters to the Royal Society describing the spermatozoa of many species, including those of man. Niklaas Hartsoeker, in his *Essai de diotropique*, 1694, drew his idea of a human spermatozoon (Plate 1.6). He admitted that it represented not what he had actually seen, but what he presumed would be visible if the sperm could be viewed sufficiently clearly. Once again there is no recognition of the changes of embryological development, only a vision of a little man or homunculus. It was not until 1827 that Von Baer described the mammalian embryo in detail (Speert, 1973).

Chromosomes were described in 1888 by Waldeyer but it was not until 15 years later that Sutton (1903) and Boveri (1904), independently recognised the role of chromosomes in reproduction. Even as a postgraduate I was taught that there were 48 human chromosomes and felt betrayed when the technique of cell culture (Ford and Hamerton, 1956; Tijo and Levan, 1956) showed that there were only 46.

The most fundamental discovery about the structure and function of the cell came with the description by Watson and Crick (1953) of the structure of DNA, which explained the mechanism of genetic inheritance and laid the foundation for modern molecular biology.

OBSTETRICS AND CLINICAL OBSERVATION

Early Attempts at Palpation and Auscultation

In Britain, women were delivered in the left lateral position and palpation of the abdomen was considered to be improper. The French, who were less prudish, were experienced at palpation, and in 1889 Pinot wrote a manual on palpation of the pregnant abdomen and on the ability to correct malpresentation by external manipulation, which gave an impetus for the practice of prenatal care (Radcliffe, 1967).

Fetal Monitoring

The French were also the first to identify heart sounds, and in 1822 Jean LeJumeau read a monograph to the Royal Academy of Medicine in Paris on the application of auscultation of the study of pregnancy (Patel, 1989). A number of other publications from Ireland and Germany, based entirely on clinical observations, demonstrated a surprisingly sophisticated understanding of fetal heart patterns. Changes in heart rate, and especially slowing, were recognised as indicating fetal compromise. It was also observed that the fetal heart often slowed during uterine contractions and that a delayed return to normal was a cause for concern.

Mechanical Recording

The first attempts at mechanical recording of the fetal heart used an acoustic microphone attached to the abdomen, but the signal-to-noise ratio was very poor and phonocardiography was soon superseded by other methods. Electrocardiograms (ECG) of the fetus were successfully obtained through external electrodes placed on the mother's abdomen, but it is necessary to subtract the maternal signal electronically and, although the technical problems have been overcome, the method is difficult and expensive. Fetal ECGs during labour are obtained by placing a small electrode on the fetal scalp through the partly dilated cervix but this method is not applicable during the antenatal period.

Doppler Ultrasound

Ultrasound has simplified the whole process of fetal heart recording. The Doppler principle states that a wave form is distorted by relative movement between the source and observer, the best example being the change in pitch of an ambulance siren as it moves towards and then away from the listener. A beam of high frequency sound (2 megahertz) is aimed at the fetus and the movement of the heart or great vessel creates a frequency shift in the reflected wave, which is easily translated electronically into audible sound. Computer logic is necessary to eliminate extraneous signals and to measure the time between successive beats in order to display an instantaneous heart rate.

As soon as commercial instantaneous fetal heart rate monitors became available, monitoring the fetal heart during labour became an established practice, although there had been no serious scientific trial of its value. As a result, there has been an increased intervention in labour, based on the assumption that cardiotocograph (CTG) changes were infallible. The enormous increase in litigation on behalf of brain damaged infants, supported by CTG changes as evidence of negligence, has encouraged defensive obstetrics, put a considerable strain on the finances of the NHS, and made the fetus the centre of legal controversy (Ennis *et al.*, 1991).

ADVANCES IN MEDICAL SCIENCE

Our perceptions of the fetus over the past forty years have been greatly influenced by four important advances in medical science:

The invention of ultrasound imaging
The greatly improved survival of very premature babies
The development of assisted reproduction and *in vitro* fertilisation
Molecular biology and the new genetics.

Imaging the Fetus

X-rays
The early attempts to X-ray the fetus failed because of the poor equipment
which required prolonged exposure, and the first radiographs of the fetal
skeleton were not obtained until 1902. Although quality improved, the
value of X-rays was limited to conditions affecting the bony skeleton.
Finally, the suggestion that ionising radiation increased the risks to the fetus
(Stewart and Kneale, 1970), which coincided with the development of
sonar, put an end to the routine use of X-rays in pregnancy.

Ultrasound
It is no exaggeration to say that the development of ultrasound has been one
of the most important advances in obstetrics. SONAR (SOund NAvigation
and Ranging) was developed during the Second World War as a method of
detecting submarines by means of echoes transmitted through water. The
echo principle, using pulses of very high frequencies, was also able to detect
flaws in metal plates in the Vickers shipyard and Ian Donald, the Professor
of obstetrics in gynaecology in Glasgow, applied the technology to the fetus
in utero in 1958 (Donald and Brown, 1961). At first, the echo was used only
for measuring the diameter of the fetal head, but the use of electro-mechani-
cal linkage systems made it possible to build up a series of echoes into a
crude picture on a long persistence television screen (Plate 1.7). Although
there were slow improvements in the quality of the images, the great leap
forward came in about 1975 with the use of real-time imaging. By means of
a small array of ultrasound transducers, which fired in sequence like the
cylinders of a motor car, it became possible to obtain moving images at
about 20 frames a second, which have been refined, by computer technology, to provide details of remarkable quality.

A further refinement of sonar has come with the combination of real-time
imaging with Doppler frequency shift which makes it possible to demonstrate flow within a structure, such as the heart, or the umbilical vessels, as
a colour change.

Magnetic Resonance Imaging (MRI)
Still relatively new, the technique of MRI promises new insights into fetal
diagnosis. The image produced depends on stimulating molecular reso-

nance by means of very high density magnetic fields. As well as producing a detailed physical image it is also possible to depict the concentration of certain elements such as hydrogen or phosphorus, which reflects function as well as structure. The exposure time needed makes the technique difficult to apply to the fetus, but if the history of X-ray imaging is a precedent that difficulty will soon be overcome.

The Management of the Very Premature Infant

Until ten years ago the outlook for the very premature infant was bleak. An infant born at 28 weeks weighs about a kilogram, and in 1965 the survival chance of any baby weighing less than a kilogram was about 10 per cent. Active resuscitation and management of the tiny newborn became a practical possibility with the development of electronic equipment which monitored respiration, oxygenation and external environment of the incubators in which the babies were nursed. Neonatal Intensive Care Units were established, at no little expense, but as a result of these advances in paediatric care the outlook for the very small infants, especially those under 1500 g at birth, has improved greatly (Alberman and Botting, 1991) (Figure 1.1).

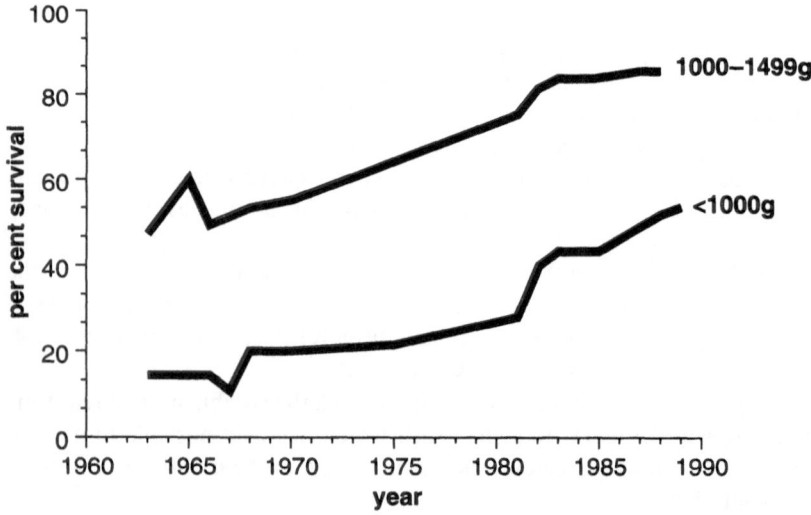

Figure 1.1   Survival of very low birth weight infants in England and Wales

Source: Based on data from Alberman and Botting (1991) and *Birth Statistics* OPCS series DH3.

The resultant improvement in survival, to the present level of about 50 per cent, has had a major impact on obstetric practice. In situations where maternal well-being is compromised, such as severe hypertension, obstetric practice has always aimed to postpone birth as long as possible. With the improved prognosis for the fetus, premature delivery became a practical alternative, thereby adding to the number of these very small babies.

A further advance in the management of very small infants is the use of extra corporeal membrane oxygenation (ECMO) which is a development of the cardiopulmonary by-pass used in open heart surgery. The baby's circulation is diverted to a pump/oxygenator which substitutes for poorly functioning lungs. The technique is both expensive and dangerous and is at present used only for severely ill neonates (Pearson *et al.*, 1992). There is however the potential for nurturing tiny fetuses before the lungs mature at 24 weeks.

Assisted Reproduction

The practice of *in vitro* fertilisation has been established in commercial farming since 1942, but it was not until 1978 that Steptoe and Edwards (1978) reported the birth of Louise Brown, the first child conceived as the result of what has become known as IVF. Quite apart from the technical difficulties and the hope that the new technique offered to infertile couples, the advent of IVF, and to a lesser extent of artificial insemination by donor, has undermined many moral, religious and ethical assumptions.

The basis of most of the moral and religious codes governing sexual conduct was to protect women from conception outside the framework of marriage, to prevent consanguineous union and to protect the nuclear family unit. Effective contraception provided women with what Baird called 'The Fifth Freedom' from unwanted pregnancies (Baird, 1965), but has also undermined the traditional family unit.

It has become possible to examine and even change the fertilised zygote before implantation. It has become possible to store, in a frozen state, an embryo which can be implanted later to become a fetus after the death of one or both of its parents, raising the spectre of ownership, custody and security of this frozen, potential fetus (Anonymous, 1989).

Thus at a stroke, most of the assumptions about sexual morality held for thousands of years have been undermined. The conception of an embryo is now possible without the act of intercourse, even within marriage. The biological and genetic mother need no longer be the same person and this raises further questions about legitimacy, custody and inheritance. A woman can have her own biological child even after a hysterectomy by donating ova, or can bear her husband's child long after his death.

Science had rushed ahead of the law and ethics and the Warnock Committee (Department of Health and Social Security, 1984) was set up to consider how to cope with the new situation. After much debate, the Human Fertilisation and Embryology Act 1990 was passed and a statutory Authority created to supervise certain aspects of assisted reproduction.

Gene Therapy

The possibility of research on the human zygote caused alarm because of the theoretical danger of selective breeding and cloning, forecast by Aldous Huxley in *Brave New World* (Huxley, 1932).

The introduction of a normal gene into a fetus with a specific defect, such as haemophilia-A, promises a major new advance in fetal medicine and in the view of many is no different in principle from the use of a hormone such as thyroxin to replace a congenital deficiency. The possibilities of gene therapy (see Pembrey, pp. 114–32) increase daily as a result of the staggering advances in the understanding of genetics at the molecular level. There has been public concern at the unpredictable effect of changing a gene, particularly in a germ cell where the change would be passed on to the fetus. As a result, the Clothier Committee was formed and its Report (Clothier, 1992) has recommended that all gene therapy should be confined to a few special centres, be supervised by a central body, and that germ line therapy should not yet be attempted.

ADVANCES IN MEDICAL TREATMENT

Sampling Fetal Tissues

Amniocentesis
The sampling of amniotic fluid has always been easy to do, requiring only a local anaesthetic and a sterile aspiration needle. Chemical analysis is performed for bile pigments, in the case of fetal haemolytic anaemia due to rhesus immunisation, and for alpha fetoprotein in cases of suspected open neural tube lesions.

Amniotic fluid also contains desquamated fetal cells which after separation can be cultured. With tissue culture came the first important step in the diagnosis of chromosomal abnormalities of the fetus and from that came the introduction of screening tests for Down's syndrome in high-risk mothers. In order to obtain samples suitable for cell culture it was necessary to wait until 16 weeks gestation and by the time the results became available the pregnancy had reached 18 to 20 weeks gestation.

Chorionic villus sampling
Although amniocentesis is now being undertaken as early as 12 weeks, there are other techniques available for obtaining fetal tissue, of which the most important is chorionic villus sampling (CVS) carried out at about 10 weeks gestation. Since chorionic tissue is actively dividing, prior tissue culture is unnecessary before chromosome analysis, so that delay is minimised. There are great advantages in the early diagnosis of chromosomal abnormality but CVS also has a number of drawbacks, including a 2 per cent risk of miscarriage and the occasional false diagnosis of polyploidy arising in trophoblastic cells (Lilford, 1991).

As imaging of the fetus improved, it has become possible to biopsy the fetus directly. The most useful material is fetal blood, obtained from cordocentesis or percutaneous blood sampling (PBS). This is particularly useful for haematological studies but also provides leucocytes for chromosome analysis.

Fetoscopy
The technique of fetoscopy involved the insertion into the uterus of a very fine telescopic endoscope which gave a limited view of the fetus. It was used for obtaining umbilical blood samples and also for skin biopsy. The method is now superseded by ultrasound guided methods.

Diagnosis of Fetal Anomalies and Selective Abortion

Many of the fetal abnormalities which are now detectable cannot yet be treated and the only available options are continuation of the pregnancy or induced abortion. Some conditions, such as anencephaly, are fatal and the decision to abort is not difficult. On the other hand, conditions such as Turner's syndrome (45XO) are only mildly disabling but the knowledge that the child is affected may cause great parental anxiety and pose a very difficult dilemma for the parents.

Selective abortion can also be difficult when the inherited condition is known to be sex-linked. Fortunately, advances in diagnosis using recombinant DNA techniques now make it possible to diagnose muscular dystrophy or haemophilia A for an individual fetus. But there are still cases of sex-linked disorder where it may be necessary to offer abortion if the fetus is male, even though only 50 per cent will be affected.

Even more difficult is the use of selective abortion of female babies for social or economic reasons especially in communities where an excessive importance is attached to having a male child (Young, 1991).

The Use of Fetal Organs for Transplant

In 1987, neural tissue from an aborted fetus was implanted in the brain of a patient with Parkinson's disease (Hitchcock, 1991). The report created a vigorous debate centred around the possibility that a woman might bear a fetus for the express purpose of allowing it to be aborted as a source of an organ for transplant. Examples given were to provide bone marrow for an existing child suffering from leukaemia or neural tissue to benefit a parent with Parkinson's disease.

The Polkinghorne Committee, which was set up to review the use of fetal tissue, suggested that a live fetus whether *in utero* or *ex utero* should be treated on principles broadly similar to those which apply to treatment and research in children. Tissue should only be taken from a dead fetus or abortus (Polkinghorne Report, 1989).

Attempts at Prenatal Treatment

It is possible to treat the fetus indirectly by administering drugs or hormones to the mother. A good example is the use of corticosteroids given to a woman in premature labour. The steroids cross the placenta and by inducing the production of surfactant in the fetal lung help to prevent respiratory distress syndrome. Another example is the use of digoxin to treat fetal heart arrhythmias.

Haemolytic anaemia due to allo-immunisation to the rhesus antigen is an early example of a condition recognised and treatable in the fetus. Attempts were made to carry out an exchange transfusion of the fetus by means of an open operation. The uterus was incised and the leg exteriorised, but these operations were not successful. Liley (1963) had described the ability of the newborn to absorb blood from its peritoneal cavity and suggested the idea of intra-peritoneal transfusion *in utero*. The procedure is carried out at about 31 weeks gestation, originally using X-ray localisation. Now, by means of ultrasound directed cordocentesis, direct intravenous transfusion and even limited exchange transfusion can be carried out (Barron and Reid, 1992).

The advances that have been made in fetal surgery are discussed by Dr Nakayama (see pp. 94–103). The technical and ethical problems are great and the practice of fetal surgery is still confined to a very small number of specialist centres.

LEGAL AND MORAL PROTECTION OF THE FETUS

Aristotle (384–322 BC) observed that the fetus changed as it grew from a vegetative being to an animal, finally becoming a recognisable human. To these three stages he attributed a nutritive soul which was replaced in turn by a sensitive soul and finally a rational soul.

Professor Dunstan has reviewed the evolution of religious thinking on the status of the fetus (Dunstan, 1984). Much was made of the distinction between the child which was not yet fully formed and one that was *formatus et animatus*. The male was visibly formed by 40 days and was given protection from that time, whilst the female, showing no external signs of gender, was not so protected until 90 days.

Pope Innocent III issued a canon in 1211 which determined the punishment for a priest who had been party to a miscarriage. In it, he prescribed a lesser penalty when the fetus had not yet quickened. It was 300 years later in 1588, that Pope Sixtus V declared that abortion whether of the formed or unformed fetus was equivalent to murder. The Bull was promptly revoked by his successor Pope Gregory XIV in 1591.

In the nineteenth century improvements in scientific medicine made abortion less hazardous and its incidence increased. Pope Pius IX, in 1869, issued a Bull *Apostolicae Sedis* which declared excommunicate all who procured abortion regardless of gestation. The claim to absolute protection of the human embryo is therefore relatively recent. The current Roman Catholic position on when life begins is one of agnosticism, assuming that life begins with conception and always giving the benefit of the doubt to the embryo (Dunstan, 1984). Most clinicians find it difficult to apply such a doctrine to an ectopic pregnancy, to a hydatidiform mole (which is a conceptus without a fetus), or to an anencephalic fetus which has no forebrain.

The Common and Statute Law

Canon and common law developed in parallel, and in 1387 the execution of a woman condemned to death for aiding the murder of her husband was postponed because she was pregnant and the baby had quickened. Once the baby was born, capital punishment was duly carried out and the woman was executed (Harvey, 1982).

Offences Against the Person Act 1861

The fetus was protected in law by the Offences Against the Person Act 1861 which made it a criminal offence to procure an abortion or to supply any substance for that purpose. That law, which was never debated in the Commons, was mainly concerned with the pregnant woman herself, or her lay friends, rather than the medical profession and still remains the basis of statute law in England, Wales and Ireland. The accepted medical practice in England and Wales, based on counsel's opinion to the Royal College of Physicians in 1896, was that abortion was permitted to save the life of the mother (Potts *et al.*, 1977).

Infant Life Preservation Act 1929

The law makes a *prima facie* presumption that any child born after 28 weeks gestation was capable of independent life and therefore 'viable'. What the Act did *not* say was that a child born before 28 weeks was incapable of life. The Act laid down the law on infanticide but also clarified the position of the obstetrician who had to perform the destructive operation on the fetus *in utero*, in order to save the life of the mother. It was followed by the Infanticide Act 1937 which softened the law against women who killed a baby during the emotional disturbance of the puerperium.

Abortion Act 1967

The change in the law on abortion came about as part of the world-wide change in attitude. The English law had already been challenged in 1938 by a distinguished obstetrician, Alec Bourne, who informed the police that he had carried out an abortion on a 14-year-old girl who had been raped by two guardsmen (Potts *et al.*, 1977). The court ruled that abortion was justified to save the health, as well as the life, of the mother (*R v. Bourne*, 1939) and on the basis of that Case Law a small but increasing number of legal abortions were carried out in the succeeding years. There were many unsuccessful attempts at parliamentary reform until 1967 when the present Act was passed. Among other provisions, the Act permitted abortion where there was a substantial risk of fetal abnormality.

One of the ambiguities of the 1967 Act was its failure to define an abortion and the time limit was based on the Infant Life (Preservation) Act which implied viability at 28 weeks. The Abortion Act has now been amended by the Human Embryology and Fertilisation Act 1990, and abortion beyond 24 weeks is only permitted in special circumstances, but without an upper limit. The effect of the change is to permit abortion for severe fetal abnormality at any gestation.

Registration of Stillbirths

Under the compulsory registration of births and stillbirths, a baby which shows signs of life after birth, whatever the gestation, must be registered as a live birth. It must be registered as stillbirth if, after 28 weeks and complete expulsion from the mother, it shows no sign of life; before 28 weeks if it shows no sign of life it is deemed to be an abortion, need not be registered and does not have to be formally buried. The definition caused problems in twin pregnancies, when one premature infant survived and the other twin was dead-born and not registered. When a tiny singleton fetus was born at, say, 22 weeks with equivocal signs of life, it was common to regard the fetus as an abortion, thus avoiding the distress of registration of birth and death and burial.

The improvement in prognosis has resulted in an increase in the number of registered births of very low birth weight babies as attempts are made to salvage the previously hopeless (Fenton *et al.*, 1990). In Scotland, where records of all pregnancies ending after 24 weeks have been kept, the number of pregnancies ending before 28 weeks has increased, and there has been a significant rise in the proportion of such pregnancies registered as a live birth (Macfarlane *et al.*, 1988) (Figure 1.2).

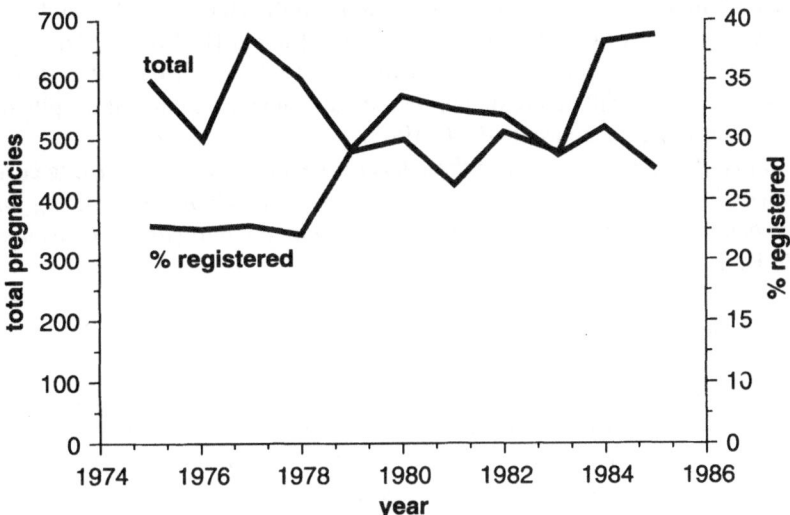

Figure 1.2   Abortions and live births between 20 and 27 weeks in Scotland, with proportion of pregnancies registered as live births

Source: Based on data in Macfarlane *et al.* (1988).

The improvement in survival has also rendered the definition of stillbirth, with its presumption of viability, out of date. From October 1992, the Still-birth (Definition) Act 1992 has reduced the gestation for compulsory regis-tration of stillbirth from 28 to 24 weeks. This is still not as low as the WHO recommendation of 22 weeks or 500 g weight.

The Difficulty of Consent

Informed consent is required before carrying out any medical procedure involving risk. The population has become well-informed about medical matters, and expectations have increased correspondingly. Obtaining in-formed consent has therefore become increasingly important and more difficult. There is a legal ruling (*Sidaway*, 1984) about how much informa-tion should be given and there are now legal precedents on consent to operations for minors and the mentally incompetent. Procedures which interfere with the fetus can only be carried out by means of an invasive procedure on the mother, to which she has to give consent. What is the position of the fetus who does not have a voice? What is the position of the fetus which is thought by a competent doctor to require some kind of intervention, for example an intra-uterine transfusion, but which the mother refuses? A minor can be made a ward of court, although that is now more difficult under the new Children Act, but no adult can be forced to undergo treatment except under the provisions of the Mental Health Act. There is, however, a recent precedent in that the Court of Appeal has ruled that a 16-year-old girl with anorexia nervosa should undergo treatment in spite of her refusal to give consent (*Re J.*, 1992).

Since this lecture was given there has been an even more disturbing case in which the President of the Family Division of the High Court, acting for the benefit of the fetus, overruled a mother's objection to caesarian section (In Re S., *1992).*

The Fetus as Litigant

It has been suggested that a disgruntled child might be able to sue its mother for her unsatisfactory life style during pregnancy, but in England such an action has been dismissed on the grounds that the fetus has no independent *locus standi* from its mother (Brahams, 1991).

There is provision under the Congenital Disabilities (Civil Liability) Act for an infant to sue for damage it received as a result of negligence while a fetus, but the Act does not permit an infant to sue its own mother except as the driver of a motor vehicle. In a recent case (Morgan, 1991) the judge ruled that an infant could sue for damage done while an embryo in the course of an ill-judged curettage (D&C)! As the law evolves, so the status of the fetus changes. The fetus is already a litigant, although retrospectively; the next step might be for someone to act on behalf of the fetus whilst still *in utero* (but see *Re F.* (1988)).

Human Fertilisation and Embryology Act 1990

This Act has created the Human Fertilisation and Embryology Authority, and with it an unpronounceable acronym HFEA. It has given the artificially induced embryo a status and degree of protection previously afforded to the fetus and certainly greater than that of a spontaneous or naturally conceived embryo. It has resulted in an amendment to the Abortion Law and ruled on the particularly difficult issue of selective reduction where more than three artificially implanted embryos have developed within the uterus, thereby threatening the continuation of the pregnancy.

ETHICS OF INDUCED ABORTION

No consideration of the status of the fetus would be complete without considering the ethics of induced abortion. There are surprisingly few people who take an absolute stand for or against abortion and very few who would advocate infanticide. Most agree that there are some circumstances where abortion is indicated especially where the mother's life is at risk. Even in Ireland, one of the very few countries in Europe where abortion is forbidden under the constitution, the Supreme Court allowed a young girl who was the victim of rape to seek an abortion overseas (Francombe, 1992). At the other extreme, there are very few who would allow abortion on demand whatever the gestation.

The majority view is that abortion should be permitted, within the law, under certain circumstances; the general perception is one of 'gradualism' but there is wide disagreement about where to draw the line. As the embryo and fetus becomes more recognisably human and as the fetus becomes increasingly autonomous, so the acceptability of abortion declines. Coupled with the fact that mortality and morbidity increase sharply after 16 weeks gestation, late abortions are performed uncommonly and most of these performed within the NHS are for congenital malformations (Barron, 1984).

The experience in Western Europe and USA has been that legalising abortion has reduced maternal mortality, especially from illegal induction procedures (Figure 1.3). Mortality and morbidity increase for abortions

S. L. Barron

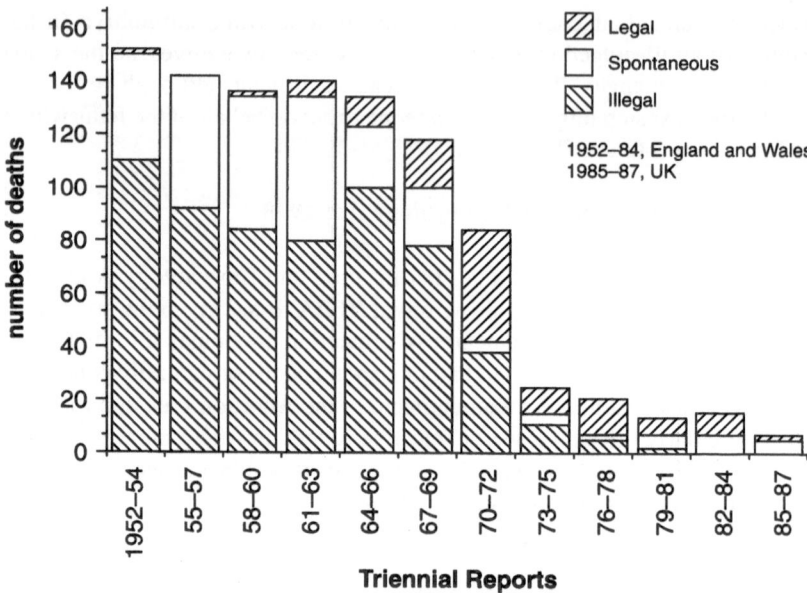

Figure 1.3   Maternal deaths due to abortion in England and Wales

Source: Data from successive Triennial Reports on Confidential Enquiries into
Maternal Deaths (1952–1987) HMSO. Taken from Barron, 1991.

beyond 16 weeks gestation and there is a general reluctance to induce
abortion beyond that time. This is particularly relevant to abortion carried
out for congenital malformations, some of which are often not diagnosed
until 16 weeks gestation. The advances in technique which enable abnormalities such as Trisomy 21 to be diagnosed early are therefore to be greatly
welcomed because, apart from the increased morbidity, later abortions can
be very distressing to the woman.

   In Eastern Europe under communism, there has been either a very liberal
regime, as in Hungary or Poland, or a very repressive one as in Ceausescu's
Romania. Information now emerging from Romania demonstrates how
suppression of previously legal abortion led to a rise in maternal mortality
(Barron, 1991). I hope that the more repressive laws about to be introduced
in Poland do not have a similar effect.

   Although distinctions are made between 'medical' and 'social' indications for abortion, such distinctions are highly subjective because there are
very few purely medical indications for terminating a pregnancy unless the

patient wants it. Take, for example, a woman who has had a successful kidney transplant, but who is taking numerous drugs to prevent rejection, most of which are potentially dangerous to the fetus. There would be the strongest indication for abortion, if the woman wished, but when she wants to continue with pregnancy, despite the risks, few would argue against her right to do so with the support of her doctors. In my view, it is the woman's attitude to the pregnancy which is crucial and the doctor's role is to give advice, assess the risks and, in the last resort, exercise the right to refuse.

CONCLUSION

For nearly fifteen hundred years our knowledge of the fetus was limited to anatomical drawings of doubtful accuracy without very much idea of how an embryo resulted from coitus. Protected by civil and religious codes, the fetus remained inaccessible until the major scientific advances of this century. The recognition of the human chromosomes in 1923 did not assume practical importance until it was possible to culture the cell and examine individual chromosomes. The understanding of DNA chemistry and use of molecular biology is advancing so rapidly that a daily update is necessary to keep track of new knowledge about the relationship between the nature of genes and disease.

Innovations in scientific knowledge have interacted with other changes in society. The emancipation of women, which started with the political changes in two world wars, produced a spirit of independence which rejected the traditional role of the woman as being subjugated to that of her husband, restricted to childbearing and child rearing, and being confined to work in the home.

The development of a reliable contraceptive pill gave women, for the first time in history, control over their own fertility and freed them from dependence on the male. There appears to have been an increase in sexual activity, especially among the young, and a decline in importance of the institution of marriage. The idea of legitimising a teenage pregnancy by marriage is less acceptable than it was in the 1960s and abortion or single parenthood is preferred to a 'shotgun marriage' (Figure 1.4) (Barron, 1991). As a result, illegitimacy has increased to 30 per cent although many of these babies are registered by both parents. The trend to use divorce as a solution to marital problems was accelerated by the Divorce Act 1969, and it is estimated that one in three marriages now end in divorce. The old family patterns are breaking up.

S. L. Barron

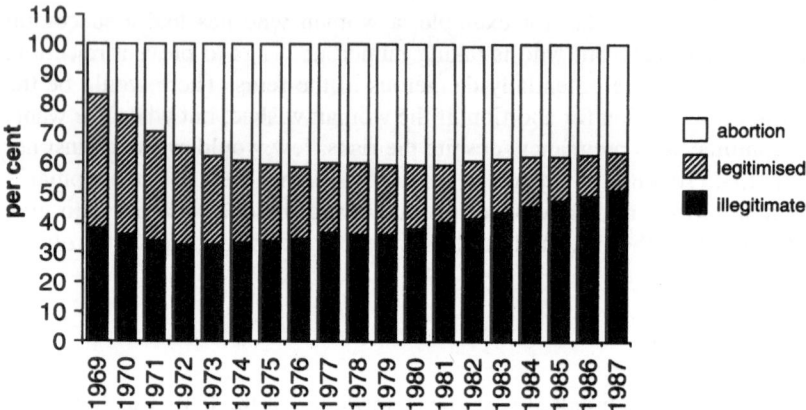

Figure 1.4   Outcomes of known conceptions in women under 20 years of age,
England and Wales

Source: Data from *Birth Statistics*, OPCS series DH3. Taken from Barron, 1991.

So, at a time when women have experienced an increased control over their fertility, they also expect medical science to provide new treatments for infertility and for avoiding or preventing congenital malformations. These apparently contradictory expectations are not inconsistent and represent a form of consumerism. Doctors claim to be able to turn fertility on and off and to divine what is happening to the fetus, and women expect to take advantage of what is on offer. But I fear that the level of expectation for medical care is becoming unrealistic. The fetus has become the focus for litigation to such an extent that it threatens the financial basis of the NHS (Symonds, 1991). The law is trying hard to keep up with these changes in medical science. Surrogacy for payment to a third party is now illegal under the Surrogacy Arrangements Act, some aspects of assisted reproduction are strictly controlled by a statutory body, the law on registration of stillbirths has been revised, and a fetus is now in some circumstances able to sue its own mother!

The wheel has turned full circle! After centuries of being jealously hidden away, the fetus has been exposed to all that modern science can offer it. It has become emancipated and its origins and development protected in law. Over two hundred years ago Laurence Sterne in the character of Tristram Shandy reflected on the importance of his conception, 'since so much depended on it!' and went on to speculate about the Homunculus '*a BEING guarded and circumscribed with rights . . . a being of such activity, – and in all senses of the word, as much and as truly our fellow-creature as my Lord Chancellor of England . . . . in a word he has all the claims and rights of humanity . . .'* (Sterne, 1759).

There remains one very important caveat: there is still a potential conflict between the interests of the mother and her fetus, but the fetus cannot give informed consent!

References

Alberman, E. and B. Botting (1991) 'Trends in prevalence and survival of very low birthweight infants, England and Wales: 1983–7', *Archives of Diseases in Childhood*, vol. 66, pp. 1304–8.

Anonymous (1989) 'Frozen Embryos: life or property?', *Bulletin of Medical Ethics*, no. 53, p. 9.

Baird, D. (1965) 'A fifth freedom?', *British Medical Journal*, vol. 2, p. 1141.

Barron, S. L. (1984) 'Service aspects of abortion', in E. Alberman and K. J. Dennis (eds), *Late Abortions in England and Wales* (London: RCOG) pp. 84–101.

Barron, S. L. (1991) 'Epidemiology of Induced Abortion', in D. R. Bromhan, M. E. Dalton, J. C. Jackson and P. J. R. Millican (eds), *Ethics in Reproductive Medicine* (London: Springer) pp. 145–60.

Barron, S. L. and M. M. Reid (1992) 'Fetal haemolytic disease', in A. A. Calder and W. Dunlop (eds), *High Risk Pregnancy* (London: Butterworth) pp. 411–34.

Boveri, T. (1904) *'Ergebnisse uber die Konstitution der chromatischen. Substanz des Zellkerns'* (Jena: G. Fischer).

Brahams, D. (1991) 'Australian mother sued by child injured *in utero'*, *The Lancet*, vol. 338, pp. 687–8.

Clements, R. V. (1991) 'Litigation in obstetrics and gynaecology', *British Journal of Obstetrics and Gynaecology*, vol. 98, pp. 423–6.

Clothier, C. (1992) *Report of the Committee on the Ethics of Gene Therapy.* Cm 1788 (London: HMSO).

Department of Health and Social Security (1984) *Report of the Committee of Inquiry into Human Fertilisation and Embryology* (Warnock). Cmnd 9314 (London: HMSO).

Donald, I. and T. G. Brown (1961) 'Demonstration of tissue interfaces within the body by ultrasonic echo sounding', *British Journal of Radiology*, vol. 34, p. 539.

Dunstan, G. R. (1984) 'The moral status of the human embryo: a tradition recalled', *Journal of Medical Ethics*, vol. 1, pp. 38–44.

Ennis, M., A. Clark and J. G. Grudzinkas (1991) 'Change in obstetric practice in response to fear of litigation in the British Isles', *Lancet*, vol. 338, pp. 616–8.

Fenton, A. C., D. G. Fields, E. Mason and M. Clarke (1990) 'Attitudes to viability of preterm infants and their effects on figures for perinatal mortality', *British Medical Journal*, vol. 300, pp. 434–6.

Ford, C. E. and J. L. Hamerton (1956) 'The chromosomes of man', *Nature*, vol. 178, pp. 1020–3.

Francome, C. (1992) 'Abortion in Ireland', *British Medical Journal*, vol. 305, p. 436.

Harvey, B. F. (ed.) (1982) *Westminster Chronicle 1381–1394*,.quoted by Dunstan 1984.

Hitchcock, E. R. (1991) 'Neural transplantation in degenerative disease', in D. F. Roberts and R. C. Chester (eds), *Molecular Genetics in Medicine* (London: Macmillan and The Galton Institute) pp. 97–123.

Huby, P. M. (1990) 'Soul, life, intellect: some thirteenth-century problems', in G. R. Dunstan (ed.), *The Human Embryo* (Exeter: Exeter University Press) pp. 115–8.

Huxley, A. (1932) *Brave New World* (London: Chatto & Windus).

Liley, A. W. (1963) 'Intrauterine transfusion of foetus in haemolytic disease', *British Medical Journal*, vol. 2, pp. 1107–9.

Lilford, R. J. (1991) 'Fetal tissue sampling', in D. F. Roberts and R. C. Chester (eds), *Molecular Genetics in Medicine* (London: Macmillan and The Galton Institute) pp. 51–72.

Macfarlane, A., S. Cole, A. Johnson and B. Botting (1988) 'Epidemiology of birth before 28 weeks of gestation', *British Medical Bulletin*, vol. 44, pp. 861–91.

Middleton, D. (1982) *Sir Francis Galton, 1822–1911* (London: Eugenics Society).

Morgan, D. (1991) 'When a fetus has legal standing', *Bulletin of Medical Ethics*, no. 66, pp. 33–4.

Patel, N. (1989) 'Fetal assessment by biophysical methods: cardiotocography', in A. Turnball and G. Chamberlain (eds), *Obstetrics* (Edinburgh: Churchill) pp. 373.

Pearson, G. A., D. J. Field, R. K. Firmin and A. S. Sosnowski (1992) 'UK experience in neonatal extracorporeal membrane oxygenation', *Archives of Disease in Childhood*, vol. 67, pp. 822–5.

Polkinghorne, J. (1989) *Review of the Guidance on the Research Use of Fetuses and Fetal Material*. Cm 762 (London: HMSO).

Potts, M., P. Diggory and J. Peel (1977) *Abortion* (Cambridge: Cambridge University Press) pp. 277–331.

Radcliffe, W. (1967) *Milestones in Midwifery* (Bristol: Wright) p. 91.

R. v. Bourne [1939] 1 KB 687.

Re F. (in utero) [1988] 2 All England Law Reports, 192.

Re J. [1992] *The Times Law Report*, 15.7.92.

Re S. (Adult: refusal of medical treatment) [1992] 4 All England Law Reports, 671.

Seller, M. (1990) 'Some fallacies in embryology through the ages', in G. R. Dunstan (ed.), *The Human Embryo* (Exeter: Exeter University Press) pp. 222–7.

Sidaway v. Board of Governors of the Royal Bethlem Hospital and the Maudsley Hospital [1984] 2 WLR, 778, 790 and 2 WLR [1985] 480.

Speert, H. (1973) *Iconographia Gyniatrica* (Philadelphia: Davis).

Steptoe, P. and R. G. Edwards (1978) 'Birth after the reimplantation of a human embryo', *Lancet*, vol. ii, p. 366.

Sterne, Laurence (1759) '*The Life and Opinions of Tristram Shandy, Gentleman*' (in edition published 1949, London: Macdonald) pp. 42–3.

Stewart, R. and G. W. Kneale (1970) 'Radiation dose effects in relation to obstetric x-rays and childhood cancers', *Lancet*, vol. i, pp. 1185–8.

Sutton, W. S. (1903) 'Chromosomes in heredity', *Biological Bulletin*, vol. 4, pp. 213–51.

Symonds, E. M. (1991) 'Obstetrics and gynaecology', in J. P. Jackson (ed.), *A Practical Guide to Medicine and the Law* (London: Springer-Verlag) pp. 163–170.

Tijo, J. H. and A. Levan (1956) 'The chromosome number of man', *Hereditas*, vol. 42, pp. 1–6.

Watson, J. D. and F. H. C. Crick (1953) 'The structure of DNA', Cold Harbor Springs Symposium, *Quantitative Biology*, vol. 18, pp. 123–31.

Young, R. (1991) 'The ethics of selecting for fetal sex', *Ballière's Clinical Obstetrics and Gynaecology*, vol. 5, pp. 575–90.

Acts of Parliament cited in text

Abortion Act 1967
Births and Deaths Registration Act 1953
Children Act 1989
Congenital Disability (Civil liability) Act 1976
Human Fertilisation and Embryology Act 1990
Infant Life (Preservation) Act 1929
Infanticide Act 1937
Mental Health Act 1983
Offences Against the Person Act 1861
Stillbirth (Definition) Act 1992
Surrogacy Arrangements Act 1985

Part I
Fetal Diagnosis

2 Applications of Recent Advances in DNA Techniques to Diagnosis in the Fetus

Ann Curtis

INTRODUCTION

In Britain, about 14 000 infants each year are born with a genetic disorder. The area covered by the Northern Regional Health Authority has a population of 3.1 million and 40 000 annual live births of which 1200 are genetically abnormal. However, there are about 60 000 people in the region who are known carriers of single gene defects and a very much larger number who are at risk of being carriers. Such genetically determined diseases cause chronic disability, and often the fear of early death and handicap leads to unnecessary abortion of normal fetuses, lifelong anxiety and childlessness. Molecular genetic techniques are advancing at a rapid rate and now offer hope to many people by demonstrating that they are not carriers of a particular defective gene or that their fetus is normal. In the minority of cases where a fetal abnormality which will cause chronic illness, either in childhood or in later life, is detected, early selective abortion can be offered.

The earliest routine investigations are carried out on DNA isolated from nine to twelve-week gestation chorionic villus (cv) biopsies with a view to obtaining a result within the first trimester. Amniocytes are also an ideal source of fetal DNA though tests may take longer if the cells have to be cultured. DNA can also be obtained following fetal blood sampling or placentesis, although placenta is not ideal as some chromosomal rearrangements which arise in the placental DNA are not true reflections of fetal abnormalities.

CATEGORISATION OF GENETIC DEFECTS

Genetic defects can simply be divided into microscopic and sub-microscopic changes at the chromosomal level.

Microscopic Mutations

The human karyotype consists of 46 chromosomes: 22 pairs of autosomes and two sex chromosomes (XX in females and XY in males). Each chromosome can be identified by size and banding pattern when stained in metaphase (Casperson *et al.*, 1971; Seabright, 1971; Sumner, 1972). Microscopic mutations are those which can be detected under the microscope as alterations in the normal banding patterns. Such changes will generally involve at least five million base pairs (bp) of DNA and will be recognised as a deletion, insertion, inversion or translocation of a part of one chromosome to another. Other forms of microscopic mutations involve whole chromosome such as trisomies and monosomies. Trisomy 21 for example gives rise to Down's syndrome and the loss of one X chromosome in a female causes Turner's syndrome.

Sub-Microscopic Mutations

Sub-microscopic changes in DNA cannot be visualised under the microscope as no gross chromosomal change is involved. Such mutations range from a simple substitution of one base by another to removal or insertion of several thousand base pairs which may involve the whole, or a large part, of a gene. As shown in Figure 2.1 a simple base substitution may cause a wrong amino acid to be incorporated into the protein product or it may create a stop codon and thus alter, reduce or totally destroy the protein's function. A deletion may alter the reading frame of the triplet code, creating a scrambled amino acid sequence and possibly a premature stop codon. When simple base substitutions occur in non-coding parts of the genome they usually have no consequential effect on the phenotype and may become established as neutral polymorphisms. When these polymorphisms alter the recognition site of a restriction endonuclease (restriction fragment length polymorphisms or RFLPs) they may be very useful as markers in the diagnosis of genetic disorders.

DIAGNOSIS OF GENETIC DISEASE

Introduction

There are currently in excess of twenty diseases, which are caused by defects in single genes *and* which have been located to a specific area of a

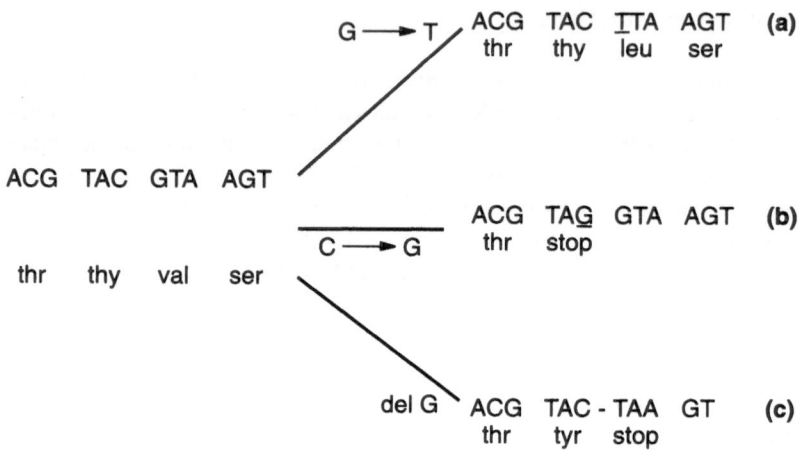

Figure 2.1   Effects of sub-microscopic mutations. Three possible effects are
shown. Simple base substitutions may (a) alter an amino acid in the
protein or, (b) cause a premature stop codon to be introduced into
the sequence. Small deletions (c) may cause the triplet reading
frame to shift and premature stop codons could occur.

chromosome *and* which lend themselves to investigation at the DNA level,
for which prenatal diagnosis can be offered. DNA-based diagnosis is only
possible for disorders where the causative gene has been localised to a
specific region of a chromosome, some examples of which are shown in
Table 2.1. The type of investigation depends upon whether the gene has
been isolated and sequenced and disease-causing mutations identified. In
these cases, it may be possible to analyse DNA directly for the presence of
such mutations. However, no disease-causing gene has yet been isolated in
which the same mutation is responsible for the disorder in all unrelated,
affected individuals. For example, about 230 different mutations, some of
which are reviewed by Tsui (1992) have been identified in the causative
gene for cystic fibrosis which was isolated in 1989 (Rommens *et al.*, 1989;
Riordan *et al.*, 1989; Kerem *et al.*, 1989). With the exception of four or five
of these mutations (Tsui, 1992), all are extremely rare and some may even
be family specific. When causative defects are unknown, an indirect gene-
tracking approach is used where closely linked RFLP or other polymorphic
DNA markers, such as variable dinucleotide repeats, are tracked through
families.

Table 2.1   Some important diseases with DNA markers useful in fetal diagnosis

Disease	Chromosome location
Huntington's disease	4p16.3
Adenomatous polyposis coli	5q21–22
Cystic fibrosis	7q31
β-Thalassaemia, sickle cell disease	11p
Phenylketonuria	12q22–24.1
Polycystic kidney disease	16pter
Alpha thalassaemia	16p13.3
Neurofibromatosis 1	17q11.2
Myotonic dystrophy	19q13.3
Duchenne/Becker muscular dystrophy	Xp21
Choroideremia	Xq21.1–21.2
Fragile X syndrome	Xq27.3
Haemophilia A	Xq28.
Haemophilia B	Xq26.3–27.1
Marfan syndrome	5q21.1
Alpha-1 antitrypsin deficiency	14q32.1

Direct Mutation Analysis

Delta 508 Mutation Analysis and Prenatal Diagnosis of Cystic Fibrosis
CF is one of the most common single gene disorders with about one person
in 25 carrying a defective CF gene (Boat *et al.*, 1989). The disease is
inherited as an autosomal recessive condition where parents are carriers of
a defective gene but do not manifest the disease themselves. One quarter of
their children will be affected, having inherited a defective gene from each
parent, one quarter will be normal, and one half will be symptomless
carriers like their parents. It would be impossible to search for all 230 CF
mutations in 'at risk' fetal DNA samples but one mutation called delta 508
(Riordan *et al.*, 1989; Kerem *et al.*, 1989), which is particularly common in
northern Europe (EWGCFG, 1990) and makes up approximately 70 per
cent of defective CF genes in Britain (Harris *et al.*, 1990; McIntosh *et al.*,
1990; Schwarz *et al.*, 1990; Watson *et al.*, 1990) can be screened for
routinely. At the DNA level, delta 508 is a deletion of three bases (CTT) in
exon ten of the gene which has the effect of removing a phenylalanine
residue at amino acid position 508 in the encoded protein (the cystic fibrosis
transmembrane regulator) (Riordan *et al.*, 1989) as shown in Figure 2.2.
    Delta 508 is detected directly using the **polymerase chain reaction**
(PCR) (Saiki *et al.*, 1985; Saiki *et al.*, 1988) and polyacrylamide gel

Normal	ATC	AT<u>C</u>	<u>TT</u>T	GGT
	Ile	Ile	Ple	Gly
	506	507	508	509
delta 508	ATC	ATT	GGT	
	Ile	Ile	Gly	
	506	507	509	

Figure 2.2   Molecular nature of the delta 508 mutation. The gene sequence and amino acid sequence around the delta 508 mutation show the CTT deletion which is in exon 10 of the gene and the subsequent removal of a phenylalanine residue at position 508 in the cystic fibrosis transmembrane regulator protein (CFTR).

electrophoresis. The PCR technique allows DNA from a particular chromosomal region to be amplified many times *in vitro* as shown schematically in Figure 2.3. The process involves continuous heat denaturation, primer annealing and DNA synthesis which is repeated 30 times to produce millions of copies of the particular DNA sequence.

In the diagnosis of CF, exon ten of the gene is amplified using the PCR. The fragment of DNA created from the normal allele is 98 bp long and from the allele carrying the delta 508 mutation (deletion of CTT) is 95 bp long. This three base pair difference can be detected using 10 per cent polyacrylamide gel electrophoresis. The example of prenatal diagnosis using these techniques, shown in Figure 2.4 demonstrates this size separation. Here both parents are heterozygous carriers of the delta 508 mutation, and the fetus is predicted to be normal.

Analysis of Mutations in X-Linked Muscular Dystrophy
A gene which has been extensively characterised is that which codes for the protein dystrophin (Hoffman *et al.*, 1987). Defects in this gene cause the disease Duchenne (DMD) and Becker (BMD) muscular dystrophy which have been shown to map to the short arm of the X chromosome at Xp21 (Davies *et al.*, 1983; Boyd *et al.*, 1986; Francke *et al.*, 1985). Both disorders are progressive with muscle wasting which, except on very rare occasions (Boyd *et al.*, 1986; Yoshioka *et al.*, 1990) only affect males. Females carry the defective gene but due to the presence of a normal gene do not manifest the disease. Half the sons of carrier females will be affected while half of their daughters will be carriers. The incidence of DMD is one in 3500 newborn males and of BMD is one in 40 000 males.

The dystrophin gene is the largest so far isolated covering 2.3 million base pairs of DNA (Koenig *et al.*, 1987; Burmeister *et al.*, 1988) and over 70 exons (Koenig *et al.*, 1989) with a messenger RNA transcript of fourteen

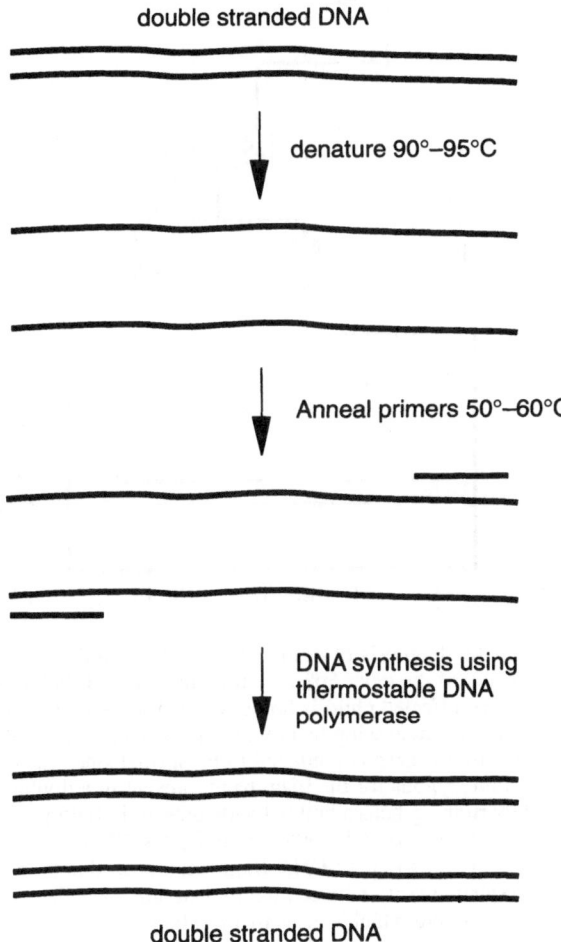

Figure 2.3   The polymerase chain reaction. Double-stranded DNA is denatured
into its single stranded form using temperatures of 90–95 °C.
Complementary oligonucleotide primers are then allowed to anneal
under specific temperature conditions to each single strand such that
they flank the region of interest. A thermostable DNA polymerase is
then able to catalyse the synthesis of a second strand of
complementary DNA from the 3′ end of each primer. The result is
two double strands of a specific sequence where originally there was
one. This process of heat denaturation, primer annealing, and DNA
synthesis is repeated 30 times to produce millions of copies of a
particular DNA sequence.

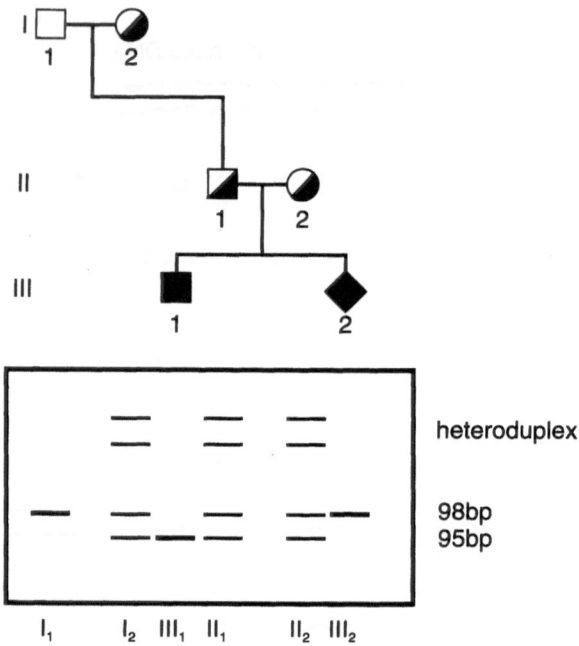

Figure 2.4   Prenatal diagnosis of cystic fibrosis. Both parents are heterozygous
carriers of the delta 508 mutation, having both 98bp and 95bp bands
and the affected child is homozygous for the delta 508 mutation,
having a single 95bp band which is present in a double dose. The
fetus in this case is predicted to be normal since the cv biopsy DNA
is homozygous for the 98bp band, present in a double dose. The
slow running heteroduplex bands present in both parents are
characteristic of delta 508 heterozygotes. They are formed when a
normal and a mutant DNA fragment anneal due to the high level
complementarity between the two strands. It is the small amount of
mismatching which causes them to be retarded in the electrophoretic
gel.

kilobases (Koenig *et al.*, 1987). The most common type of disease-causing
mutation is a sizeable deletion of part of the gene sequence. Approximately
65 per cent of affected boys have such a defect and in the majority of these
it is the mid-part of the gene, called the 44–1 region, which is affected
involving exons 45–54 (Koenig *et al.*, 1987). In about 50 per cent of boys
affected with DMD and over 80 per cent of males with BMD who show a
deletion (Bushby *et al.*, 1993), it is the 44–1 region which is involved.
Southern blotting (Darras *et al.*, 1988) or PCR (Chamberlain *et al.*, 1988;
Hentemann *et al.*, 1990) can be used to detect deletions. Figure 2.5 shows

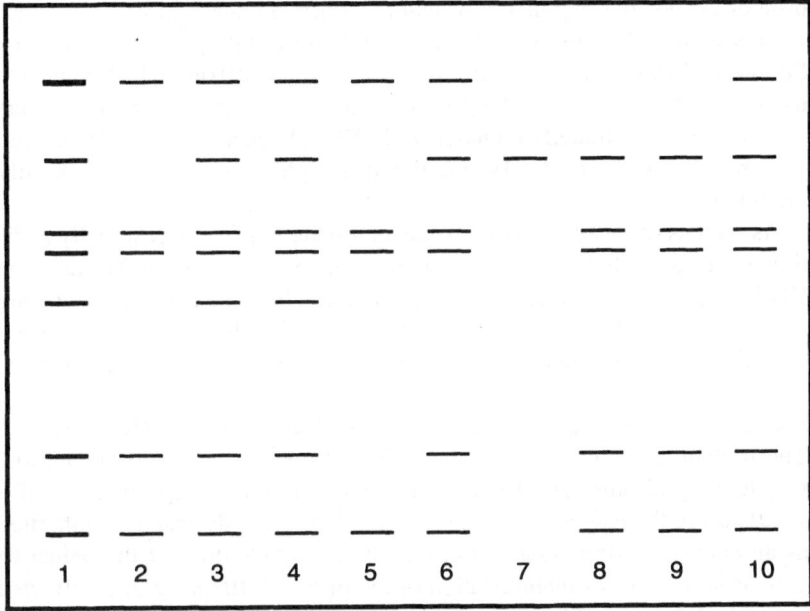

Figure 2.5   DMD deletion screening. A Southern blot containing DNA, digested
with Hind III, from eight boys affected with Duchenne muscular
dystrophy (lanes 2–9), and two unaffected controls (lanes 1 and 10)
showing the normal pattern of bands. The blot has been probed with
the 44–1 cDNA. The absent bands in lanes 2, 5, 7, 8 and 9,
represent deletions in this part of the dystrophin gene.

a Southern blot containing DNA samples from eleven boys affected with
DMD. Several of these boys have part of the 44–1 region of the gene
deleted, identified as bands which are missing when compared with the
normal pattern. When there is a family history of DMD or BMD and a
previous molecular investigation has identified a deletion in an affected
member, female carriers may request screening of male fetuses for the same
defect.

A more difficult task with X-linked muscular dystrophy is determination
of which females in a family are carriers of a defective dystrophin gene.
Those females at highest risk of producing affected sons are the sisters and
aunts of affected boys. Since females have two X chromosomes, the presence of the normal dystrophin gene masks the presence of the abnormal
gene and a complete pattern of bands will be present on a Southern blot
deletion screen. However, with precise loading of DNA quantities it is
possible to determine which females are carriers, because they have a single

dose of the deleted region, equivalent to a normal male, and which females are not carriers because they have a double dose. Interpretation of dosage Southern blots is often very difficult, however, and carrier detection is now usually carried out by tracking dinucleotide repeat polymorphic markers which are closely linked to (Oudet *et al.*, 1990; Feener *et al.*, 1991), or even within (Clemens *et al.*, 1991), the dystrophin gene, through family members.

As well as observing deleted bands in affected males, occasionally additional bands, called junction fragments, arise. These occur because the DNA fragments which flank the deleted region become contiguous and are detected on the blot as a single band of altered size. Junction fragments are very useful both in the diagnosis of male fetuses and in carrier prediction.

Mutations which Cause Fragile X Syndrome and Myotonic Dystrophy

The mutations responsible for the X-linked mental retardation condition, fragile X syndrome, and for myotonic dystrophy are amplifications of a small part of the respective gene sequence. Myotonic dystrophy is inherited as an autosomal dominant condition where a single dose of the defective gene is sufficient for manifestation of the disease. Offspring of an affected individual have a 50 per cent chance of having inherited the defect themselves.

In the case of fragile X syndrome, a triplet of bases, CGG, near the 5' end of the gene is present in between 6 and 52 copies in the normal gene, but becomes amplified to hundreds, or even thousands of copies when abnormal (Kremer *et al.*, 1991; Verkerk *et al.*, 1991). Asymptomatic female carriers and normal transmitting males have a premutation which involves an intermediate number of CGG repeats in the region of 70–200 (Fu *et al.*, 1991).

In the case of myotonic dystrophy, the amplified region is a CTG triplet of bases in the 3' untranslated part of the gene (Brook *et al.*, 1992; Mahadevan *et al.*, 1992; Fu *et al.*, 1992). In normal individuals the repeat sequence is present in between five and 27 copies but in affected individuals one gene has an increased number of repeats (52–2500) which appears to correlate with the severity of the disease (Harley *et al.*, 1992; Buxton *et al.*, 1992; Brook *et al.*, 1992; Mahadevan *et al.*, 1992; Fu *et al.*, 1992). For example, the defective genes in patients with minimal symptoms and late age of onset (over 40 years) have an amplification of 52 to 500 copies of the CTG, whereas those with the classical adult form of the disease have approximately 500 to 1000 copies. Congenital cases are the most severe and it is these which have been shown to have the largest amplification of over 1000 copies of the triplet. Congenital cases are born to couples where the mother is the affected parent. Detection of a large amplification in DNA from a cv sample taken from an affected mother is likely, therefore, to indicate a congenitally affected fetus.

On a Southern blot, these amplified regions appear as larger than normal DNA fragments as shown in Figure 2.6 and may even appear as smears where the size of the somatic mutation is variable in different cells. Although the mechanisms by which these amplifications arise and the actual proteins coded for by the genes are not precisely defined, the increased sized DNA segments appear to be highly diagnostic of the two disorders and tend to increase in size both with severity of the condition and with passage from generation to generation (Fu *et al.*, 1992; Mahadevan *et al.*, 1992; Fu *et al.*, 1991).

Gene Tracking

Introduction
What about the diagnosis of disorders where the causative gene has not been isolated or fully characterised? What about diagnosis in disorders such as CF and DMD where a disease causing mutation cannot be detected? Such cases make up approximately 35 per cent of DMD boys and 15–20 per cent of CF carriers. In these situations, indirect techniques are adopted to track the defective genes through families, using linked RFLP or hypervariable repeat markers.

Prenatal Genetic Testing for Huntington's Disease
The location of the Huntington's disease (HD) gene was demonstrated to be in the telomeric region of the short arm of chromosome four in 1983 (Gusella *et al.*, 1983) and since that time many polymorphic DNA markers have been isolated from this region (see Andrew *et al.*, 1992 and Weber *et al.*, 1992 for examples) which have refined the location to 4p16.3 (Wang *et al.*, 1986). However, because the gene itself has not been isolated, disease causing mutations are unknown.

The disease is inherited as an autosomal dominant condition which shows complete penetrance. It is a neuro-degenerative disorder with late onset symptoms which are not apparent in early life. Onset generally, but not exclusively, occurs between the ages of 35 and 50 years, which is very often after the defective gene has been passed to the next generation. This means that both parent and child suffer great anxiety awaiting the onset of symptoms. Due to the effect the disease has, not only on the patient but on other members of the family, some form of prenatal testing is often sought. It is possible for individuals who are at risk of developing HD to undergo genetic testing to determine whether they carry the defective gene (Wexler *et al.*, 1985; Meissen *et al.*, 1988; Brock *et al.*, 1989) and this test is often

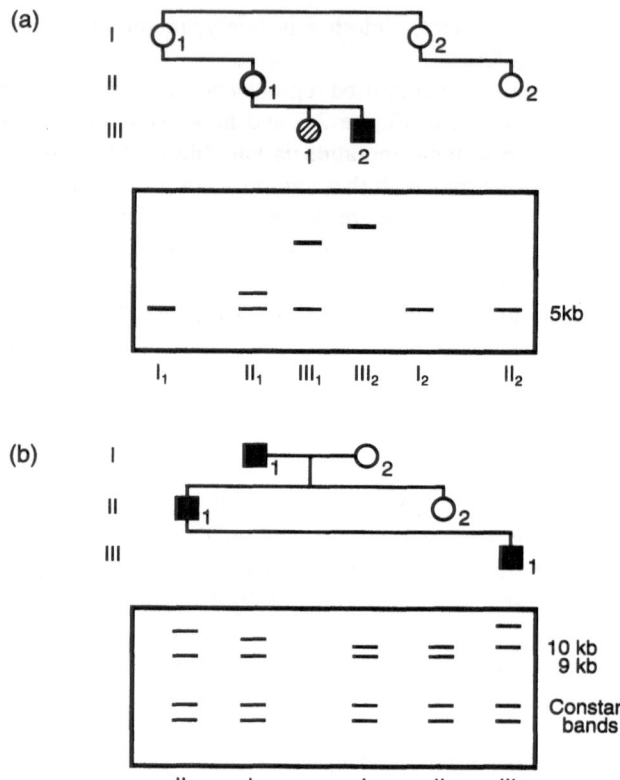

Figure 2.6   Detection of trinucleotide repeat expansions. (a) A Southern blot of
Hind III digested DNA samples from members of a fragile X
syndrome family probed with the fragile X probe OX1.9 (Nakahori
et al., 1991). The normal-sized DNA fragment of five kilobases is
present in all individuals showing that each has at least one normal
copy of the gene. The mother, II_1, has an amplification in one of her
fragile X genes as shown by the DNA fragment of increased
molecular weight. This amplified region has become larger in her
daughters, III_1 and III_2, who manifest disease symptoms, as shown
by the increased molecular weight smears (b) A Southern blot of
EcoRI digested DNA from members of a family, probed with the
myotonic dystrophy probe, pM10M6 (Brook *et al.*, 1992). The
nine and ten kilobase bands represent an allelic insertion polymorphism
at the myotonic dystrophy locus which is close to the CTG repeat
sequence. Each affected family member has an amplification of this
repeat as shown by the presence of a band of higher molecular
weight than 10 kilobases. The size of the amplification has further
increased as it has been passed from one generation to the next.

taken before deciding whether to have children (Fahey *et al.*, 1989). However, some people do not wish to have this sort of test. This places them in a dilemma, since, while not wishing to know their own carrier status, they also do not want to risk passing a devastating disease on to their children.

A prenatal test has been developed which gives some help to such people. Here, a positive diagnosis on the fetus is not made but a positive exclusion of the defective gene can be made, thus reducing some of the anxiety (Quarell *et al.*, 1987; McIntosh *et al.*, 1989; Fahey *et al.*, 1989). In this way, the risk to the future parent remains at 50 per cent and the risk to the fetus never rises above 50 per cent. A hypothetical example is shown in Figure 2.7, giving both a 'high risk' and a 'low risk' outcome, and is achieved using a gene tracking approach. Polymorphic DNA markers which lie around and very close to the HD gene are followed through families as they are passed from one generation to the next. The markers have no direct influence on the gene itself, but because the two are so closely linked physically, by following their inheritance one is effectively following the HD gene also. There is a small, but finite, risk of error here which depends on the chance of recombination occurring between the marker and the disease gene. This is between one per cent and five per cent depending upon which polymorphic DNA marker is informative in the particular family.

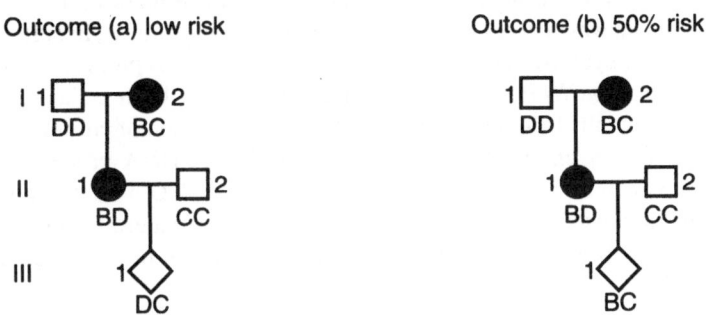

Figure 2.7   Prenatal exclusion testing in Huntington's Disease (HD). The inheritance of a linked polymorphic marker with alleles B, C and D is tracked through family members. The HD gene is linked to *either* the B allele *or* the C allele in the grandmother I_2, with a 50 per cent risk attached to each. The father II_1 has inherited B from his affected mother, and is at 50 per cent risk of developing the disease. In outcome (a) the B allele has not been passed to the fetus III_1 which is, therefore, at low risk of developing HD. In outcome (b) however, the fetus has inherited the grandmaternal B allele from its father, and therefore will be at 50 per cent risk of developing HD in later life

This test, of course, means that pregnancies which are only at a 50 per cent risk of carrying a defective gene may be terminated. Attitudes towards this vary among potential parents. To some it is the only possible option to reduce the risk of transmitting a dreadful condition, and to others it is unacceptable and the only option is not to have children at all.

In situ Hybridisation and Gene Tracking in Wolf–Hirschhorn Syndrome
A technique, recently introduced into routine service laboratories for diagnostic purposes, which incorporates the skills of both the cyto- and molecular geneticist, is that of *in situ* hybridisation (Buckle and Craig, 1986). Here, specific DNA probes are labelled with fluorescence or radioactivity and are used as tagged hybridisation markers to identify particular chromosomes or chromosomal regions. The procedure has been developed to detect carriers of DMD and BMD where hybridisation to one X chromosome and lack of hybridisation to the second X, using the appropriate DNA probe, indicates that the woman is a carrier of a deletion in one dystrophin gene (Reid *et al.*, 1990).

An *in situ* hybridisation test was carried out on the chromosomes of the mother of a child with Wolf–Hirschhorn syndrome (see Goodship *et al.*, 1992). The features of this syndrome begin prenatally when growth is retarded and go on to include mental retardation, seizures and, in some cases, congenital heart defects after birth. The facial features are a prominent glabella which gives a characteristic Greek helmet profile, hypertelorism, high arched eyebrows, sagging lower eyelids and a short philtrum. The gene responsible for Wolf–Hirschhorn syndrome has not been isolated but the condition results from monosomy of the terminal region of chromosome 4p (Hirschhorn *et al.*, 1965; Johnson *et al.*, 1976). A DNA probe from this region which is also useful in the diagnosis of HD was fluorescently labelled and used to demonstrate a translocation of material from chromosome 4 to chromosome 10 in the asymptomatic mother of the affected child (Goodship *et al.*, 1992).

Molecular techniques using Southern blotting and terminal 4p DNA probes showed (Figure 2.8) that the child had inherited from the mother the abnormal chromosome 4 which had material missing but had not inherited the material translocated from chromosome 4 to chromosome 10. This suggests that translocated part of the chromosome contains the Wolf–Hirschhorn gene, the abnormality having arisen due to monosomy of this region.

The woman became pregnant again and requested prenatal diagnosis but unfortunately, as shown in Figure 2.8a, the fetus had the same pattern of markers as the affected child and the pregnancy was terminated. In a third

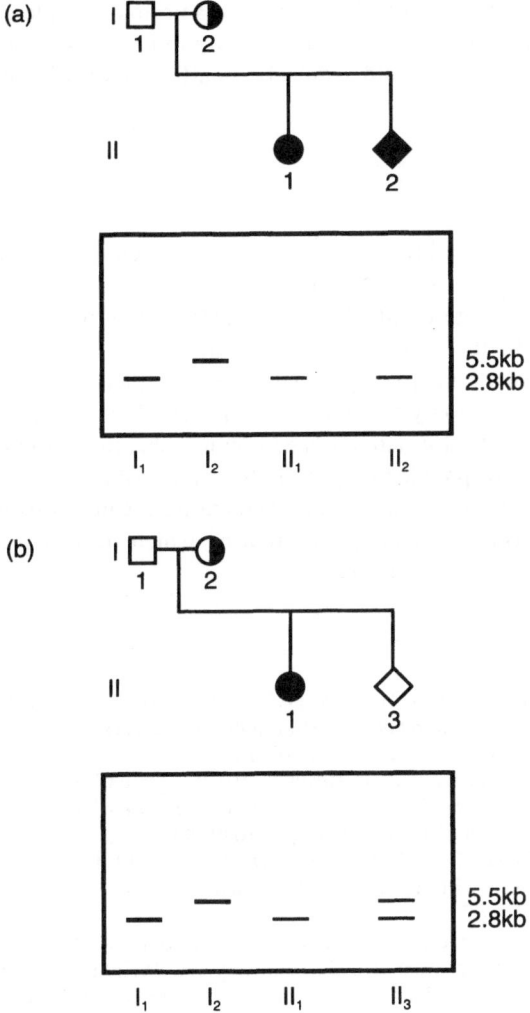

Figure 2.8   Prenatal diagnosis in a family with Wolf–Hirschhorn Syndrome. Southern blots of MspI digested DNA, probed with the chromosome 4p probe H5.52 from members of a family with a child affected with Wolf–Hirschhorn Syndrome of showing that the child has inherited a 4p allele from her father but not from her mother. In a second pregnancy (a), the chorionic villus biopsy DNA showed that the fetus had also not inherited a maternal allele and was, therefore, at high risk of also being affected with the disorder. In a third pregnancy (b), however, the fetus had inherited alleles from both mother and father

pregnancy however, the cv biopsy showed a normal complement of alleles inherited from both parents as can be seen in Figure 2.8b and therefore, it was predicted that the child would be unaffected with Wolf–Hirschhorn syndrome.

CONCLUSION

Whether using the indirect gene tracking approach or the direct mutation analysis approach to genetic testing in the fetus with DNA probes, it is usually an advantage to all (that is, the patient and his or her family, the laboratory staff, the genetic counsellor, the obstetrician and the general practitioner) for a family study to have been completed prior to pregnancy. The procedures are only efficient if the defect which is segregating in the family or the most informative linked polymorphic marker has been identified in advance of prenatal diagnosis. It is impossible to screen all fetuses for all defects in the genes thus far characterised. Current technology only allows this form of screening for fetuses which have a prior risk of a disorder through family history.

References

Andrew, S., J. Theilman, A. Hedrick, D. Mah, B. Weber and M. R. Hayden (1992) 'Non random association between Huntington's disease and two loci separated by about 3 Mb on 4p16.3', *Genomics*, vol. 13, pp. 301–11.
Boat, T. F., M. J. Welsh and A. L. Beaudet (1989) 'Cystic fibrosis', in C. L. Scriver, A. L. Beaudet, W. S. Sly and D. Valle (eds), *The Metabolic Basis of Inherited Disease* (New York: McGraw-Hill) pp. 2649–80.
Boyd, Y., V. Buckle, S. Holt, E. Munro, D. Hunter and I. Craig (1986) 'Muscular dystrophy in girls with X; autosome translocations', *Journal of Medical Genetics*, vol. 23, pp. 484–90.
Brock, D. H. J., A. Curtis, L. Barron, D. Dinwoodie, A. Crosbie, M. Mennie, F. A. Millan, J. A. Raeburn, S. Holloway, A. Wright and I. Pullen (1989) 'Predictive testing for Huntington's disease with linked DNA markers', *Lancet*, vol. ii, pp. 463–6.
Brook, J. D., M. E. McCurrach, H. G. Harley, A. J. Buckler, D. Church, H. Aburanti, K. Hunter, V. P. Stanton, J. P. Thirion, T. Hudson, R. Sohn, B. Zemelman, R. G. Snell, S. A. Rundle, S. Crowe, J. Davies, P. Shellbourne, J. Buxton, C. Jones, V. Juvonen, K. Johnson, P. S. Harper, D. J. Shaw and D. E. Housman (1992) 'Molecular basis of myotonic dystrophy: expansion of a trinucleotide (CTG) repeat at the 3' end of a protein kinase family member', *Cell*, vol. 68, pp. 799–808.
Buckle, V. J. and I. W. Craig (1986) '*In situ* hybridisation', in K. E. Davies (ed.), *Human Genetic Diseases – A Practical Approach* (Oxford: IRL Press) pp. 85–100.

Burmeister, M., A. J. Monaco, E. F. Gillard, G. J. B. van Ommen, N. A. Affara, M. A. Ferguson-Smith, L. M. Kunkel and H. A. Lehrach (1988) 'A 10 megabase physical map of human Xp21, including the Duchenne muscular dystrophy gene', *Genomics*, vol. 2, pp. 189–202.

Bushby, K. M. D., D. Gardner-Medwin, L. V. B. Nicholson, M. A. Johnson, I. D. Haggerty, N. J. Cleghorn, J. B. Harris and S. S. Bhattacharya (1993) 'The clinical, genetic and dystrophin characteristics of Becker muscular dystrophy', *Journal of Neurology*, vol. 240, pp. 105–12.

Buxton, J., P. Shelbourne, J. Davies, C. Jones, T. van Tongeren, C. Aslanidis, P. J. de Jong, G. Jansen, M. Anvret, B. Riley, R. Williamson and K. Johnson (1992) 'Detection of an unstable fragment of DNA specific to individuals with myotonic dystrophy', *Nature*, vol. 355, pp. 547–8.

Casperson, T. G., G. Lomakka and L. Fech (1971) 'The 24 fluorescence patterns of the human metaphase chromosomes – distinguishing characteristics and variability', *Hereditas*, vol. 67, pp. 89–102.

Chamberlain, J. S., R. A. Gibbs, J. E. Ranier, P. N. Nguyen and C. T. Caskey (1988) 'Deletion screening of the Duchenne muscular dystrophy locus via multiplex DNA amplification', *Nucleic Acids Research*, vol. 23, pp. 11141–56.

Clemens, P. R., R. G. Fenwick, J. S. Chamberlain, R. A. Gibbs, M. de Andrade, R. Chakraborty and C. T. Caskey (1991) 'Carrier detection and prenatal diagnosis in Duchenne and Becker muscular dystrophy families using dinucleotide repeat polymorphisms', *American Journal of Human Genetics*, vol. 49, pp. 951–60.

Darras, B. T., J. F. Blattner, P. Harper, A. J. Spiro, S. Alter and U. Francke (1988) 'Intragenic deletions in 21 Duchenne muscular dystrophy (DMD)/Becker muscular dystrophy (BMD) families studied with the dystrophin cDNA: Location of breakpoints on Hind III and Bgl II exon-containing fragment maps, meiotic and mitotic origin of mutations', *American Journal of Human Genetics*, vol. 43, pp. 612–9.

Davies, K. E., P. L. Pearson and P. S. Harper (1983) 'Linkage analysis of two cloned DNA sequences flanking the Duchenne muscular dystrophy locus on the short arm of the human X chromosome', *Nucleic Acids Research*, vol. 11, pp. 2303–12.

European working group on cystic fibrosis genetics (EWGCFG) (1990) 'Gradient of distribution in Europe of the major CF mutation and its associated haplotype', *Human Genetics*, vol. 85, pp. 436–42.

Fahey, M., C. Robbins, M. Bloch, R. W. Turnell and M. R. Hayden (1989) 'Different options for prenatal testing for Huntington's disease using DNA probes', *Journal of Medical Genetics*, vol. 26, pp. 353–7.

Feener, C. A., F. M. Boyce and L. M. Kunkel (1991) 'Rapid detection of CA polymorphisms in cloned DNA: Application to the 5' region of the dystrophin gene', *American Journal of Human Genetics*, vol. 48, pp. 621–7.

Francke, U., H. D. Ochs and B. de Martinville (1985) 'Minor Xp21 chromosome deletion in a male associated with expression of Duchenne muscular dystrophy, chronic granulomatous disease, retinitis pigmentosa and McLeod syndrome', *American Journal of Human Genetics*, vol. 37, pp. 250–67.

Fu, Y-H., D. P. A. Kuhl, A. Pizzuti, M. Pieretti, J. S. Sutcliffe, S. Richards, A. J. M. H. Verkerk, J. J. A. Holden, R. G. Fenwick, S. T. Warren, B. A. Oostra, D. L. Nelson and C. T. Caskey (1991) 'Variation of the CGG repeat at the Fragile X site results in genetic instability: Resolution of the Sherman paradox', *Cell*, vol. 67, pp. 1047–58.

Fu, Y-H., A. Pizzuti, R. G. Fenwick, J. King, S. Rajnarayan, P. W. Dunne, J. Dubel, G. A. Nasser, T. Ashizawa, P. J. de Jong, B. Wieringa, R. Korneluk, M. B. Perryman, H. F. Epstein and C. T. Caskey (1992) 'An unstable triplet repeat in a gene related to myotonic muscular dystrophy', *Science*, vol. 255, pp. 1256–8.

Goodship, J., A. Curtis, I. Cross, J. Brown, J. Emslie, J. Wolstenholme, S. S. Bhattacharya and J. Burn (1992) 'A sub-microscopic translocation t(4;10) responsible for recurrent Wolf–Hirschhorn syndrome identified by allele loss and fluorescent *in situ* hybridisation', *Journal of Medical Genetics*, vol. 29, pp. 451–4.

Gusella, J. F., N. S. Wexler, P. M. Conneally, S. L. Naylor, M. A. Anderson, R. E. Tanzi, P. C. Watkins, K. Ottina, M. R. Wallace, A. Y. Sagaguchi, A. B. Young, I. Shoulson, E. Bonilla and J. B. Martin (1983) 'A polymorphic DNA marker genetically linked to Huntington's disease', *Nature*, vol. 306, pp. 234–8.

Harley, H. G., J. D. Brook, S. A. Rundle, S. Crowe, S. A. Reardon, A. J. Buckler, P. S. Harper, D. E. Housman and D. J. Shaw (1992) 'Expansion of an unstable DNA region and phenotypic variation in myotonic dystrophy', *Nature*, vol. 355, pp. 545–6.

Harris, A., F. Beards and C. Mathew (1990) 'Mutation analysis at the cystic fibrosis locus in the British population', *Human Genetics*, vol. 85, p. 408.

Hentemann, M., J. Reiss, M. Wagner and D. N. Cooper (1990) 'Rapid detection of deletions in the Duchenne muscular dystrophy gene by PCR amplification of deletion probe exon sequences', *Human Genetics*, vol. 84, pp. 228–32.

Hirschhorn, K., H. L. Cooper and I. L. Firschein (1965) 'Deletion of short arms of chromosome 4–5 in a child with defects of midline fusion', *Humangenetik*, vol. 1, pp. 479–82.

Hoffman, E. P., R. H. Brown and L. M. Kunkel (1987) 'Dystrophin: The protein product of the Duchenne muscular dystrophy locus', *Cell*, vol. 51, pp. 919–28.

Johnson, V. P., R. D. Mulder and R. Hosen (1976) 'The Wolf–Hirschhorn (4p-) syndrome', *Clinical Genetics*, vol. 10, pp. 104–12.

Kerem, B.-S., J. M. Rommens, J. A. Buchanan, D. Markiewicz, T. K. Cox, A. Chakravarti, M. Buchwald and L.-C. Tsui (1989) 'Identification of the cystic fibrosis gene: genetic analysis', *Science*, vol. 245, pp. 1073–80.

Koenig, M., E. P. Hoffman, C. J. Bertelson, A. J. Monaco, C. Feener and L. M. Kunkel (1987) 'Complete cloning of the Duchenne muscular dystrophy (DMD) cDNA and preliminary genomic organisations of the DMD gene in normal and affected individuals', *Cell*, vol. 50, pp. 509–17.

Koenig, M., A. H. Beggs and M. Moyer (1989) 'The molecular basis for Duchenne versus Becker muscular dystrophy: Correlation of severity with type of deletion', *American Journal of Human Genetics*, vol. 45, pp. 498–506.

Kremer, E. J., M. Pritchard, M. Lynch, S. Yu, K. Holman, E. Baker, S. T. Warren, D. Schelssinger, G. R. Sutherland and R. I. Richards (1991) 'Mapping of DNA instability at the Fragile X to a trinucleotide repeat sequence p(CCG)n', *Science*, vol. 252, pp. 1711–4.

McIntosh, I., A. Curtis, F. A. Millan and D. H. J. Brock (1989) 'Prenatal exclusion testing for Huntington's disease using the polymerase chain reaction', *American Journal of Medical Genetics*, vol. 32, pp. 274–6.

McIntosh, I., A. Curtis, M-L. Lorenzo, M. Keston, A. J. Gilfillan, G. Morris and D. J. H. Brock (1990) 'Haplotype distribution of delta 508 mutation in cystic fibrosis families in Scotland', *Human Genetics*, vol. 85, pp. 419.

Mahadevan, M., C. Tsilfidis, L. Sabourin, G. Shutler, C. Amemiya, G. Jansen, C. Neville, M. Narang, J. Barcelo, K. O'Hoy, S. Leblond, J. Earle-Macdonald, P. J. de Jong, B. Wieringa and R. Korneluk (1992) 'Myotonic dystrophy mutation: An unstable CTG repeat in the 3' untranslated region of the gene', *Science*, vol. 255, pp. 1253–5.

Meissen, G. J., R. Myers, C. A. Mastromauro, W. J. Koroshetz, K. W. Klinger, L. A. Farrer, P. A. Watkins, J. F. Gusella, E. D. Bird and J. B. Martin (1988) 'Predictive testing for Huntington's disease with use of a linked DNA marker', *New England Journal of Medicine*, vol. 318, pp. 535–42.

Nakahori, Y., S. J. L. Knight and J. Holland (1991) 'Molecular heterogeneity of the fragile X syndrome', *Nucleic Acids Research*, vol. 19, pp. 4355–9.

Oudet, C., R. Heilig and J. L. Mandel (1990) 'An informative polymorphism detected by polymerase chain reaction at the 3' end of the dystrophin gene', *Human Genetics*, vol. 84, pp. 283–5.

Quarell, O. W. J., A. Tyler, M. Upadhyaya, A. L. Meredith, S. Youngman and P. S. Harper (1987) 'Exclusion testing for Huntington's disease in a pregnancy with a closely linked DNA marker', *Lancet*, vol. ii, pp. 1281–3.

Reid, T., V. Mahler, P. Vogt, L. Blonden, G. J. B. van Ommen, T. Cremer and M. Cremer (1990) 'Direct carrier detection by *in situ* hybridisation with cosmid clones of the Duchenne/Becker muscular dystrophy locus', *Human Genetics*, vol. 85, pp. 381–6.

Riordan, J. R., J. M. Rommens, B-S. Kerem, N. Alon, R. Rozmahel, Z. Grzelczak, S. Lok, N. Plavsic, J.-I. Chou, M. L. Drumm, M. C. Iannuzzi, F. S. Collins and L.-C. Tsui (1989) 'Identification of the cystic fibrosis genes: Cloning and characterisation of complimentary DNA', *Science*, vol. 245, pp. 1066–73.

Rommens, J. M., M. C. Iannuzzi, B-S. Kerem, M. L. Drumm, G. Melmer, M. Dean, R. Rozmahel, J. L. Cole, D. Kenmedy, N. Hidaka, M. Zsiga, M. Buchwald, J. R. Riordan, L.-C. Tsui and F. S. Collins (1989) 'Identification of the cystic fibrosis gene: Chromosome walking and jumping', *Science*, vol. 245, pp. 1059–65.

Saiki, R. K., S. Scharf, F. Faloona, K. B. Mullis, G. T. Horn, H. A. Erlich and N. Arnheim (1985) 'Enzymatic amplification of B globin genomic sequences and sequences and restriction site analysis for diagnosis of sickle cell anaemia', *Science*, vol. 230, pp. 1350–4.

Saiki, R. K., D. H. Gelfand, S. Stoffel, S. J. Scharf, R. Higuchi, G. T. Horn and K. B. Mullis (1988) 'Primer directed amplification of DNA with a thermostable DNA polymerase', *Science*, vol. 239, pp. 487–91.

Schwarz, M. J., M. Super, C. Wallis, P. Beighton, C. Newton, L. E. Heptinstall, C. Summers, A. Markham, G. Hambleton, K. W. Webb, D. Bilton, D. Heaf and M. Dalzell (1990) 'Delta 508 testing of the DNA bank of the Royal Manchester Children's Hospital', *Human Genetics*, vol. 85, p. 428.

Seabright, M. (1971) 'A rapid banding technique for human chromosomes', *Lancet*, vol. ii, pp. 971–2.

Sumner, A. T. (1972) 'A simple technique for demonstrating centrometric heterchromatin', *Experimental Cell Research*, vol. 75, pp. 302–6.

Tsui, L.-C. (1992) 'The spectrum of cystic fibrosis mutations', *Trends in Genetics*, vol. 8, pp. 392–8.

Verkerk, A. J. M. H., M. Pieretti, J. S. Sutcliffe, Y.-H. Fu, D. P. A. Kuhl, A. Pizzuti, O. Reiner, J. S. Richards, M. A. Victoria, F. Zhang, B. E. Eussen, G. J. B. van Ommen, L. A. J. Blonden, G. J. Riggins, J. L. Chastain, C. B. Kunst, H. Calijaard,

C. T. Caskey, D. L. Nelson, B. A. Oostra and S. T. Warren (1991) 'Identification of a gene (FMR-1) containing a CGG repeat coincident with a breakpoint cluster region exhibiting length variation in Fragile X syndrome', *Cell*, vol. 65, pp. 905–14.

Wang, H. S., C. R. Greenberg, J. Hewitt, D. Kalousek and M. R. Hayden (1986) 'Subregional assignment of the linked marker G8 (D4S10) for Huntington's disease to chromosome 4p16.1–16.3', *American Journal of Human Genetics*, vol. 39, pp. 392–6.

Watson, E. K., E. S. Mayall, L. Simova, E. M. Thompson, J. O. Warner, R. Williamson and C. Williams (1990) 'The incidence of delta 508 CF mutation and associated haplotypes in a sample of English CF families', *Human Genetics*, vol. 85, p. 435.

Weber, B., A. Hedrick, S. Andrew, O. Reiss, C. Collins, D. Kowbel and M. R. Hayden (1992) 'Isolation and characterisation of new highly polymorphic DNA markers from the Huntington's disease region', *American Journal of Human Genetics*, vol. 50, pp. 382–93.

Wexler, N. S., P. M. Conneally, D. Housman and J. F. Gusella (1985) 'A DNA polymorphism for Huntington's disease marks the future', *Archives of Neurology*, vol. 42, pp. 20–4.

Yoshioka, M., Y. Yamamoto and J.-I. Furuyama (1990) 'An isolated case of Duchenne muscular dystrophy (DMD) in a female with a deletion of DND cDNA', *Clinical Genetics*, vol. 38, pp. 474–8.

3 Normal Fetal Development and the Time of Origin of Some Structural Abnormalities

Mary J. Seller

INTRODUCTION

One branch of contemporary Fetal Medicine is 'to search out and see': that is, to use ultrasound scanning to visualise the embryo and fetus *in utero* to determine whether it is developing normally, both temporally and structurally. Structural anomalies, or congenital malformations, can affect all systems of the body and many of them originate in the very early stages of embryonic development during organogenesis. However, a few do originate later in pregnancy when a normally formed structure is altered in some way. Ultrasound scanning is becoming increasingly refined and excellent views of the fetus can now be obtained. By using vaginal probes, good views may now be obtained at very early stages of pregnancy, right back to the embryo. However, no imaging technique yet provides the equivalent of a photograph of the embryo or fetus.

From a study of normal early development of the embryo, it is possible to suggest the stage at which specific developmental abnormalities originate, and thereby indicate when they may first be diagnosed by ultrasound scanning in pregnancy. In practice it is not feasible to make detailed studies of organogenesis in the human embryo; the basic developmental stages have been determined from museum collections of embryos, e.g. that of the Carnegie Institute. Fortunately the mouse, which can be very easily studied, is very similar to the human in the overt processes of development and the scanning electron microscope is a particularly useful tool in such studies. This paper illustrates specific common developmental abnormalities found in humans, and briefly reviews the normal development of the organ system involved, as shown by scanning electron micrographs of mouse embryos at comparable stages.

NEURAL TUBE DEFECTS

Neural tube defects – anencephaly and spina bifida – are amongst the most common congenital malformations affecting children of the United Kingdom. The defects involve the brain and spinal cord and the immediately surrounding mesodermal tissue; they often occur as a single lesion localised to one area of the body.

Neurulation, or formation of the neural tube, is fundamental to the entire development of the embryo. It starts around eighteen days after conception when the embryo is little more than a flattened disc consisting of three layers of cells, each a single layer thick: an upper layer of ectoderm and a lower layer of endoderm, are separated by a mass of mesoderm cells. Chemical messages from the paraxial elements of the mesoderm induce the ectoderm above to thicken and become the neural plate, the precursor of the central nervous system. Forces both extrinsic and intrinsic to the neural plate cause the edges of the neural plate to rise up and form the neural folds, which grow higher and higher on either side of the central neural groove, and eventually overarch and join up to form a tube. The neural folds juxtapose and fuse first in the lower cervical region around day 22, and then fusion occurs concurrently from this, in both a cranial and a caudal direction (Figure 3.1).

During this, other crucial morphogenetic processes are going on; the embryo is growing and elongating so that the body bends to accommodate the increasing length, the heart is forming, somites are appearing and the body cavities are created. The neural tube is completed by fusion of the anterior neuropore on day 24 and the posterior neuropore on day 26. Thus, the foundation of the central nervous system, the brain and the spinal cord, is completed by the 26th day after conception.

Forces which drive the process of neurulation include a change in the shape of the neuroepithelial cells themselves, from being flat to being tall and spindle shaped. From the surface, the neural plate seems to consist of tiny cells, but they are simply the apices of very elongate cells. This change in shape may be partially brought about by the synthesis of the cytoskeleton within the cell: for instance, microtubules are formed paraxially in the cytoplasm. Also, the neural folds are largely composed of mesoderm cells, underneath the neural plate, and these multiply and condense during neurulation. Fusion of the neural folds involves, amongst other things, formation of projections of the outer cell membrane in specific areas of the juxtaposing neural folds, as does closure of the neuropores.

Although it is not known exactly how or why neural tube defects arise, it is believed that the neural folds somehow fail to fuse, rather than that they

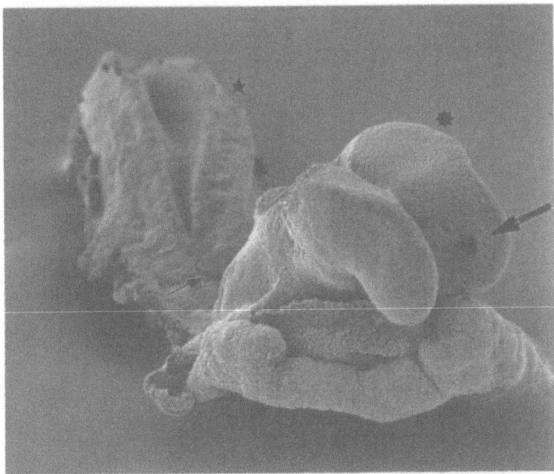

Figure 3.1   The embryo at neurulation. Fronto-lateral view of embryo with
neural plate still open cranially (asterisk) and caudally (star). The
neural folds have overarched and fused in the mid-line in the lower
cervical region and fusion (small arrow) has taken place from that
site. At the extreme rostral end the optic sulcus can be seen
evaginating from the neural plate (large arrow).

fuse and then burst open again. This can be observed in mice (the mutant
curly-tail) which are genetically predisposed to NTD. Human anencephaly
and spina bifida are localised lesions, for most of the neural tube closes
properly. However, failure of the whole length of the neural tube to close –
total craniorachischisis – does also occur.

Since this primary form of neurulation is normally completed by day 26,
potentially, neural tube defects could be detected by imaging techniques
from the end of the fourth week onwards.

CLEFT LIP

Another common abnormality is cleft lip: again, an abnormality not restricted to humans – mice, and other animals, can also be affected.

At the end of the fourth week, the cranial neuropore is closed and on
either side of the head are the facial swellings (Figure 3.2). These lie above
the stomodeum, the future mouth, beneath which are the mandibular swellings arising from the mandibular arch which will form the lower jaw;
however, they are not yet fused in the mid-line. On either side of the

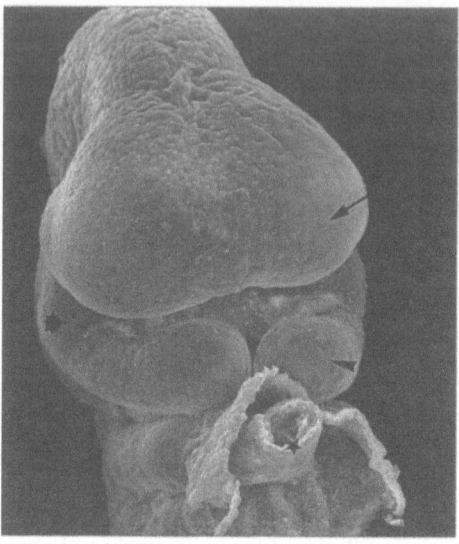

Figure 3.2   Frontal view of the head. The neural tube is closed and there are
paired frontal processes (arrow) above the stomodeum, beneath
which are the paired mandibular processes (arrowhead) which have
not yet fused in the mid-line. On either side are the maxillary
swellings (asterisk). The heart had been removed, leaving the stump
of the truncus arteriosus (star) surrounded by the cut edge of the
pericardium.

stomodeum are the maxillary swellings, small at this stage, which will
contribute to the upper jaw and upper lip.

On each side of the facial swellings, just above the stomodeum, the nasal
placode forms, first as a thickening of the surface, and then as an invagination
(Figure 3.3). During the fifth week this becomes deeper, and on either side,
two rapidly growing ridges of tissue, the lateral and medial nasal swellings,
enlarge and grow down around the nasal placode to convert it to the nasal
pit (Figure 3.4). During the next two weeks, the maxillary swellings begin
to increase in size, and grow medially. In so doing they push the medial
nasal swellings together in the mid-line. Then the maxillary swelling fuses
with the outer part of the medial nasal swelling (Figure 3.5), and the inner
parts of the two medial nasal swellings fuse medially and grow down. Thus
the upper lip is formed. The lateral nasal swellings do not contribute to the
lip but form the alae of the nose.

Failure of fusion of the maxillary, and the outer part of the medial, nasal
swellings will give rise to cleft lip. This may be right or left sided, or
bilateral, and, depending on the extent of the non-fusion, may involve only

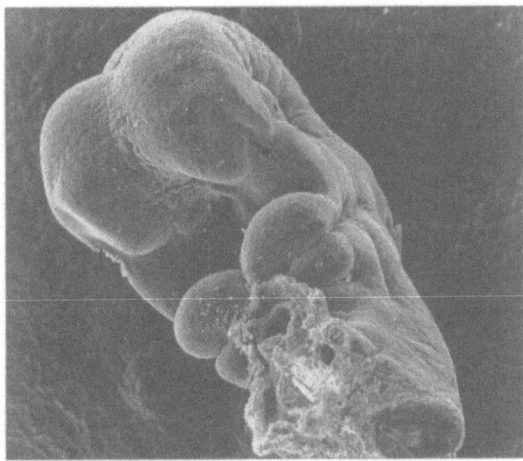

Figure 3.3   Early development of the head. Inferior view of the head showing the nasal placodes indenting on the inferior aspect of the two frontal processes (arrowheads), and Rathke's pouch (arrow) in the mid-line of the roof of the stomodeum.

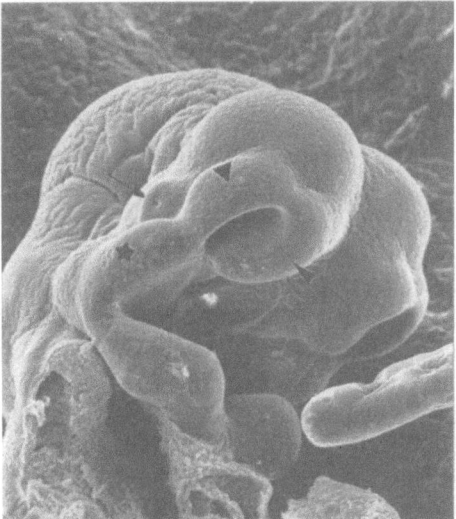

Figure 3.4   The head showing the formation of the nostrils. Latero-frontal view of the head. Each nasal placode has invaginated and the lateral (triangle) and medial (arrowheads) nasal processes have grown down around it converting it into the nasal pit. The mandibular processes are partially fused in the mid-line, and the maxillary processes are beginning to enlarge (star). The eye pit (arrow) is also present.

Mary J. Seller

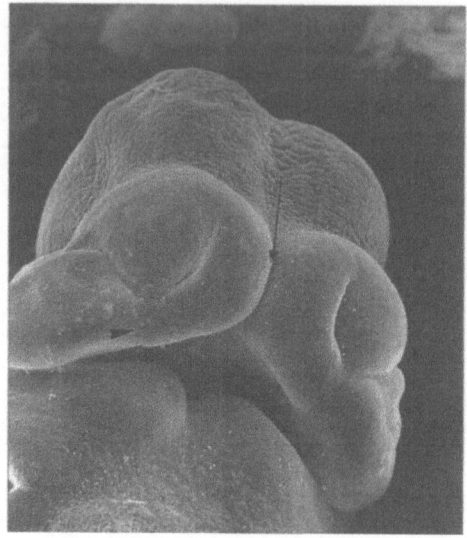

Figure 3.5   The head showing the formation of the nose and upper lip. Frontal
view of head. The lateral and medial nasal processes and the
maxillary processes have enlarged. The inner part of the maxillary
process has fused with the outer part of the medial nasal process
(arrowhead) to form the lateral part of the upper lip. The two medial
nasal processes have grown together and are fusing in the mid-line
(arrow) and will grow down to form the central part of the upper lip.

the lip or also may include the nose. The site of fusion of the two medial
nasal swellings is the philtrum of the lip and failure of fusion results in a
median cleft lip. Median cleft lip is less common than lateral clefts, and it
can be associated with mid-face hypoplasia, ocular hypotelorism and sometimes with an absent nose, which implies that both nasal processes have
failed to form, but that the maxillary processes were normal. By contrast,
the opposite facial abnormalities ocular hypertelorism and a bifid nose may
also occur, and, these could have been caused by failure of movement of the
tissues towards the mid-line.

Fusion to form the upper lip occurs at the end of the seventh week of
development, so cleft lip cannot be diagnosed before then.

CLEFT PALATE

Cleft palate may occur as an isolated lesion, or together with cleft lip. At the
time when the nasal placodes are just forming, it is possible to see in the

mid-line of the roof of the stomodeum, Rathke's pouch (Figure 3.3). This is invaginating into the head, just in front of the cephalic end of the notochord, and will come in contact with the undersurface of the forebrain. It will be constricted off to form a closed vesicle, and then join on to the brain to become the anterior lobe of the pituitary gland.

When the two median nasal processes fuse in the mid-line they do so not only anteriorly to form the lip, but posteriorly to form the medial part of the upper jaw. This is the primary palate: it is the front part of the palate which will bear the four incisor teeth (Figure 3.6). Just posterior to the primary palate are the primitive choanae, formed when the nasal sacs ruptured internally into the oral cavity.

In the sixth week, the secondary or main part of the palate is formed from two shelf-like outgrowths from the maxillary swellings. They initially lie downwards either side of the tongue, but in the seventh week, these palatal shelves elevate to a horizontal position above the tongue, and gradually move towards each other (Figure 3.7). They eventually fuse in the mid-line in the tenth week, and finally fuse anteriorly with the primary palate, closing the naso-palatine canal.

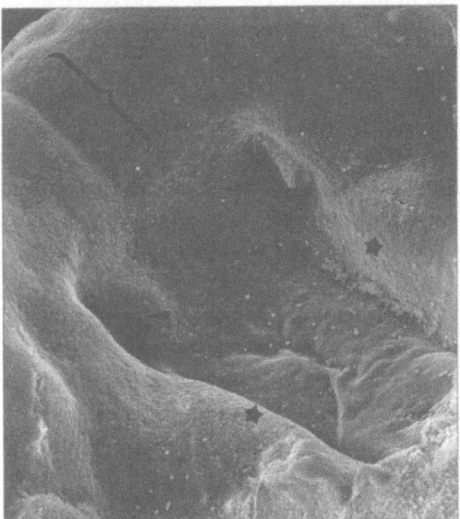

Figure 3.6   View inside the mouth before formation of the palate. The roof of the stomodeum. The nasal sacs have opened internally (arrowheads). The medial nasal processes, as well as fusing anteriorly to form the lip, have also fused posteriorly to form the primary palate (bracket). The palatal shelves (stars) are beginning to form either side of the tongue (which has been removed).

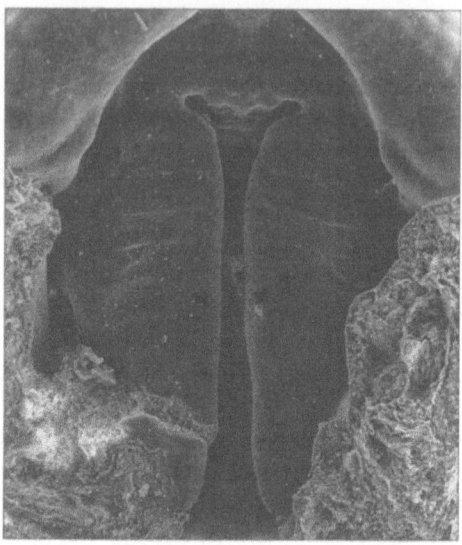

Figure 3.7　　The palatal shelves moving across to the mid-line – soon to fuse.
　　　　　　　The roof of the mouth. The palatal shelves (star) are almost apposed
　　　　　　　and will soon fuse together to form the secondary palate, and the
　　　　　　　frontal portions will fuse with the primary palate (arrow), so
　　　　　　　separating the nasal cavity from the mouth.

Cleft palate occurs when the growth or movement of the palatal shelves is impeded in some way, and does not arise until after ten weeks.

DEFECTS OF THE EXTERNAL EAR

The internal ear begins to be formed around 22 days, before the anterior neuropore has closed, when the otic placodes become visible as small circular depressions either side of the hindbrain (Figure 3.8). These invaginate rapidly, each forming a tube which then closes over externally and develops within the embryo to form the internal ear.

The external ear, or auricle, develops from proliferations from the lower part of the first branchial, or mandibular, arch, and the upper part of the second branchial arch (Figure 3.9). First, three swellings appear from the upper part of the second branchial arch (Figure 3.10), they are followed by three swellings from the lower part of the mandibular arch. All these swellings are called auricular hillocks and have formed by day 36. They will fuse and undergo differential growth, contributing the different parts

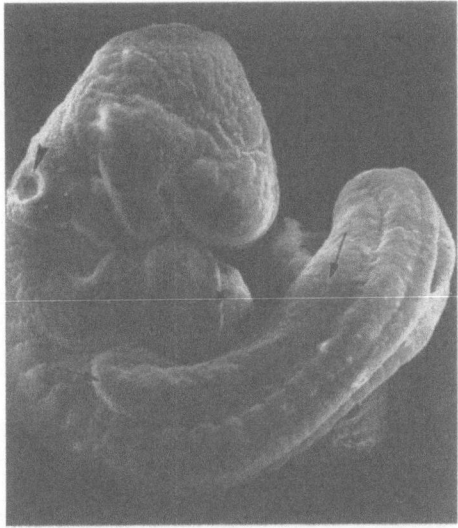

Figure 3.8　Whole embryo showing the heart and the beginning of the limb buds. Whole embryo equivalent to about a 24-day human embryo. The otic vesicle (arrowhead), heart within the pericardium (star) and anterior and posterior limb buds (arrows) are evident.

which will form the external ear. The external auditory meatus develops from the dorsal part of the first pharyngeal cleft. Initially the external ears are located low in the neck, but with development of the jaws they move upwards to the side of the face: and do not reach their final position until the mid-trimester. Fusion of the auricular hillocks is a complicated process, and abnormalities of the external ear are relatively common.

EYE DEFECTS

The eye too begins to develop at about twenty days, before closure of the anterior neuropore. First a groove, the optic sulcus, appears laterally at the cranial end of the open neural plate on either side of the neural groove. The optic sulci evaginate (Figure 3.1) to form the optic vesicle and project from the sides of the forebrain into the mesenchyme. Soon the optic vesicles induce the ectoderm over them to thicken to form the lens placode, the central portion of which, together with the opticle vesicle, invaginate, forming the optic cup and lens pit (Figures 3.4 and 3.9). When the surface ectoderm fuses over the lens pit, it separates from the lens vesicle beneath

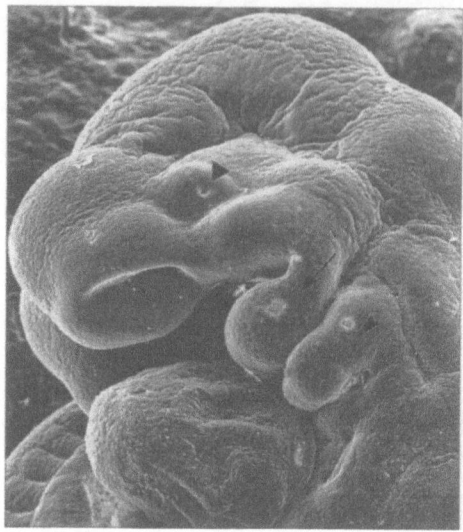

Figures 3.9 and 3.10 Side view of head showing formation of external ear.
Lateral view of head showing mandibular (arrow) and
second branchial (arrowhead) arches from which the
external ear will form. The lens pit (triangle) is present,
and the invaginating nasal placode and heart covered by
pericardium can also be seen.

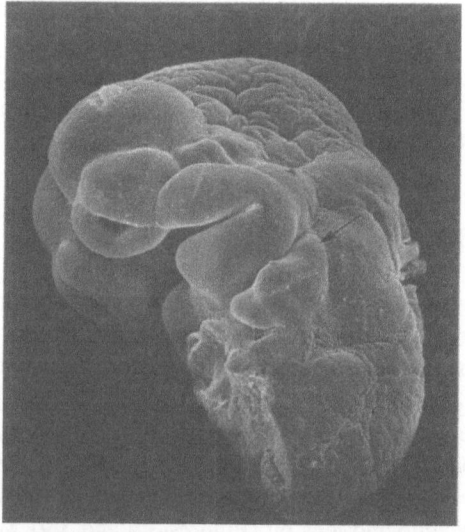

Figure 3.10 Lateral view of head showing three auricular hillocks formed from
the upper part of the second branchial arch (arrow).

it and restores the ectodermal covering of the future eye. The various components of the eye develop beneath. Pigment first appears at about six weeks. With time, eyelids form above and below, from surface ectodermal folds containing cores of mesoderm. They grow over the eye and will meet and fuse by the tenth week. The eyes start at the side of the head and move around to the front of the face later on.

There are many congenital abnormalities affecting the eye including anophthalmia, a complete absence. Cyclopia, that is, partial or complete fusion to form a single eye within one orbit, usually has a supervening proboscis, but the nose is absent. This malformation appears to derive from failure of the establishment of two separate cerebral hemispheres rostrally. It occurs very early and is potentially detectable.

LIMB ABNORMALITIES

The limb buds are not present around day 23, but by day 25–26 they can be observed as small elevations within the ventrolateral body wall (Figure 3.8). The upper limb buds are more advanced than the lower ones. Overall, the upper buds appear to be very low on the trunk, but this is because at this stage, the head, neck and upper thoracic regions have priority in development over the lower part of the body. It is particularly necessary for the heart to be established early on, in order to circulate blood containing nutrients and oxygen to the rapidly enlarging body, which can no longer be supplied by simple diffusion.

The limb buds elongate by the proliferation of mesenchyme within them (Figure 3.11). At the tip of each limb bud is the apical ectodermal ridge, a specialised group of ectodermal cells, which induces the mesenchyme to develop. In the sixth week the distal ends of the limb buds flatten to form paddle-like foot and hand plates. By the end of the sixth week digital rays can be observed on them, formed by condensation of mesenchyme within. Then cells within the mesenchyme between the rays die: this is first seen as notches at the periphery (Figure 3.12). Soon, cell death in the interdigital region becomes total, so separating the fingers and toes. This is an example of a surprising fact, that cell death is a normal component of the developmental process. It is programmed cell death, and if it does not take place, then syndactyly results – that is, cutaneous fusion of the fingers or toes. Other digital abnormalities include the wrong number of digital rays being formed – either polydactyly, too many fingers or toes, or hypodactyly – too few. Sometimes there is a combination of the two abnormalities – polysyndactyly.

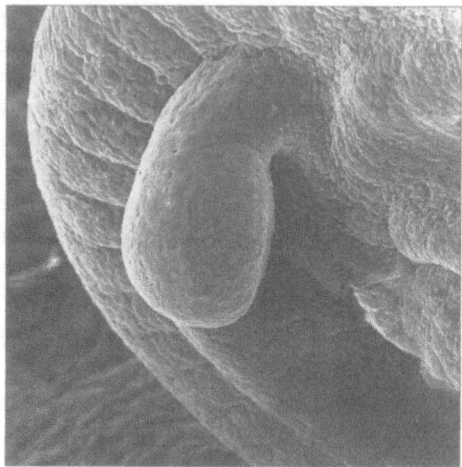

Figure 3.11 Upper limb beginning to elongate. Upper limb bud elongating; the distal portion has not yet flattened with the hand plate.

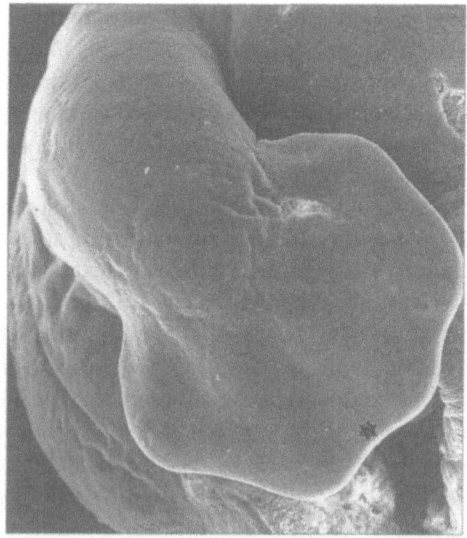

Figure 3.12 Hand plate with digital rays visible. Developing limb – the flattened hand plate has developed distinct digital rays and cell death is beginning to take place between them peripherally (asterisk) producing notches.

Secondary abnormalities of the limbs are also common. In this case the limb is normally formed, but is altered by a subsequent event. An example is intrauterine amputation which is thought to arise because strands of amnion aberrantly separate from the membranes and become twisted around a limb, constricting and eventually amputating it. The extremities alone, that is fingers or toes, may be affected. The amniotic strands may sometimes be observed still attached to the remnants of the extremities in aborted fetuses.

The digits should separate and the fingers become distinct in the eighth week, but intrauterine amputations must presumably occur later.

INTERNAL ORGANS

Whilst the features of the body which are visible externally are completed, the internal organs are being formed at the same time, but they are, of course, far less accessible to the scanning electron microscopist.

Heart

The heart begins to appear around day 21, when paired tubes on the underside of the embryo beneath the stomoderm come together and fuse. This tube then thickens and folds up on itself (Figure 3.13) within the covering pericardium. It develops various constrictions and dilations which are the foundations for the various parts of the future four-chambered heart – two ventricles and two atria. Spasmodic contractions begin on day 22, and a more co-ordinated beat producing a regular flow of blood occurs by day 28.

Gut

The beginning of the gut forms during the fourth week, as the head fold, the tail fold and the lateral folds close inwards to the mid-line and engulf the upper part of the yolk sac. Successful closure of the lateral folds in the mid-line completes the formation of the anterior body wall and encloses the body cavity. The endoderm within produces the intestine, liver, pancreas and the respiratory organs. Congenital malformations of the intestines are common, particularly omphalocoele. In the normal course of development, part of the abdominal mid-gut actually develops within the proximal part of the umbilical cord until the tenth week when it returns to the abdominal cavity. This is called a physiological hernia, and if it fails to resolve

Mary J. Seller

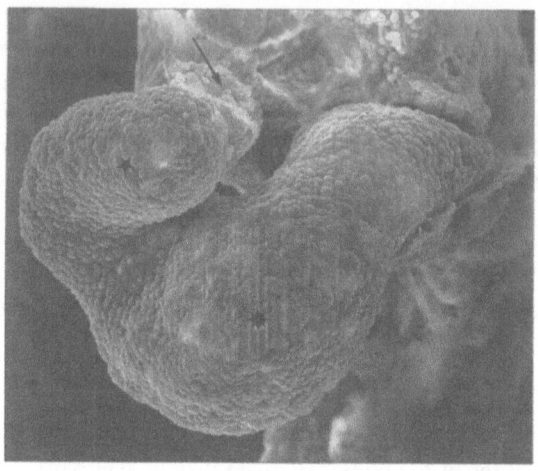

Figure 3.13 The developing heart. The developing heart with the pericardium removed. Paired tubes have fused to form a single tube which is now folding up on itself and thickening locally. Bulbus cordis (star), ventricle (asterisk), truncus arteriosus (arrow).

normally, then omphalocoele results. Omphalocoele cannot, therefore, be diagnosed until after ten weeks.

Urogenital System

The urogenital system develops from a longitudinal ridge of mesoderm which forms on either side of the dorsal mid-line within the body cavity. This urogenital ridge gives rise to both the kidney system and the genital system. Three successive sets of kidneys form: the first two degenerate, the final, permanent kidneys develop in the fifth week and produce urine around the eleventh week. Kidney abnormalities are common: for example, absent kidneys, horseshoe kidneys, and abnormally sited or ectopic kidneys.

GENETIC CONTROL OF DEVELOPMENT

This chapter has been entirely about anatomy, but the course of development from the single celled fertilised egg to the mature multicellular form is under genetic control. It is a complicated system; there are master genes which control the action of other genes in a co-ordinated and hierarchical manner. Some genes specify the overall pattern and others specify particular parts. It has long been thought that mutations in those genes which control normal development must underlie the cause of many of the human congenital malformations which occur. For instance, in Treacher-Collins syndrome, there are abnormalities of the external ear, deafness and hypoplasia of the facial bones and the lower jaw. The disorder affects tissues which derive from the first and second branchial arches. These tissues develop through the immigration of cells which have, in turn, emigrated from the neural crest. It appears that the migration process is under genetic control, and one possibility is that a mutation in one of the genes controlling this process could be the underlying defect in this malformation. We are only just beginning to be able to study and understand the molecular basis of development. It is producing the most exciting results and it is one of the most important and fascinating areas of research today.

4 Preimplantation Diagnosis of Genetic Disease

P. R. Braude

INTRODUCTION

A number of diseases are genetic, that is to say inherited (Milunsky, 1986). Some of these will manifest themselves early in childhood resulting in severe physical and mental handicap, and sometimes in the demise of the child before its teens. Many couples who carry such genetic diseases already have one affected child and are eager to take advantage of methods which will allow antenatal diagnosis of the condition during a subsequent pregnancy. However a number of women, whether for religious or personal reasons, cannot accept abortion of an affected pregnancy and would rather avail themselves of methods to diagnose the genetic disease prior to conception. The clinical and laboratory procedures for *in vitro* fertilisation (IVF) which were originally developed for the treatment of tubal infertility (Edwards *et al.*, 1980), now enable diagnosis of genetic disorders before the pregnancy is established, thus obviating the need for repeated and often late therapeutic abortions (McLaren, 1985; Verlinsky *et al.*, 1990b). This technique of preimplantation diagnosis requires the taking of a single cell or group of cells, from the egg or early cleavage stage embryo *in vitro*, as a biopsy on which a diagnostic test can be performed for the particular genetic lesion (Figure 4.1). Only those preimplantation embryos which have been found to be free of the particular genetic disease are selected for replacement into the woman's uterus. Thus the couple can continue with the pregnancy safe in the knowledge that their baby will not be affected by the disease for which they are carriers.

SOURCE OF GENETIC SAMPLE

A sample of cells or tissue suitable for diagnosis can be taken at one of three distinct periods during preimplantation *in vitro* culture (Figure 4.2).

(a) From the *oocyte* – the polar body can be removed from the oocyte shortly after retrieval but prior to insemination (Verlinsky *et al.*, 1990a);

(b) from the *cleavage stage embryo* between the 4-cell and 16-cell stage (early morula) (Handyside *et al.*, 1989);

(c) from the trophectoderm of the *blastocyst* (Monk *et al.*, 1988).

Each of these stages is associated with specific practical and theoretical advantages and limitations.

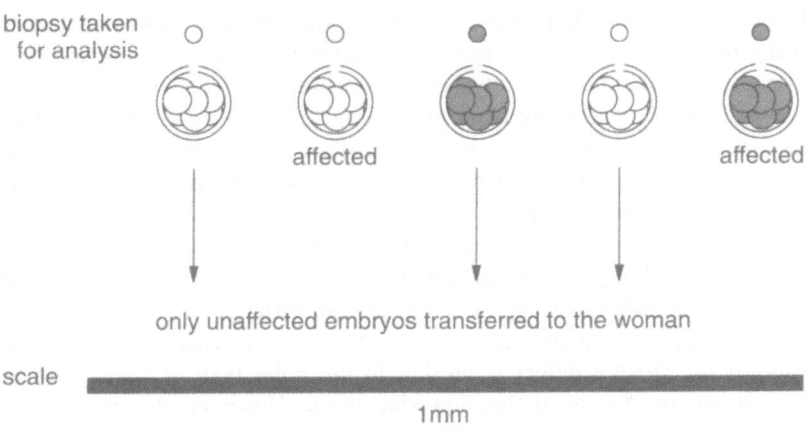

Figure 4.1   Principles of preimplantation diagnosis

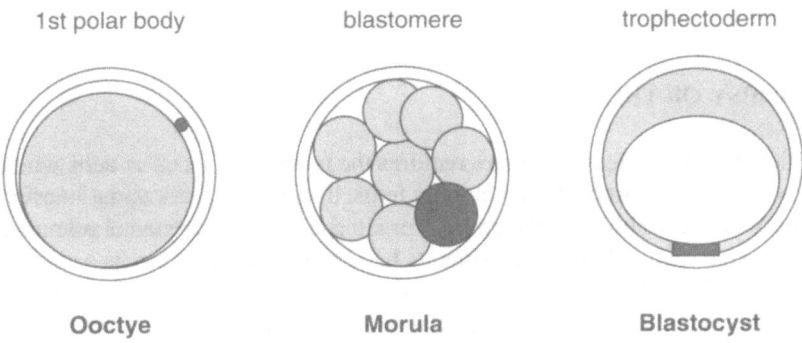

Figure 4.2   Stages of development and tissues suitable for preimplantation biopsy

Biopsy of Polar Body

Biopsy of the polar body is relatively easy as there is a defined cell to be removed, and experience of the technique can be gained by the use of oocytes which have failed to fertilise after IVF (Verlinsky *et al.*, 1992). Polar body biopsy also confers the advantage that the cell sample is taken before fertilisation, a time which may be acceptable to those who find interference with the developing embryo, however early, unethical. The formation of a small hole in the zona pellucida in order to remove the polar body, may make it easier for sperm to reach the oocyte membrane and thus increases the likelihood of polyspermic fertilisation which would render the oocyte/embryo genetically abnormal and unsuitable for later replacement. In contrast, as not all oocytes will be fertilised after insemination *in vitro*, more procedures, which of necessity are delicate and time consuming, will have been performed than are necessary. However, the main disadvantage is that the genetic diagnosis that can be made from the polar body is limited. The first polar body contains only half of the woman's alleles. As the carrier woman from whom the egg derives is a heterozygote, theoretically the alleles in the polar body will be 'opposite' to those remaining in the egg. Thus if the genetic defect is present in the polar body it should not be present in the oocyte alleles and vice versa. However, during meiosis, areas of genetic crossing over form (chiasmata), making it possible that the polar body and the egg are themselves heterozygous for the genetically relevant allele. Thus a useful clinical diagnosis can only be made if the polar body is found to be homozygous for the presence or absence of the genetic locus of interest, and relies on the fact that the oocyte is homozygous as well.

BIOPSY OF THE ZYGOTE

Biopsy at early cleavage stages requires the removal of a cell or cells which could become part of the developing fetus, thus raising fears about interfering with the viability of the embryo or altering its developmental potential. Although relatively few experiments have been conducted on the safety of removal of cells from human preimplantation embryos, there is a substantial literature about micromanipulation of embryos from both laboratory and domestic animal species (First, 1991; Willadsen, 1982). It is clear from experiments in cattle and sheep, that individual blastomeres of the cleaving embryo retain their developmental totipotentiality up to the 8-cell stage of development, as 8-cell ovine morulae disaggregated into their constituent blastomeres and transferred individually to recipient ewes have produced identical lambs and comparable experiments have been conducted using bovine 4-cell embryos. These experiments demonstrate (i) that the individual blastomeres of the preimplantation embryo are totipotent and identical during the early cleavage stages, and (ii) that micromanipulation of cleavage stage embryos and removal of blastomeres is compatible with continuing normal development. Although for obvious reasons such experiments have not been conducted in humans, pregnancies have derived from frozen cleavage stage embryos where up to 50 per cent of the blastomeres have not survived the thawing process, confirming the potential of early cleavage human embryos to survive substantial mechanical damage (Trounson, 1986).

Experiments which have used spare preimplantation human embryos, surplus to a therapeutic IVF programme, have demonstrated that removal of one or two blastomeres from human 8-cell embryos is compatible with development to the blastocyst stage (Hardy *et al.*, 1990), although a reduction in the total number of cells was found. However, the proportion of cells contributing to the inner cell mass (ICM – from which the fetus is derived), was not reduced. This is not the case for 4-cell stage embryos where removal of blastomeres retards cleavage and reduces the ratio of ICM to trophectoderm (Tarin *et al.*, 1992). As with polar body biopsy, the major disadvantage of cleavage stage biopsy is the availability of only one or perhaps two cells on which the diagnosis is to be made, which stretches the current technology for genetic diagnosis to its limits, and allows a substantial chance of misdiagnosis (see below). Notwithstanding these limitations, the only pregnancies which have been reported so far following biopsy for therapeutic diagnoses, have been performed at the morula stage (Handyside *et al.*, 1990; Handyside *et al.*, 1993).

BIOPSY OF THE BLASTOCYST

Biopsy at the blastocyst stage holds a number of advantages over biopsy at earlier cleavage stages (Dokras *et al.*, 1990). First, since there are more cells present at this stage (over 50) (Hardy *et al.*, 1989; Winston *et al.*, 1991), a larger biopsy can be removed without jeopardising further development (Muggleton-Harris and Findlay, 1991; Summers *et al.*, 1988). Second, the biopsy can be removed from the abembryonic pole of the blastocyst, tissue which usually gives rise to placental and extraembryonic membranes rather than from cells likely give rise to the embryo proper. One of the major disadvantages of blastocyst biopsy is that development from fertilised egg to this stage *in vitro* is extremely limited, with less than 50 per cent of fertilised oocytes reaching the fully expanded blastocyst stage by day 5 (Bolton *et al.*, 1988). However, blastocyst biopsy can be applied not only to embryos obtained *in vitro* by IVF, but also to embryos which derive from fertilisation *in vivo* and are flushed from the uterine cavity (uterine lavage). Although this method has only been used for the purposes of embryo donation (Buster *et al.*, 1985; Formigli *et al.*, 1990) theoretically it could overcome the difficulties of obtaining blastocysts *in vitro*, although there are substantial difficulties still to be resolved including the potential for the retention of an embryo *in vivo* despite uterine lavage. It is also still unclear whether embryo transfer at the blastocyst stage will be as successful as cleavage stage embryo transfer (Bolton *et al.*, 1991).

The premise of preimplantation diagnosis is that the biopsy to be analysed is representative of the remaining cells of the embryo. Although experiments on animal embryos have demonstrated retained totipotentiality of blastomeres at early cleavage stages (see above), there is now mounting evidence that not all the cells in the human cleavage stage embryo are identical. Examination of embryos spare to therapeutic programmes has demonstrated a high rate of nuclear abnormalities, including the presence of multinucleated and anucleate cells (Winston *et al.*, 1991). It is also clear that there is a high rate of chromosomal abnormality detectable in the blastomeres of embryos developed *in vitro* and that these abnormalities need not be consistent between blastomeres of the same embryo (Plachot *et al.*, 1989). Thus caution should be exercised in the interpretation of the analysis from single blastomeres biopsied from early cleavage stages (Pickering *et al.*, 1992). Further experiments are being conducted currently to test the incidence of this type of discrepancy.

METHODS FOR DETECTING GENETIC DISEASE

Genetic disease can be diagnosed at one of two levels – directly from the DNA, or from the synthesised product of the gene (Figure 4.3). Diagnosis at a DNA level requires a knowledge of the defective gene and tools (probes) to identify its presence or absence. If the exact structure of the defective portion of the gene is unknown, an area near the gene may be identifiable whose size or sensitivity to restriction enzyme digestion is altered by the presence of the defective gene (restriction enzyme analysis and gene linkage). However, since only one or very few cells can be taken safely for analysis, the amount of DNA that is available from the tiny biopsy is miniscule. Thus the techniques employed for analysis have to be exquisitely sensitive.

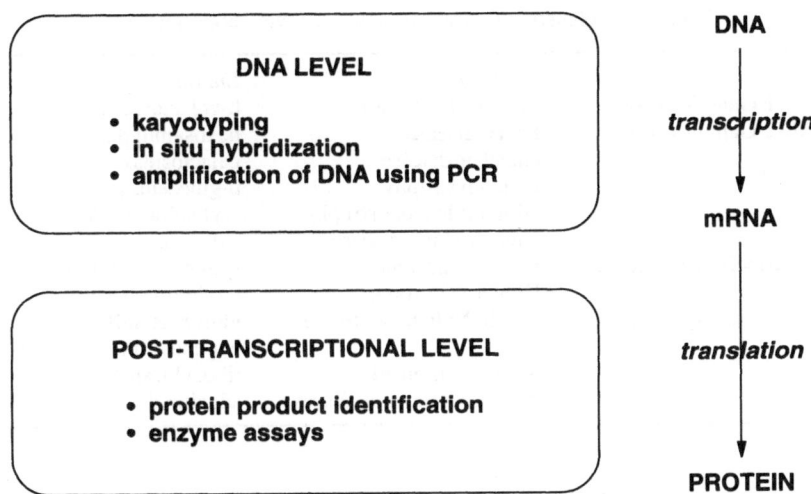

Figure 4.3   Methods for detection of organic disease

Until relatively recently, direct analysis was not possible other than by use of *in situ* hybridisation (Grifo *et al.*, 1991; West *et al.*, 1988) where the presence of the relevant genetic locus is identified by the presence of developed photographic grains or fluorescence over the interphase nucleus or the particular chromosome. Now, however, the polymerase chain reaction (PCR) can be used to achieve a manyfold amplification of minute amounts of DNA (Erlich *et al.*, 1988). Using PCR, areas of the DNA containing defective genes can be amplified after extraction from single cells in sufficient amounts to be characterised using standard laboratory techniques (Li *et al.*, 1988). Although amplification of the DNA using the polymerase chain reaction can overcome this difficulty, faithfulness of amplification and contamination are serious confounding problems (see below).

Alternatively, the genetic disease may be diagnosed at a post-transcriptional level by measuring the intracellular product of messenger RNA (mRNA) translation (Braude, 1991). In general due to the small size of the biopsy, the protein product synthesised by the relevant gene is present in such small amounts that it cannot be identified directly. However, if the protein is an enzyme, microassays are available which enable their detection, provided that the appropriate substrate for the enzyme reaction is known. A number of genetic disorders are caused by defective or deficient enzymes (Table 4.1). However, these enzyme assays would be useful for preimplantation diagnosis of disease only if the embryonic enzyme activity

Table 4.1   Genetic diseases caused by enzyme abnormalities

Group	Syndrome	Enzyme
GM1 Gangliosidoses	Tay–Sachs disease	ß-galactosidase
GM2 Ganglisidoses	Fabry disease	hexosaminidase
	Gaucher disease	galactosidase A
	Leucodystrophy	ß-glucosidase
	Globoid leucodystrophy	aryl sulfatase A
	Nieman–Pick disease	gal-cerase
Mucopolysaccharidoses	Hurler syndrome	sphyngomyelinase
	Hunter syndrome	a-L-iduronidase
Purine salvage diseases	Lesch–Nyhan syndrome	iduronate sulfatase
		hypoxanthine-phospho-
	Severe combined	ribosyl transferase
	immunodeficiency disease	adenine deaminase

could be distinguished clearly from the activity of any maternal enzyme carried over in the egg.

Two disorders (Lesch–Nyhan syndrome, deficiency of HPRT [hypoxanthine phosphoribosyltransferase] and Tay–Sachs disease, a deficiency of ß-hexosaminidase) have been investigated extensively with a view to preimplantation diagnosis in the human (Braude *et al.*, 1989; Sermon *et al.*, 1993). Although experiments in mice have suggested that embryonic enzyme activity should be distinguishable from the background level of maternal enzyme activity (Monk *et al.*, 1987), equivalent measurements of HPRT and hexosaminidase in preimplantation human embryos have not been able to verify this, probably due to a substantial enzyme activity carried over in the oocyte which masks any embryonically synthesised activity (Braude, 1991; Sermon *et al.*, 1993). Currently, this technique looks unlikely to be useful for preimplantation diagnosis of inherited enzyme deficiencies.

The availability of such tiny amounts of material for genetic diagnosis requires the use of techniques of exquisite sensitivity. Inherent in this sensitivity is the potential for failure of the method itself, or for contamination of the analysis by extraneous DNA (Navidi and Arnheim, 1991). Despite its relatively recent introduction, methods for the amplification of DNA using PCR have improved substantially in the past few years. Automated machines are now available which control precisely the rapid temperature changes that are required to achieve reliable melting of DNA, annealing of primers and enzymic extension in multiple identical cycles. However different primer sets are required for the identification of each specific disease locus, and the conditions needed for optimal working differ for each set of primers, and the extraction of DNA may be different for different tissues and cells. Thus, although conditions may be worked out using animal models, or using human cells of similar type, there is no guarantee that extraction or amplification will work equivalently when human blastomeres or trophectodermal tissue is used (Pickering *et al.*, 1992). Meticulous and repeated experiments are required to establish the optimum working conditions for each specific tissue (Varawalla *et al.*, 1991).

EFFECT OF BIOPSY ON SUBSEQUENT DEVELOPMENT

Once the biopsy has been performed, what are the chances of conception following? The prospects for pregnancy following IVF have been improving steadily year on year. Although overall national figures may give the impression that assisted conception by IVF is largely unsuccessful, there is a wide variation between centres which correlates largely with experience and the number of cycles being conducted annually by the centre (HFEA, 1992). Larger, more established centres can achieve pregnancy success rates of over 35 per cent per replacement cycle where three embryos are replaced. Although it would be unwise to replace in excess of two embryos following preimplantation biopsy, as later confirmatory diagnosis by CVS or amniocentesis would be both hazardous and unreliable in the presence of a high multiple pregnancy, pregnancy rates with two embryos have been shown to be almost, if not as successful as three embryo replacements (Bennett *et al.*, 1989). Although interference with the cellular content of the embryo is likely to reduce the chances of viability, the breach of the zona pellucida required for the purposes of biopsy may confer advantages for implantation. Deliberate drilling or incision of the zona pellucida in preimplantation embryos *in vitro* has been associated with an enhanced ability to implant and is being tested as a routine method to improve conception following IVF. It is suggested that the breach in the zona pellucida may assist hatching of the blastocyst (Cohen, 1992). Furthermore, the patients on whom preimplantation diagnosis is being undertaken are generally normally fertile and may have an increased chance of conception when compared with patients on whom IVF is usually practised. Thus the prospects for implantation following embryo biopsy are good provided they take place within a robust and successful IVF programme.

CONCLUSION

Preimplantation diagnosis is a powerful new technique of antenatal genetic diagnosis which is currently under evaluation. Although it may hold many advantages for the couple who are at substantial risk of passing on a severe genetic disease, there are still many problems to be resolved including its reliability and accuracy, the effects of biopsy upon the embryo and fetus, and its success in comparison with other prenatal diagnostic techniques. With these limitations and the need for IVF in order to practise it, it should not be seen as a method of general screening for genetic disease.

References

Bennett, S. J., J. H. Parsons and V. N. Bolton (1989) 'Two-embryo transfer', *Lancet*, vol. ii, pp. 215.
Bolton, V. N., S. M. Hawes, C. T. Taylor *et al.* (1988) 'Development of spare human preimplantation embryos *in vitro*: An analysis of the correlations among gross morphology, cleavage rates and development to the blastocyst', *Journal of In Vitro Fertilisation and Embryo Transfer*, vol. 6, pp. 30–5.
Bolton, V. N., M. E. Wren and J. H. Parsons (1991) 'Pregnancies after *in vitro* fertilization and transfer of human blastocysts', *Fertility and Sterility*, vol. 55, pp. 830–2.
Braude, P. R. (1991) 'Preimplantation diagnosis of genetic disease using enzyme assays', in Y. Verlinsky and A. Kuliev (eds), *Preimplantation Genetics* (New York: Plenum) pp. 113–9.
Braude, P. R., M. Monk, S. J. Pickering *et al.* (1989) 'Measurement of HPRT activity in the human unfertilized oocyte and pre-embryo', *Prenatal Diagnosis*, vol. 9, pp. 839–850.
Buster, J. C., M. Bustillo, I. A. Rodi *et al.* (1985) 'Biologic and morphologic description of donated human ova recovered by non-surgical uterine lavage', *American Journal of Obstetrics and Gynecology*, vol. 153, pp. 211–7.
Cohen, J. (1992) 'Zona Pellucida micromanipulation and consequences for embryonic development and implantation', in J. Cohen, H. E. Malter, B. E. Talansky *et al.* (eds), *Micromanipulation of Human Gametes and Embryos* (New York: Raven York) pp. 191–222.
Dokras, A., I. L. Sargent, C. Ross *et al.* (1990) 'Trophectoderm biopsy in human blastocysts', *Human Reproduction*, vol. 5, pp. 821–5.
Edwards, R. G., P. C. Steptoe and J. M. Purdy (1980) 'Establishing full term human pregnancies using cleaving embryos grown *in vitro*', *British Journal of Obstetrics and Gynaecology*, vol. 87, pp. 737–56.
Erlich, H. A., D. H. Gelfand and R. K. Saiki (1988) 'Specific DNA amplification', *Nature*, vol. 331, pp. 461–2.
First, N. (1991) 'Manipulation techniques with potential use in animal agriculture', in Y. Verlinsky and A. M. Kuliev (eds), *Preimplantation Genetics* (New York: Plenum Press) pp. 49–61.

Formigli, L., C. Roccio and G. Belotti *et al.* (1990) 'Non-surgical flushing of the uterus for pre-embryo recovery: possible clinical applications', *Human Reproduction*, vol. 5, pp. 329–35.

Grifo, J. A., D. C. Ward and A. Boyle (1991) '*In situ* hybridization of blastomeres from embryo biopsy', in Y. Verslinsky and A. M. Kuliev (eds), *Preimplantation Genetics* (New York: Plenum) pp. 147–52.

Handyside, A. H., E. H. Kontogianni, K. Hardy *et al.* (1990) 'Pregnancies from human preimplantation embryos sexed by Y-specific DNA amplification', *Nature*, vol. 344, pp. 768–70.

Handyside, A. H., J. G. Lesko and J. J. Tarin (1993) 'Birth of a normal girl after *in vitro* fertilization and preimplantation diagnostic testing for cystic fibrosis', *New England Journal of Medicine*, vol. 327, pp. 905–9.

Handyside, A. H., J. K. Pattinson, R. J. A. Penketh *et al.* (1989) 'Biopsy of human pre-embryos and sexing by DNA amplification', *Lancet*, vol. ii, pp. 347–9.

Hardy, K., A. H. Handyside and R. M. L. Winston (1989) 'The human blastocyst: cell number, death and allocation during late preimplantation development *in vitro*', *Development*, vol. 107, pp. 597–604.

Hardy, K., K. Martin, H. Leese *et al.* (1990) 'Human preimplantation development *in vitro* is not adversely affected by biopsy at the 8-cell stage', *Human Reproduction*, vol. 5, pp. 708–14.

HFEA (1992) *Annual Report of the Human Fertilisation and Embryology Authority*. (London: Human Fertilisation and Embryology Authority, Paxton House, 30 Artillery Lane, London E1 7LS).

Li, H., U. B. Gyllensten, X. Cui *et al.* (1988) 'Amplification and analysis of DNA sequences in single human sperm and diploid cells', *Nature*, vol. 335, pp. 414–7.

McLaren, A. (1985) 'Prenatal diagnosis before implantation: opportunities and problems', *Prenatal Diagnosis*, vol. 5, pp. 85–90.

Milunsky, A. (1986) *Genetic Disorders and the Fetus* (New York: Plenum) 992 pages.

Monk, M. *et al.* (1988) 'Preimplantation diagnosis of HPRT deficient male and carrier female mouse embryos by trophectoderm biopsy', *Human Reproduction*, vol. 3, pp. 377–81.

Monk, M., A. Handyside, K. Hardy *et al.* (1987) 'Preimplantation diagnosis of HPRT-deficiency in mice', *Human Reproduction*, vol. 2, pp. 65–6.

Muggleton-Harris, A. L. and I. Findlay (1991) '*In vitro* studies on "spare" human preimplantation embryos in culture', *Human Reproduction*, vol. 6, pp. 85–92.

Navidi, W. and N. Arnheim (1991) 'Using PC in preimplantation diagnosis', *Human Reproduction*, vol. 6, pp. 836–49.

Pickering, S. J., P. R. Braude, J. C. McConnell *et al.* (1992) 'Reliability of detection by PCR of the sickle cell containing region of the ß-globin gene in single human blastomeres', *Human Reproduction*, vol. 7, pp. 630–6.

Plachot, M., J. Mandelbaum, A. M. Junca *et al.* (1989) 'Cytogenetic analysis and developmental capacity of normal and abnormal embryos after IVF', *Human Reproduction*, vol. 4, pp. 99–103.

Sermon, K., W. Lissens, B. Tarlatzis *et al.* (1993) 'ß-N-acetylhexosaminidase activity in human oocytes and preimplantation embryos', *Human Reproduction*, vol. 7: 1278–80.

Summers, P. M., J. M. Campbell and M. W. Miller (1988) 'Normal *in vivo* development of marmoset monkey embryos after trophectoderm biopsy', *Human Reproduction*, vol. 1, pp. 89–94.

Tarin, J. J., J. Conaghan, R. M. L. Winston *et al.* (1992) 'Human embryo biopsy on the 2nd day after insemination for preimplantation diagnosis: removal of a quarter of embryo retards cleavage', *Fertility and Sterility*, vol. 58, pp. 970–6.

Trounson, A. (1986) 'Preservation of human eggs and embryos', *Fertility and Sterility*, vol. 46, pp. 1–12.

Varawalla, N. Y., A. Dokras, J. M. Old *et al.* (1991) 'An approach to preimplantation diagnosis of ß-thalassaemia', *Prenatal Diagnosis*, vol. 11, pp. 775–85.

Verlinsky, Y., N. Ginsberg, A. Lifches *et al.* (1990a) 'Analysis of the first polar body: preconception genetic diagnosis', *Human Reproduction*, vol. 5, pp. 826–9.

Verlinsky, Y., E. Pergament and C. Strom (1990b) 'The preimplantation diagnosis of genetic diseases', *Journal of In Vitro Fertilisation and Embryo Transfer*, vol. 7, pp. 1–5.

Verlinsky, Y., S. Rechitsky, S. Eviskov *et al.* (1992) 'Preconception and pre-implantation diagnosis for cystic fibrosis', *Prenatal Diagnosis*, vol. 12, pp. 103–10.

West, J. D., J. R. Gosden, R. R. Angell *et al.* (1988) 'Sexing whole human pre-embryos by *in-situ* hybridization with a Y-chromosome specific DNA probe', *Human Reproduction*, vol. 3, pp. 1010–9.

Willadsen, S. M. (1982) 'Micromanipulation of embryos of the large domestic species', in C. E. Adams (ed.), *Mammalian Egg Transfer* (Florida: CRC Press).

Winston, N. J., P. R. Braude, S. J. Pickering *et al.* (1991) 'The incidence of abnormal morphology and nucleo-cytoplasmic ratios in 2, 3 and 5 day human pre-embryos', *Human Reproduction*, vol. 6, pp. 17–24.

5 Clinical Methods of Prenatal Diagnosis

Stephen A. Walkinshaw

INTRODUCTION

There are now available many methods of diagnosing fetal illness which range from simple clinical examination, through detailed anatomical examination to procedures directly accessing the fetus *in utero*. Diagnosis is no longer confined to structural abnormality but can include the diagnosis of infection, anaemia or starvation. However, because of the unique situation of the fetus, there are three major problems specific to fetal diagnosis. First, there are problems of adequate visualisation, making diagnostic accuracy less certain than in paediatrics. Secondly, there is the problem of obtaining normal ranges for fetal variables, since the normal fetus is rarely sampled. Thirdly, and uniquely, simple procedures such as obtaining fetal urine or blood actually carry a risk of death to the fetus.

Methods of fetal diagnosis can be considered as non-invasive or invasive, according to whether or not the uterine cavity is broached. Most methods of diagnosis will be discussed with reference to their role in malformation.

NON-INVASIVE METHODS

Ultrasound

Ultrasound can be used at any stage of pregnancy to detect malformation. It can be used to screen all women. It can be used selectively for women identified pre-pregnancy as being at risk of malformation either because of previous anomaly, a medical problem such as diabetes, or because of therapeutic drug usage such as lithium or anticonvulsant medication. It can be used where there is a complication of pregnancy, such as hydramnios or viral infection, known to be associated with malformation.

It is now recommended that all pregnant women should be offered a detailed examination between 18 and 20 weeks gestation (Joint Study Group on Fetal Abnormalities, 1989). The main purpose of this examination is to detect structural malformation. Detection of such abnormalities achieves several objectives. It allows couples choice with respect to termination of pregnancy for major defects. It identifies anomalies requiring other investigations. It identifies a small group of malformations which might benefit from antenatal intervention. Finally, it will identify abnormalities where changes in place of delivery, mode of delivery or timing of delivery may be of benefit. It will alert neonatal and specialist paediatric staff to possible problems, allowing rapid and appropriate use of investigations postnatally.

However, the public perception of abnormality may differ from that of specialists. Once a couple has been informed of a structural malformation in their fetus, the concept that many detectable malformations are of a non-threatening nature and may need little action, is one which is difficult to explain in lay terms. This may be particularly true where information is given by generalists or by junior medical staff. It has become increasingly clear that routine ultrasound screening is not perceived as being an anomaly screen and that the information given to women prior to screening and the organisation of how to deal with an abnormal result are inadequate in many centres. With current levels of expertise and equipment ultrasound has proven an effective diagnostic tool. Single centres have reported detection rates of 85 per cent (Chitty *et al.*, 1991; Luck, 1992) of all major anomalies although larger studies have suggested detection rates much less than this (Levi *et al.*, 1991; Northern Regional Survey Steering Group, 1992). Composite figures disguise the fact that for some abnormalities, such as anencephaly or renal dysgenesis, diagnostic rates are very high, but for others, such as cardiac defects or diaphragmatic hernia, detection rates are disappointing (Northern Regional Survey Steering Group, 1992; Cullen *et al.*, 1992).

Failure to diagnose is only one of the limitations of ultrasound diagnosis. Because therapeutic termination is likely to be an option in many cases, diagnostic accuracy must be high and the false positive rate extremely low. Incomplete or erroneous diagnoses are not uncommon even in highly skilled hands (Davis *et al.*, 1990; Walkinshaw *et al.*, 1992) and can cause considerable problems in counselling. The erroneous diagnosis of exomphalos rather than gastroschisis would, for example, result in the offer of unnecessary invasive procedures to diagnose trisomy, worrying discussion about other major anomalies including serious congenital heart disease, and an overall gloomy view of survival associated with exomphalos. It would not raise the concerns of intrauterine growth retardation or postnatal feeding problems more associated with gastroschisis. False positive rates exist for virtually all groups of malformation, and for many these are more than 10 per cent (Northern Regional Survey Steering Group, 1992). Although in many cases such errors may make little material difference to the pregnancy or the infant, at worst it could result in the termination of a pregnancy with a healthy fetus.

Practitioners need to be aware of the limitations of ultrasound as a method of diagnosis of malformation. They must also be aware that the prognosis of detectable major defects may be different from that of those detected postnatally. This appears especially true of cardiac defects and of diaphragmatic hernia (Adzick *et al.*, 1985; Crawford *et al.*, 1988) which carry a much worse prognosis if diagnosed early. Data provided from paediatric sources may therefore not be relevant, as it pertains solely to infants born with a given anomaly. Surgical treatment for posterior urethral valves has a survival in excess of 90 per cent. However, the overall survival of a group of fetuses with this diagnosis may be only 60 per cent (Reuss *et al.*, 1988).

These sorts of difficulties are especially acute where minor malformations or variants are detected. The controversies over mild renal pyelectasis and particularly over choroid plexus cysts (Benacerraf and Laboda, 1989) illustrate the potential harm that ultrasound, as a diagnostic tool, can generate. Whilst the main topic of discussion revolves round the role of ultrasound in malformation, ultrasound has a central role in the diagnosis of fetal growth problems (Neilson, 1992). This involves not only fetal measurement, but also a range of ultrasound techniques which provide information about fetal well-being. These include examination of amniotic fluid volume (Chamberlain *et al.*, 1984), examination of placental morphology (Proud and Grant, 1987), fetal biophysical activity and behaviour (Manning *et al.*, 1980; Pillai and James, 1990) and doppler ultrasound (Trudinger *et al.*, 1987).

Biochemical Screening for Abnormality

Currently, it is possible to screen serum from all pregnant women to identify a fetus at especial risk of either neural tube defect or autosomal trisomy.

Neural Tube Defects

The use of maternal serum alphafetoprotein in screening and the use of amniotic fluid AFP for diagnosis of open neural tube defects is well-established (see Wald and Cuckle, 1984). A refinement using gel acetylcholinesterase (Peat and Brock, 1984) can distinguish between open neural tube and anterior wall defects.

In recent years, especially since the description of the ultrasonographic cranial and cerebellar signs of open spina bifida (Nicolaides *et al.*, 1986a) AFP has had less of a role in actual diagnosis; the diagnostic sequence now tending to be maternal serum AFP screening and high resolution ultrasound of those at risk. Very high detection rates are achieved in the specialist centres (Campbell *et al.*, 1987) using this approach. However, results reported from the Northern Regional Survey (Northern Regional Survey Steering Group, 1992) where serum screening is not widely utilised, suggest caution in using ultrasound alone as a screening or a diagnostic tool.

Autosomal Trisomy

The use of age-related screening for trisomy 21 has proven disappointing in terms of a reduction in the birth incidence of Down's syndrome. At best, such screening appears to reduce birth prevalence by around 15 per cent (Walker and Howard, 1986). Over the last few years, there has been growing interest in the use of serum markers in the identification of the at-risk fetus. Preliminary data (see Wald and Cuckle, 1987) demonstrated that the median maternal serum AFP in pregnancies where the fetus had trisomy 21 was approximately 0.7 multiples of the population median (MoM).

These low AFP results were independent of maternal age. Calculations suggested that the theoretical detection rate for trisomy 21 could be increased to 35 per cent (Cuckle *et al.*, 1987) using a combination of age and AFP. Subsequently maternal serum oestriol and B-HCG levels were correlated with trisomy 21 (Bogart *et al.*, 1987; Wald *et al.*, 1988a). Theoretical detection rates of around 60 per cent were felt possible by using 'triple screening' (Wald *et al.*, 1988b). Subsequently, many areas have introduced screening based on combinations of serum markers and age. Recent evidence (Wald *et al.*, 1992) has shown that detection rates in practice are between 50 and 60 per cent.

Alterations in screening protocols to include the total obstetric population have been fraught with problems, in particular in ensuring that women understand the process of screening, a statistically complex system. Introduction of trisomy screening has re-emphasised the need for adequate antenatal counselling before any prenatal test but such sophisticated counselling is not universally available. The psychological trauma caused by the knowledge of being 'at risk' of trisomy 21 cannot be underestimated, especially in the younger age groups who traditionally have not considered this problem before.

It remains to be seen whether these programmes will prove to be worthwhile within a more global context of maternity care.

INVASIVE FETAL DIAGNOSIS

There is now a vast array of invasive fetal diagnostic procedures, ranging from embryo biopsy through to fetal tissue biopsy. The choice of test will depend on a number of factors including gestation, the indication for the test, other information likely to be useful, urgency of diagnosis, operator experience, availability of tests, risks of tests and finally maternal preference.

Amniocentesis

Amniocentesis remains the commonest diagnostic test and it is available in every maternity unit. The recommended method is the insertion of a 20 to 22 gauge needle into the amniotic fluid cavity under direct ultrasound visualisation. It is undoubtedly the safest prenatal invasive test, although its precise risks are still controversial. Where the procedure is being undertaken for karyotyping at between 15 and 20 weeks gestation, the published evidence suggests an excess risk of miscarriage of around 1 per cent (NICHD, 1979; Tabor *et al.*, 1986). However, with increasing use of simùltaneous ultrasound, the risks may be lower, and many groups would claim an excess risk of only 0.5 per cent.

The commonest indication for amniocentesis is the risk of autosomal trisomy, whether screening is by age, by serum factors, or by ultrasonically detected anomaly. Amniocentesis still has a small role in the diagnosis of neural tube defects and can be used for genetic diagnosis, especially with the development of new molecular biology techniques, such as the polymerase chain reaction. Later in pregnancy it retains a role in the management of red cell allo-immunisation (Welch and Walkinshaw, 1993). Diagnostically, amniocentesis still forms part of the assessment of fetal viral infection as the virus can be cultured from fluid or viral particles seen on direct electron microscopy. Again with modern molecular techniques, amniocentesis may replace fetal blood sampling as the test of choice for the diagnosis of fetal toxoplasmosis. Increasing availability, on delivery suites, of good ultrasound facilities has resulted in the use of amniocentesis in the diagnosis of bacterial infection in pre-term labour or pre-term rupture of the membranes, allowing more appropriate clinical management. The decision to use amniocentesis following detection of malformation by ultrasound, is generally based on the preference of individual couples and lack of available expertise to perform more specialist testing. Alterations in the legislation governing termination of pregnancy allow termination for major malformation at any gestation. There is therefore less pressure of time to reach a karyotypic diagnosis from a strictly clinical viewpoint. Practitioners need to be aware that quickest is not necessarily best, especially where the indication for karyotyping is not robust. Traditional teaching regards 15 weeks as the lower limit for amniocentesis. Concerns over the safety of chorion villus sampling (see below) have led to an examination of early amniocentesis, prior to 14 weeks and improvements in cytogenetic culture techniques have made this feasible. It is still a developing area, but preliminary work has suggested it is safe (Nevin, 1990) and that culture failures are rare (Byrne *et al.*, 1991a). Concerns over neonatal lung function following removal of a high proportion of the total amniotic fluid volume have not been realised in follow-up studies (Thompson *et al.*, 1991). Despite these reassuring data, attempts continue to develop methods of filtering amniotic fluid at early amniocentesis (Byrne *et al.*, 1991b) in order to reduce the total volume removed.

It remains to be demonstrated that early amniocentesis is safer than chorion villus sampling, or indeed safer than conventional amniocentesis. It must be remembered that early amniocentesis may require more ultrasound skill than conventional techniques, and this may limit its use.

Chorion Villus Sampling

Although first described over 20 years ago (Hahnemann and Mohr 1969), first trimester chorionic villus sampling (CVS) has only become established as a diagnostic technique in the last decade. There are two main groups of pregnancies for whom early CVS is an appropriate option. First, there are women with a risk of specific genetic disease, such as cystic fibrosis or muscular dystrophy, in whom a biochemical or, more commonly, a DNA diagnosis can be made using cells from the developing chorion. It was for this purpose that the technique was developed in Western countries. Secondly, there are women at more general risk of chromosomal anomaly, including families with known chromosomal rearrangements or previously affected abnormal children. However, women are increasingly requesting CVS on the basis of age-perceived risk. There are two methods of obtaining samples, both carried out under direct ultrasound control. Transcervical or transvaginal CVS was developed initially, using a range of different sampling instruments. The commonest in general use is the Portex cannula (Ward *et al.*, 1983). The procedure is carried out in much the same way as a cervical smear, with appropriate attention to sterility. Initial experience showed acceptably low fetal loss rates of a few per cent (Jackson and Wapner, 1987).

The alternative technique is to perform the procedure as for amniocentesis, transabdominally. This can be done freehand or using a needle guide. Again there are a number of different sampling devices, including simple 20g needles, a double needle system (Lilford *et al.*, 1987) or biopsy forceps.

The major advantages of CVS, compared with amniocentesis, are the ability to provide sufficient DNA for a molecular diagnosis, and the speed with which a cytogenetic diagnosis can be obtained. Generally a result is available in 24 hours to two weeks. An abnormal result can, therefore, be obtained at a time when simple first trimester surgical termination is an option. This is more acceptable both in terms of its physical risk and in terms of its long-term psychological sequelae (Faden *et al.*, 1987).

The issues around the use of CVS in routine practice centre round its safety, the choice of route, and cytogenetic reliability. A number of large trials have been reported (Canadian Collaborative Group, 1989; Rhoads *et al.*, 1989; MRC Working Party on the Evaluation of CVS, 1991). The US and Canadian studies suggested an excess risk of around 1 per cent greater than that of amniocentesis, with upper confidence limits, i.e. the maximum possible excess, of just under 3 per cent. In contrast, the MRC trial demonstrated that women having CVS had 5 per cent less likelihood of delivering a live infant than one having amniocentesis. All three studies had methodological and analysis problems, but the certain conclusion is that CVS is less safe than amniocentesis. The MRC trial is likely to overestimate the risk, as many centres were offering CVS for the first time when women entered the trial, and there is an association between operator experience and loss rates (Jackson and Wapner, 1987).

Disagreement still remains regarding the safest route for sampling. Experienced operators using a single technique are likely to have similar loss rates. Randomised studies appear to show that transabdominal CVS is safer (Smidt-Jensen *et al.*, 1991), but doubt remains. What is clear is that sampling should be deferred until 10 weeks because there appears to be a risk of severe limb abnormalities earlier in pregnancy (Firth *et al.*, 1991).

The other problems around CVS are related to its ultimate accuracy. Although accuracy is acceptable, more women will require additional tests than those undergoing amniocentesis. Confined placental mosaicism is commoner in CVS samples (Gosden, 1991) as is maternal contamination.

Where then is the place of first trimester CVS? It still has a role in the diagnosis of inherited disease and this role is increasing with the rapid advances in the identification of the location of many genes. Its role in the early diagnosis of trisomy must be increasingly questioned, especially with the advent of serum screening. It is unlikely that a woman undergoing early

CVS will ever have the same expectations of a successful pregnancy as a woman waiting and having amniocentesis, and counselling must ensure that all the facts are made available.

Late CVS (Placental Biopsy)

Using the transabdominal approach, a karyotype can be obtained rapidly from chorionic villi at any gestation (Nicolaides *et al.*, 1986b). The greatest use of this technique is where there has been an ultrasound diagnosis of a fetal malformation after 18 weeks gestation. Although there may be problems with the analysis in the third trimester (Pijpers *et al.*, 1988), rapid third trimester diagnosis is possible (Constantine *et al.*, 1992). Technically such a technique, with appropriate links with a regional cytogenetics laboratory, may well be feasible in most district general hospitals. Its risks are largely unknown, but may be in the order of 1–1.5 per cent (Holzgreve *et al.*, 1990).

Fetal Blood Sampling

The final diagnostic technique available is that of antenatal fetal blood sampling (cordocentesis, percutaneous umbilical blood sampling/PUBS, funipuncture). Accessing the fetal circulation opens up a vast range of diagnostic and therapeutic options in fetal medicine, and therefore, the indications for cordocentesis are wide. They include karyotyping, assessment and therapy in allo-immunisation, investigation of growth retardation and non-immune hydrops and the investigation of fetal infection. This procedure should probably be confined to specialist centres to maintain competence (Whittle, 1989). Again there are a number of methods of obtaining fetal blood and blood is most commonly obtained from the placental cord insertion (Daffos *et al.*, 1985) but sampling can be carried out safely within the intrahepatic portion of the umbilical vein (Nicolini *et al.*, 1990a). Some workers (Antsaklis *et al.*, 1992) have safely used direct cardiac puncture. Overall, the risk of procedure-related loss for uncomplicated procedures is 1–2 per cent (Daffos *et al.*, 1985, Maxwell *et al.*, 1991). However, in the presence of anomaly, severe growth retardation or hydrops the mortality directly attributable to the procedure is much higher (Maxwell *et al.*, 1991). The incidence of pre-term labour or fetal distress requiring early delivery has not been properly evaluated, but may be as high as 12 per cent (Chueh and Golbus, 1989).

The overall risks of the procedure are poorly understood and its precise role is yet to be established. The use of invasive fetal assessment in IUGR has been challenged (Nicolini *et al.*, 1990b) and placental biopsy may be an equally useful and technically more acceptable test if simple karyotyping is required. The vascular approach is preferred in the assessment and treatment of allo-immunisation (Harman *et al.*, 1990) and is mandatory in the evaluation of non-immune hydrops. The use of cordocentesis in karyotyping remains unclear. It gives a rapid answer (in 24 to 48 hours) and is free of the risk of mosaicism associated with late CVS, but it may be riskier than late CVS in the presence of structural malformation.

Other Invasive Diagnostic Tests

Other body fluids can be obtained for diagnostic purposes. Most commonly this involves the drainage of pleural fluid or ascites for biochemical or virological assessment. Fluid can also be infused into the amniotic cavity to aid visualisation. Finally, fetal renal function in obstructive uropathy can be assessed by bladder or renal aspiration of fetal urine (Golbus *et al.*, 1985).

CHOICE OF DIAGNOSTIC TEST

The factors influencing the choice of diagnostic test are complex. Paramount must be the safety of the test for the normal fetus, given that the risk of abnormality is rarely above 10 per cent and is often much lower. Thereafter, consideration must be given to the reliability of the test in obtaining the required result. Operator experience and available laboratory support will play an important role in some cases. Finally we must approach the question of maternal or parental choice. This is an ethical and moral issue separate from the physical factors discussed above. The role of the clinician is to provide *all* the relevant information to aid parental choice. There may be times when the choice of test will set unreasonable risks for potentially normal fetuses, for example CVS prior to nine weeks in a 25-year-old woman, and fetal physicians have in part a duty to protect their 'other' patient. The final question to be addressed is whether any test is necessary. In a clearly grossly abnormal fetus, many would feel the invasive testing is inappropriate since it would not influence clinical management. However, knowledge of the karyotype may alter postpregnancy counselling. Another problem arising in late pregnancy is illustrated by the finding of duodenal atresia by ultrasound, which raises a strong possibility of trisomy 21. Most fetuses with this anomaly are chromosomally normal and fetal blood sampling or placental biopsy carry a risk of death or pre-term delivery. The question to be asked is not what information can be obtained, but whether the availability of this information would alter the clinical management for the remainder of the pregnancy. In this case the answer is likely to be no change. A fetus with trisomy 21 would be managed in exactly the same way antenatally and intrapartum as any normal fetus with this surgically correctable anomaly. The need for invasive testing at all can, therefore, be challenged. If the anomaly carried a risk of a lethal chromosomal condition such as trisomy 15, then the answer might be yes – as with that information, clinicians would hope to avoid operative intervention for fetal reasons.

There must be constant vigilance not only in assessing the type of procedure, but also in deciding whether a procedure is necessary. That is the current challenge in invasive fetal medicine.

References

Adzick, N. S., M. R. Harrison, P. L. Glock et al. (1985) 'Diaphragmatic hernia in the fetus: prenatal diagnosis and outcome in 94 cases', Journal of Pediatric Surgery, vol. 20, pp. 357–62.

Antsaklis, A. I., N. E. Papantoniou, S. A. Mesogitis, P. T. Koutra, A. M. Vintzileos and D. I. Aravantinos (1992) 'Cardiocentesis: an alternative method of fetal blood sampling for the prenatal diagnosis of haemoglobinopathies', Obstetrics and Gynecology, vol. 79, pp. 630–3.

Benacerraf, B. and L. Laboda (1989) 'Cysts of the fetal choroid plexus: a normal variant', American Journal of Obstetrics and Gynecology, vol. 160, pp. 319–21.

Bogart, M. H., M. R. Pandian and O. W. Jones (1987) 'Abnormal maternal serum chorionic gonadotrophin levels in pregnancies with fetal chromosome abnormalities', Prenatal Diagnosis, vol. 7, pp. 623–30.

Byrne D., K. Marks, G. Azar and K. Nicolaides (1991a) 'Randomised study of early amniocentesis versus chorionic villus sampling: a technical and cytogenetic comparison of 650 patients', Ultrasound in Obstetrics and Gynaecology, vol. 1, pp. 235–40.

Byrne, D. L., K. Marks, P. R. Braude and K. H. Nicolaides (1991b) 'Amnifiltration in the first trimester: feasibility, technical aspects and cytological outcome', Ultrasound in Obstetrics and Gynaecology, vol. 1, pp. 320–4.

Campbell, J., W. M. Gilbert, K. H. Nicolaides and S. Campbell (1987) 'Ultrasound screening for spina bifida: cranial and cerebellar signs in a high risk population', Obstetrics and Gynecology, vol. 70, 247–50.

Canadian Collaborative CVS-amniocentesis Clinical Trial Group (1989) 'Multicentre randomised clinical trial of chorion villus sampling and amniocentesis: first report', Lancet, vol. i, pp. 1–6.

Chamberlain, P. F., F. A. Manning and I. Morrison (1984) 'Ultrasound evaluation of amniotic fluid volume. I. The relationship of marginal or decreased amniotic fluid volume to perinatal outcome', American Journal of Obstetrics and Gynecology, vol. 150, pp. 245–9.

Chitty, L. S., G. H. Hunt, J. Moore and M. O. Lobb (1991) 'Effectiveness of routine ultrasonography in detecting fetal structural abnormalities in a low risk population', British Medical Journal, vol. 303, pp. 1165–9.

Chueh, J. and M. S. Golbus (1989) 'Diagnosis and management of the abnormal fetus', *Fetal Medicine Review*, vol. 1, pp. 61–78.

Constantine, G., A. Fowlie and J. Pearson (1992) 'Placental biopsy in the third trimester of pregnancy', *Prenatal Diagnosis*, vol. 12, pp. 783–8.

Crawford, D. C., S. K. Chita and L. D. Allan (1988) 'Prenatal detection of congenital heart disease: factors affecting obstetric management and survival', *American Journal of Obstetrics and Gynecology*, vol. 159, pp. 352–6.

Cuckle, H. S., N. J. Wald and S. G. Thompson (1987) 'Estimating a woman's risk of having a pregnancy associated with Down's syndrome using her age and serum alphafetoprotein level', *British Journal of Obstetrics and Gynaecology*, vol. 94, pp. 387–402.

Cullen, S., G. K. Sharland, L. D. Allan and I. D. Sullivan (1992) 'Potential impact of population screening for prenatal diagnosis of congenital heart disease', *Archives of Disease in Childhood*, vol. 67, pp. 775–8.

Daffos, F., M. Capella-Pavlovsky and F. Forestier (1985) 'Fetal blood sampling during pregnancy with the use of a needle guided by ultrasound: a study of 606 consecutive cases', *American Journal of Obstetrics and Gynecology*, vol. 153, pp. 655–60.

Davis, G. K., C. M. Farquar, L. D. Allan, D. C. Crawford and M. G. Chapman (1990) 'Structural cardiac abnormalities in the fetus: reliability of prenatal diagnosis and outcome', *British Journal of Obstetrics and Gynaecology*, vol. 97, pp. 27–31.

Faden, R. R., A. J. Chwalow and K. Quaid (1987) 'Prenatal screening and pregnant women's attitudes towards the abortion of defective fetuses', *American Journal of Public Health*, vol. 77, pp. 288–90.

Firth, H. V., P. A. Boyd, P. Chamberlain, I. Z. MacKenzie, R. H. Lindembaum and S. M. Huson (1991) 'Severe limb abnormalities after chorion villus sampling at 56–66 days gestation', *Lancet*, vol. 337, pp. 762–3.

Golbus, M. S., R. A. Filly and P. Callen (1985) 'Fetal urinary tract obstruction: management and selection for treatment', *Seminars in Perinatology*, vol. 9, pp. 91–7.

Gosden, C. M. (1991) 'Fetal karyotyping using chorion villus samples', in J. O. Orife and D. Donnai (eds), *Antenatal Diagnosis of Fetal Abnormalities* (London: Springer-Verlag) pp. 25–40.

Hahnemann N. and J. Mohr (1969) 'Antenatal fetal diagnosis in genetic disease', *Bulletin of the European Society of Human Genetics*, vol. 3, p. 47.

Harman, C. R., J. M. Bowman, F. A. Manning and S. M. Menticoglou (1990) 'Intrauterine transfusion – intraperitoneal versus intravascular approach: a case-control comparison', *American Journal of Obstetrics and Gynecology*, vol. 162, pp. 1053–9.

Holzgreve, W., P. Miny and R. Schloo (1990) 'Late CVS international registry compilation of data from 24 centres', *Prenatal Diagnosis*, vol. 10, pp. 159–67.

Jackson, L. G. and R. J. Wapner (1987) 'Risks of chorion villus sampling', Balliere's *Clinical Obstetrics and Gynaecology*, vol. 1, pp. 513–31.

Joint Study Group on Fetal Abnormalities (1989) 'Recognition and management of fetal abnormalities', *Archives of Disease in Childhood*, vol. 64, pp. 971–6.

Levi, S., Y. Hyjazi, J.-P. Schapps, P. Defoort, R. Coulon and P. Buekens (1991) 'Sensitivity and specificity of routine antenatal screening for congenital anomalies by ultrasound', *Ultrasound in Obstetrics and Gynaecology*, vol. 1, pp: 102–10.

Lilford, R. J., H. C. Irving, G. Linton and M. K. Mason (1987) 'Transabdominal chorion villus sampling: 100 consecutive cases', *Lancet*, vol. i, pp. 1415–7.

Luck, C. A. (1992) 'Value of routine ultrasound scanning at 19 weeks: a four year study of 8849 deliveries', *British Medical Journal*, vol. 304, pp. 1474–8.

Manning, F. A., D. D. Platt and L. Sipos (1980) 'Antepartum fetal evaluation: Development of a fetal biophysical profile', *American Journal of Obstetrics and Gynecology*, vol. 136, pp. 787–95.

Maxwell, D. J., P. Johnson, P. Hurley, K. Neales, L. Allan and P. Knott (1991) 'Fetal blood sampling and pregnancy loss in relation to indication', *British Journal of Obstetrics and Gynaecology*, vol. 98, pp. 892–7.

MRC Working Party on the Evaluation of Chorion Villus Sampling (1991) 'Medical Research Council European Trial of chorion villus sampling', *Lancet*, vol. 337, pp. 1491–9.

Neilson, J. P. (1992) 'Abnormalities of fetal growth', in A. A. Calder and W. Dunlop (eds), *High Risk Pregnancy* (Oxford: Butterworth-Heinemann) pp. 362–86.

Nevin, J., N. C. Nevin, J. C. Dornan, C. Sim and J. J. Armstrong (1990) 'Early amniocentesis: experience of 222 consecutive patients. 1987–1988', *Prenatal Diagnosis*, vol. 10, pp. 78–83.

NICHD Concensus Conference on Antenatal Diagnosis (1979) '*NIH Publication number 80*' NIH, Washington D.C.

Nicolaides, K. H., S. G. Gabbe, S. Campbell and R. Guidetti (1986a) 'Ultrasound screening for Spina bifida: Cranial and cerebellar signs', *Lancet*, vol. ii, pp. 72–4.

Nicolaides, K. H., C. H. Rodeck and C. M. Gosden (1986b) 'Rapid karyotyping in non-lethal fetal malformations', *Lancet*, vol. i, pp. 283–6.

Nicolini, U., P. Nicolaidis, N. M. Fisk, Y. Tannirandorn and C. H. Rodeck (1990a) 'Fetal blood sampling from the intrahepatic vein: analysis of safety and clinical experience with 214 procedures', *Obstetrics and Gynecology*, vol. 76, pp. 47–53.

Nicolini, U., P. Nicolaidis and N. M. Fisk (1990b) 'Limited role of fetal blood sampling in prediction of outcome in intrauterine growth retardation', *Lancet*, vol. 336, pp. 768–72.

Northern Regional Survey Steering Group (1992) 'Fetal abnormality: an audit of its recognition and management', *Archives of Disease in Childhood*, vol. 67, pp. 770–4.

Peat, D. and D. J. H. Brock (1984) 'Quantitative estimation of the density ratios of esterase bands in human amniotic fluids', *Clinica Chimica Acta*, vol. 138, pp. 319–24.

Pijpers, L., M. G. H. Jahoda, A. Reuss, J. Wladimiroff and E. Sachs (1988) 'Transabdominal chorion villus biopsy in the second and third trimesters of pregnancy to determine fetal karyotype', *British Medical Journal*, vol. 297, pp. 822–3.

Pillai, M. and D. James (1990) 'Development of human fetal behaviour – a review', *Fetal Diagnosis and Therapy*, vol. 5, pp. 15–32.

Proud, J. and A. Grant (1987) 'Third trimester placental grading by ultrasonography as a test of fetal wellbeing', *British Medical Journal*, vol. 294, pp. 1641–4.

Reuss, A., P. A. Stewart, J. W. Wladimiroff and R. J. Scholtmeiger (1988) 'Non-invasive management of fetal obstructive uropathy', *Lancet*, vol. ii, pp. 949–51.

Rhoads, G. G., L. G. Jackson and S. E. Schlesselman (1989) 'The safety and efficacy of chorionic villus sampling for early prenatal diagnosis of cytogenetic abnormalities', *New England Journal of Medicine*, vol. 320, pp. 609–17.

Smidt-Jensen, S., M. Permin and J. Philip (1991) 'Sampling success and risk by transabdominal chorion villus sampling, transcervical chorion villus sampling and amniocentesis: a randomised trial', *Ultrasound Obstetrics and Gynaecology*, vol. 1, pp. 86–90.

Tabor, A., M. Masden and E. B. Obel (1986) 'Randomised controlled trial of genetic amniocentesis in 4606 low risk women', *Lancet*, vol. ii, pp. 1287–93.

Thompson, P. J., A. Greenough and K. H. Nicolaides (1991) 'Lung function following first-trimester amniocentesis or chorion villus sampling', *Fetal Diagnosis Therapy*, vol. 6, pp. 148–52.

Trudinger, B. J., C. M. Cook, W. B. Giles, A. Connelly and R. S. Thompson (1987) 'Umbilical artery flow velocity waveforms in high risk pregnancy – randomised controlled trial', *Lancet*, vol. i, pp. 188–190.

Wald, N. J. and H. S. Cuckle (1984) 'Open neural tube defects', in N. J. Wald (ed.), *Antenatal and Neonatal Screening for Disease* (Oxford: Oxford University Press) pp. 25–73.

Wald, N. J. and H. Cuckle (1987) 'Recent advances in screening for neural tube defects and Down's syndrome', Bailliere's *Clinical Obstetrics and Gynaecology*, vol. 1, pp. 649–76.

Wald, N. J., H. S. Cuckle and J. W. Densem (1988a) 'Maternal serum unconjugated oestriol as an antenatal screening test for Down's syndrome', *British Journal of Obstetrics and Gynaecology*, vol. 95, pp. 334–41.

Wald, N. J., H. Cuckle and J. W. Densem (1988b) 'Maternal serum screening in early pregnancy for Down's syndrome', *British Medical Journal*, vol. 297, pp. 883–7.

Wald, N. J., A. Kennard, J. W. Densem, H. S. Cuckle, T. Chard and L. Butler (1992) 'Antenatal maternal serum screening for Down's syndrome: Results of a demonstration project', *British Medical Journal*, vol. 305, pp. 391–4.

Walker, S. and P. J. Howard (1986) 'Cytogenetic prenatal diagnosis and its relative effectiveness in the Mersey region and North Wales', *Prenatal Diagnosis*, vol. 6, pp. 13–23.

Walkinshaw, S. A., M. Renwick, G. Hebisch and E. N. Hey (1992) 'How good is ultrasound in the detection and evaluation of anterior abdominal wall defects?', *British Journal of Radiology*, vol. 65, pp. 298–301.

Ward, T. H. T., B. Modell, M. Petrou, F. Karagozlu and E. Douratsos (1983) 'Method of sampling chorionic villi in the first trimester of pregnancy under guidance of real time ultrasound', *British Medical Journal*, vol. 286, pp. 1542–4.

Welch, C. R. and S. A. Walkinshaw (1993) 'Management of pregnancies complicated by Rh (D) antibodies', *British Journal of Hospital Medicine* (in press).

Whittle, M. J. (1989) 'Cordocentesis', *British Journal of Obstetrics and Gynaecology*, vol. 96, pp. 262–4.

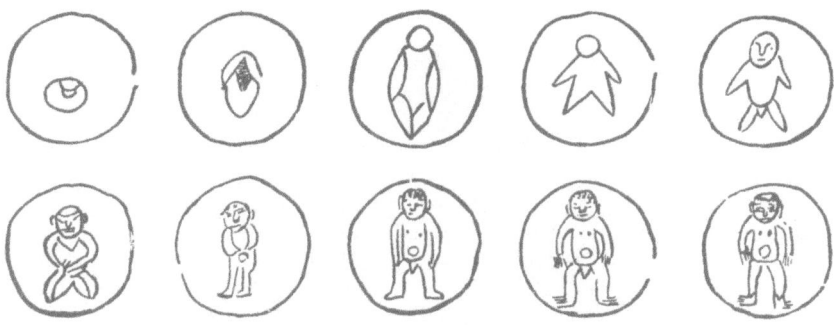

1.1 The human fetus from the first to the tenth month as illustrated in a Chinese text of 1638.

1.2 Mary and Elizabeth: *The Visitation.*

1.3 Seventeenth-century Spanish statuette of the Virgin.

dem angesicht / wie das mit dem rucken / soll die hebam wie obstaht / thün.

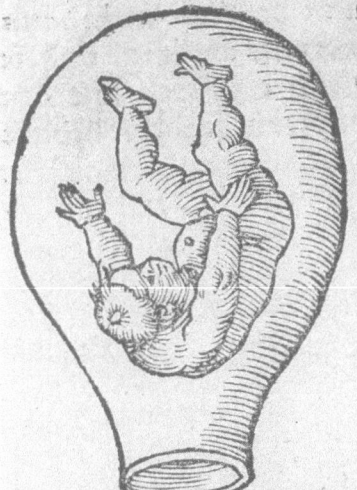

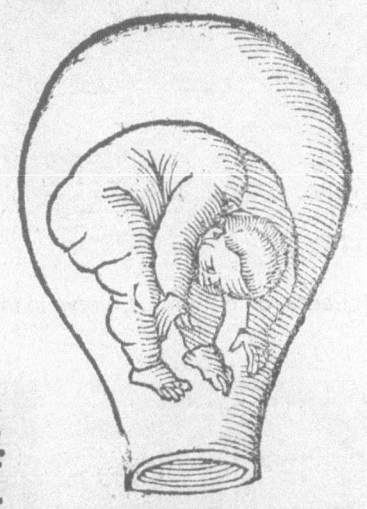

Vnnd so das kind mit eim oder beiden füssen beim kopff kem / soll die hebam das haupt begreiffen / die füß vbersich richten / vnd dem kind außhelfen.

Ob das kindt getheilt leg / oder auff seim angesicht / so sol die hebam zü der frawen greiffen / vnd gar subtil das kind in der seitten vmbkeren. Oder dz kind richten / also / Welche teil dem außgang aller nechst / die sol sie halten vnnd außfüren / am meisten doch das haupt süchen vnd außfüren.

C

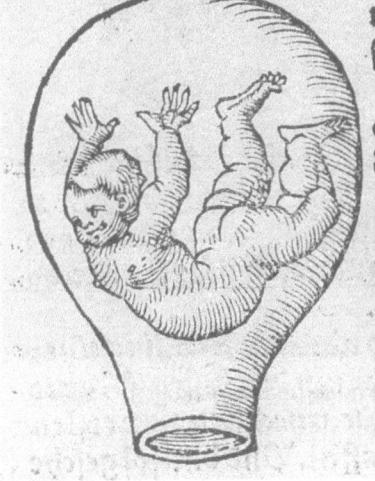

1.4 Woodcut – *Child in Womb* by Albertus Magnus (*c*.1200–80).

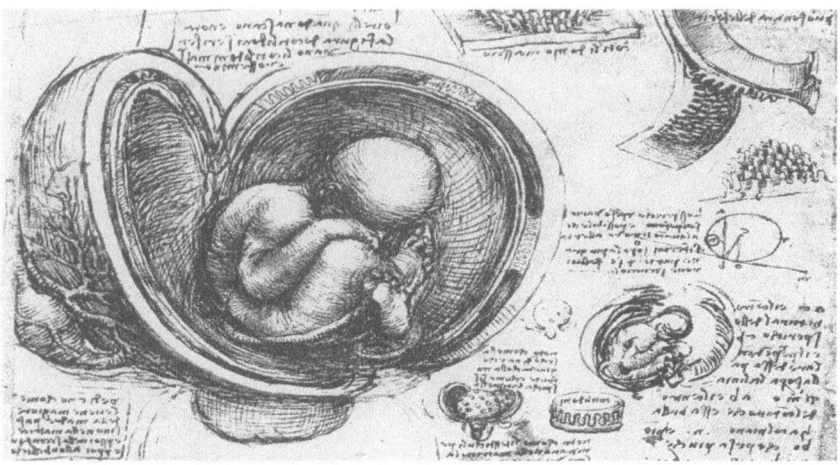

1.5 Leonardo da Vinci, *Embryo in the Uterus.*

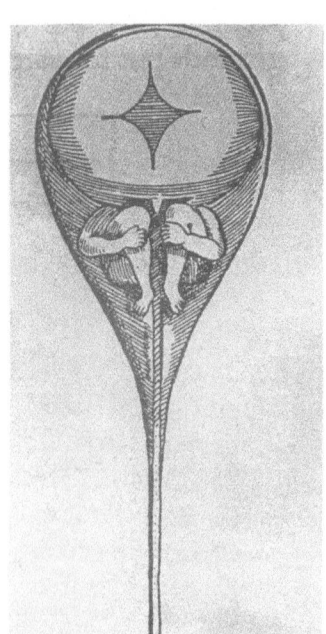

1.6 A human spermatozoon as conceived by Niklaus Hartsoeker and drawn in his *Essai de diotropique*, 1694.

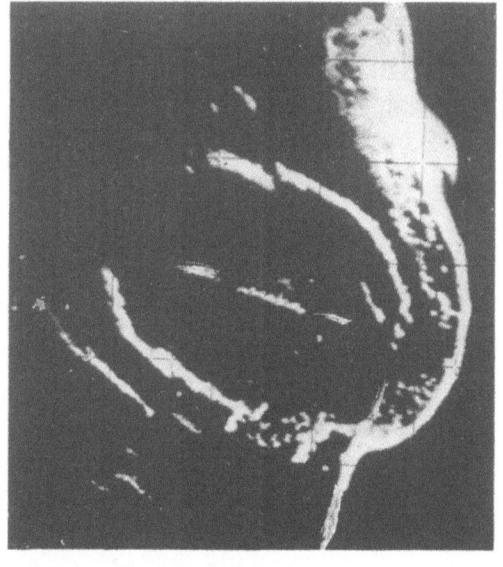

1.7 Sonar image of a fetal skull using a B scan, *c.*1973.

Part II
Management and Treatment

6 Management in a Fetal Medicine Clinic

Tom Lind

INTRODUCTION

The clinical problems which are encountered in referrals to a fetal medicine clinic vary according to the gestation, and their management will be discussed under these gestation headings: during the first trimester (usually 8–13 weeks gestation); the second trimester (usually about 19–20 weeks gestation); and the third trimester (usually 28–30 weeks gestation). To be effective, a fetal medicine clinic must have ready access to a team of experts who do not need to attend every time, but who can join the team when appropriate. The core of the team is formed by an obstetrician trained in fetal medicine, supported by a senior midwife with experience of ultrasound scanning and of counselling. Other key members of the team are the medical geneticist and the consultant radiologist who is able to offer a second opinion on difficult sonar scans. A neonatal paediatrician, paediatric cardiologist and paediatric surgeon come whenever they are needed, to advise parents on the management and prognosis of those babies likely to survive. Finally, the work of the clinic generates a great deal of administrative work and adequate secretarial support is essential.

THE FIRST TRIMESTER

Parents are referred for counselling during the first trimester of pregnancy either because of the age of the mother or of a previous history of a condition which can be investigated by chromosome, DNA, or enzyme analysis on fetal material. Such fetal material can be obtained at 9–10 weeks gestation by the technique of chorion villus biopsy (CVB) in which fragments of trophoblast, which surround the embryo, are biopsied by aspiration through a hollow needle.

Maternal Age

Referral on account of age implies that the mother is elderly but begs the question of the age at which a woman is 'elderly'. Many women who are educated, but perhaps not well informed, demand a CVB at the age of 34 or below, others at 36 and so on. Thus the perception of 'elderly' with regard to obstetric risk varies from woman to woman. One solution is to define maternal age in terms of the incidence of Down's syndrome. Thus, for example, if testing is thought to be appropriate when the risk of having an affected baby is 1 : 200, then this would equate to a maternal age of 38 years. At age 36 the Down's incidence is about 1 : 300 and at age 34 about 1 : 500. A complementary approach would be to assess the risk of a miscarriage in a particular investigation. For argument, if the risk of chorionic villus biopsy causing miscarriage is 2 per cent, then the maternal age at which the incidence of a Down's syndrome baby also reaches 2 per cent would be 43 years (Cuckle *et al.*, 1989). Personal experience suggests that the risk of amniocentesis causing miscarriage is about 1 : 200, which is equivalent to the incidence of Down's syndrome at the age of about 38. It is therefore my practice to offer screening to mothers aged 38 or more.

Once the maternal age at which diagnostic testing will be offered has been decided upon, then the possibility of CVB and amniocentesis both need to be discussed. The relative risk of causing a miscarriage is not the only basis for comparing the two techniques. Amniocentesis, which may be safer to the fetus, is usually undertaken at about 16 weeks in order to obtain sufficient fetal cells from the amniotic fluid. As it can take two weeks in culture to obtain a sufficient cell yield for chromosome analysis, termination of pregnancy (TOP) may become necessary at about 18 weeks gestation. At this stage a difficult and emotionally upsetting procedure is required, the usual methods being to stimulate the uterus to go into labour and expel the fetus.

Chorion villus biopsy can be undertaken at about 10 weeks gestation and a direct preparation from the tissue sample usually allows a chromosome report within 24 hours. Not only does this short interval to achieve a diagnosis benefit the patient emotionally, it allows her to undergo termination of pregnancy by evacuation of the uterus under general anaesthetic. Hence even on such an apparently straightforward indication as maternal age, counselling problems have begun. What might seem to be the best option for the mother may pose an unacceptable risk to the fetus, remembering that the large majority of babies are going to be normal, even in women aged over 40.

It could be argued that the risks of CVB are the same no matter what analytical procedures are undertaken on the fetal material obtained. However, there are other particular aspects which require consideration.

Chromosome Analysis

Down's Syndrome

Down's babies survive more often than those with other trisomic conditions and so the general public are aware of them; many parents are clear that if such a condition was diagnosed in their fetus, they would request termination of pregnancy. However, other chromosomal anomalies may be diagnosed, such as Turner's syndrome (45, X), in which one of the X chromosomes is missing from a phenotypically female fetus. In such a situation, a mother who had not been adequately counselled may acknowledge to herself only that the baby is 'abnormal' and thereby request TOP. But such individuals, while infertile, are usually physically well and of average or only slightly impaired intellectual capacity; termination thus hardly seems appropriate.

Klinefelter's Syndrome

A similar comment applies to male fetuses with an additional X chromosome known as Klinefelter's syndrome (47, XXY). This clinical condition is often diagnosed by gynaecologists in the course of investigating a couple for infertility where the male partner has lived a perfectly normal adult, married life. It would be hard to justify terminating such a fetus.

While it seems prudent to counsel all couples about these and other possible chromosomal anomalies, too much detail may lead to parental confusion and anxiety. Counselling must therefore be carefully tailored to individuals and hence remains as much an art as a science.

Mosaicism

Mosaicism describes the condition in which there are two types of cell in the CVB sample. Thus, for example, analysis of the cells may show a Turner mosaic, 45, X/46, XX, suggesting that the individual is intermediate between Turner's syndrome and a normal female. However, the fetus may actually be completely normal (46, XX), the mosaic condition being confined to the placenta from which the sample was obtained. To take another example, some cells display trisomy for chromosome 2, a form of mosaicism which is usually confined to the placenta. Confirmation, or otherwise, of such conditions comes from longer term cultures of the CVB-derived cells during which the mosaic features usually disappear. Offering amniocentesis or fetal cord blood sampling later in pregnancy are two ways of confirming the reality or otherwise of a mosaic condition. But should initial counselling go into this degree of detail or should a broader view be offered, i.e. that 'other' rare problems can arise but will only be discussed if the situation occurs?

DNA analysis

While the basic value of modern DNA analytical techniques is not questioned, some of its implications need to be considered. Duchenne muscular dystrophy is an X-linked recessive disorder, which implies that if the mother is a known carrier then there is a 50/50 chance that a male child will be affected by this severe illness. Until recent times it was not possible to determine which male fetuses were affected and most women elected to have all male fetuses aborted, keeping only girls. Now, if blood samples are available from other family members, particularly an affected male, analysis of a CVB sample with DNA marker techniques can achieve up to 95 per cent accuracy in determining whether or not a particular male fetus is likely to be affected, thereby avoiding the unnecessary termination of pregnancies carrying normal male fetuses.

The situation is different in a condition such as Huntington's disease (HD), an autosomal dominant condition causing mental breakdown in early middle age. A woman with a family history of Huntington's disease may seek CVB with a view to TOP if the fetus is affected, yet may not wish to know if she is affected herself. By seeking to find the defective gene in the fetus, she must face the possibility that doing so implies that she too has the same gene. It might be preferable to remain in ignorance.

Enzyme analysis

The ability to undertake specialised enzyme analysis on small amounts of tissue (perhaps 25 mg) is established in some laboratories, but the techniques must be reliable if they are to be offered as a clinical service. For conditions such as Gaucher's disease (a deficiency of the enzyme glucocerebrosidase) and Hunter's disease (iduronate sulphate deficiency) the techniques are firmly established. For others such as Menke's disease, a defect in copper metabolism causing excessive tissue uptake, the assay techniques are less well-established and require caution in interpretation. In one family of two sisters, one was said to have an unaffected baby from CVB analysis and such turned out to be the case. In the second sister, who had previously had an affected child, the fetus was said to be affected and termination was undertaken, but later review failed to substantiate the diagnosis.

With such rare conditions only a small number of laboratories will gain experience of undertaking these assay techniques and the establishment of

laboratory reference centres serving a national or international function
would be sensible.

Other problems
Twin pregnancy can cause ethical dilemmas, when a mother who attends
for CVB is found to be carrying twins. Analysis can be undertaken, but
what happens if one fetus is diagnosed, for example, as a Down's and the
other normal? Will the mother wish termination for both the fetuses, knowing that one is normal and if so, should TOP be offered? Should selective
fetocide be offered and if so, how can the operator be certain that it is the
affected fetus which is killed?

Another difficult situation arises when a couple insist on knowing the sex
of the fetus, not for the diagnosis of a sex-linked disorder but because they
only wish to have a baby of a specific sex and would otherwise request
TOP.

It should be remembered that as prenatal sampling techniques are usually
provided by the obstetricians, it is they who are faced with undertaking (or
refusing) any subsequent request for TOP. For that reason a significant part
of initial counselling must be to discuss management policies in broad
terms before the chromosome or other data have become available. Equally,
in the view of the author, if a mother would not consider having a TOP
under any circumstances, it is difficult to justify undertaking expensive
and potentially risky investigation procedures. Some couples argue that
knowing the diagnosis helps them to prepare to cope with a handicapped
baby, but no matter how low the apparent risk, CVB could cause a miscarriage and is difficult to justify for a 'need to know for information only'
indication.

THE SECOND TRIMESTER

In most maternity units a routine antenatal sonar scan is offered at about 18
weeks gestation. The timing is a compromise between sonar yielding sufficient fetal definition to offer the chance of detecting most structural de-
formities, yet early enough to offer TOP if such is deemed to be necessary.
Thus the indications for investigations are usually different from those
during the first trimester, and so are the problems of counselling.

Defects of the Abdominal Wall

Defects of the fetal abdominal wall can be detected during a scan undertaken at 18 weeks gestation, but the diagnosis is not straightforward. A true

mid-line defect (exomphalos) may be associated with heart or chromosome defects, while those off the mid-line (gastroschisis) are not usually associated with other anomalies. Both groups can be further investigated for cardiac defects by fetal echocardiography because it is a non-invasive process; but the location of an abdominal wall defect cannot be defined as gastroschisis with sufficient accuracy by sonar, to avoid the need for chromosome analysis. Does a diagnosis of either condition as early as 18 weeks warrant TOP?

Diaphragmatic Hernia

Another 'hole' problem concerns a defect in the fetal diaphragm (diaphragmatic hernia), which allows abdominal organs such as the stomach, bowel and even liver to enter the fetal chest cavity. In many such cases, the space occupied by the abdominal viscera in the chest denies lung growth and many such babies die as a consequence of severe lung hypoplasia. In the author's opinion the outlook at delivery cannot be deduced from the 18 week appearances on sonar scan, in which case, should all mothers be offered TOP knowing that about two thirds to three quarters of affected babies would not survive anyway? On the other hand, if the condition is usually lethal, should the parents not be encouraged to let the pregnancy continue so that perhaps three out of ten have the chance to survive? What is the emotional stress caused in such mothers by continuing to feel the baby grow and move, while accepting that survival is unlikely? Is such stress aggravated by the fact that some babies will subsequently be subjected to corrective surgery post-delivery yet still die? If such babies develop evidence of distress during labour, should the mother be subjected to delivery by Caesarean section? Such operative delivery is rarely to the direct advantage of the mother and is usually intended to secure a better outcome for the baby. But such babies are already severely compromised from the defect and will probably die. In which case should the parents be counselled before labour about these various difficult aspects of delivery management?

Renal Disorders

Attempts to diagnose the renal status of a fetus are beset by problems, and in the experience of the author assessment of fetal renal status is one of the most difficult and misleading aspects of sonar surveillance. Can the absence of kidneys be diagnosed by sonar scanning with sufficient confidence, before 24 weeks gestation, such that TOP can be offered? Can post-delivery renal function be accurately predicted from an antenatal scan examination of the renal tract? The presence of hydronephrosis (enlargement and dilatation of the kidneys) does not always herald kidney dysfunction postdelivery and the degree of any dysfunction cannot be accurately assessed. As the absence of both kidneys (renal agenesis) is a lethal condition, it could be argued that the mother does not need to consider TOP because the baby would not survive anyway, so why risk a possible mistake? On the other hand, should the mother be told of the presence of a lethal fetal condition? It would make the remainder of the pregnancy a major emotional burden for her if TOP is not going to be an option.

Lung Disorders

Lung appearances can also be confusing. A condition called adenomatoid lung can be evident from about mid-pregnancy. The appearance is often of a solid or cystic mass replacing a variable amount of lung tissue and in severe cases TOP would be an option. In some cases it is difficult to believe that the severity of the condition could regress so much that by term virtually no abnormality can be detected, yet such is sometimes the case. However, in the time spent waiting to see whether or not the condition resolves, the pregnancy could go beyond 24 weeks, and the option of offering TOP may have passed.

Intracranial Anomalies

Brain changes in the fetus *in utero* can be very difficult to assess. The most common conditions are cysts or an excessive amount of cerebrospinal fluid (hydrocephaly). In some instances the amount of brain tissue compressed by cyst formation or hydrocephaly is so major that the baby is likely to be severely handicapped, and TOP is an appropriate option. In other babies with mild to moderate hydrocephaly, it is difficult to give an accurate prognosis concerning the degree of any physical or mental impairment which might persist in the child. The question is not always whether or not TOP should be discussed, because the condition is usually diagnosed during late pregnancy, but in many instances it is the further investigation and management of the birth which require discussion.

Hydrops Fetalis of Unknown Origin

In hydrops fetalis, the fetus can have free fluid in its abdominal and chest cavities, around the heart and beneath the skin. Degrees of heart failure, chromosome anomalies, or conditions causing severe anaemia are all known to cause hydrops and can be excluded by suitable investigations. This leaves a residual group known as 'hydrops of unknown origin'. Such babies usually die *in utero* or shortly after birth, and autopsy seldom provides an explanation for the condition.

To make management more difficult, it has been reported that this type of hydrops may resolve spontaneously so that the option of offering TOP becomes a matter of judgement. Again the question arises: 'if a condition is likely to be lethal anyway, should TOP be part of the counselling procedure?' The end result is the same whether from TOP or spontaneous demise but termination removes any possibility of survival, no matter how remote.

THE THIRD TRIMESTER

Intrauterine Growth Retardation

One of the most common clinical conditions to cause anxiety is fetal intrauterine growth retardation (IUGR). If suspected during an antenatal examination, the clinical impression of a small baby can be checked by sonar measurements of various fetal organs from which fetal weight can be assessed. From charts of birthweight distributions at each week of gestation, the determined weight of the fetus *in utero* can be expressed as a centile. Babies in whom the estimated weight is on or below the third centile of weight for gestation would usually cause concern. The problem is what to do in terms of advising the parents; severe IUGR usually occurs for no diagnosable reason but can be associated with the presence of chromosome abnormalities. One example would be a fetus with triploidy, i.e. 69 instead of 46 chromosomes. Sometimes structural defects, such as cardiac anomalies or absence of kidneys are present. Do these possible conditions need to be diagnosed so late in pregnancy? The answer is 'yes' for two reasons. First, if the baby is thought to be normal in all respects other than size, it might be prudent to deliver the baby before term and in a hospital with neonatal intensive care facilities. Second, if major anomalies are detected such that survival of the baby is unlikely, then delivery by Caesarean section should be avoided, as discussed above.

Demands on the Clinic

To give some idea of the amount and type of work that may be undertaken at a fetal medicine clinic Table 6.1 gives some data from our clinic collected over a 3-year period. Referral rates were low initially but as colleagues became aware of the new service, they have been increasing steadily. The

Table 6.1   Reasons for referral to a fetal medicine clinic

Referrals to a fetal medicine clinic over a 3-year period are shown by the anomaly detected, the system affected or the type of investigation undertaken.

Central nervous system (CNS)	51
Neural tube defect (NTD)	18
CNS and NTD	15
Cardiovascular system	20
Gastroschisis	19
Exomphalos	23
Gastrointestinal tract	17
Abdominal cysts	8
Kidneys	57
Ureters	2
Kidneys and ureters	25
Bladder	13
Limbs	34
Lungs	19
Diaphragmatic hernia	21
Chorion villus biopsy	243
Fetal hydrops	24
Amniocentesis*	102
Cordocentesis	9
Placentesis	106
Other	86
Chromosome problems	38
Total	950

*Not for rhesus isoimmunisation.

total refers to the number of patients rather than visits. Hence some women require only one visit, many require two and a few as many as six visits.

THE BABY THAT SURVIVES

Diagnosing and discussing various fetal problems is not the end of the matter but the beginning. In circumstances where the baby can be kept alive by surgery after delivery, the parents will be subjected to seeing the baby in a very 'high tech' environment perhaps for weeks at a time. Seeing their child with an endotracheal tube to assist breathing, intravenous drips in its scalp or limbs, heated electrodes on its skin leaving small 'red spots' each time they are moved, together with the associated incubator and electronic monitoring produces considerable stress in many parents. The knowledge that this kind of care is 'all for the good of the baby' is often of little comfort; some parents later volunteer the information that if they thought future children would go through the same process, they would not have further pregnancies. Clinical success does not always equate to parental comfort and acceptance. In situations of prolonged intensive treatment the time and care demanded of the mother for the child can put an intolerable strain on the husband/wife relationship and occasionally lead to marital breakdown. Sometimes the seeds of future difficulties can be detected in the response of each parent during the pre-delivery phases. If the parents each ask questions, then spontaneously confer about the advice offered before asking further questions, then a sharing of the pregnancy and its outcome is likely. If, on the other hand, the husband begins to say 'well, I will leave it up to you as you have to go through it all', then, in the author's view, the 'togetherness' aspect may not be strong.

CONCLUSION

Running a Fetal Medicine Clinic is rewarding in the technical sense of trying to reach the correct diagnosis as often as possible and using the relatively sophisticated clinical skills of colleagues in a variety of disciplines to help to achieve a good outcome. However, at the personal level, there is a major need to be able to advise and counsel parents about the best way to manage a problem pregnancy. If such aspects are difficult for doctors and nurses, how much more difficult must it be for the parents. Usually there is no 'right' answer; the essence of counselling is to ensure that the parents remain convinced for the rest of their lives that the decisions reached and the management finally offered achieved the best outcome.

Reference

Cuckle, H. S., N. J. Wald, K. Nanchahal and J. Densem (1989) 'Repeat maternal alphafetoprotein testing in antenatal screening programmes for Down's syndrome', *British Journal of Obstetrics and Gynaecology*, vol. 96, pp. 52–60.

7 Fetal Surgery

Don K. Nakayama

THE HUMAN FETUS AS A PATIENT

During the 1970s improvements in obstetric ultrasound imaging revealed details of human fetal anatomy never previously observed during gestation. Ultrasound examination detailed body size, growth and contour. Measurement of the biparietal diameter allowed an accurate assessment of gestational age, and estimation of the date of confinement ('due date', the anticipated date of birth). Under direct observation the baby moved, breathed, and swallowed. Remarkable images for the first time showed fetal organs in all body cavities. The functioning of the fetal heart, previously assessed by a barely audible heartbeat, could now be visualised as the four chambers of the fetal heart filled and contracted, their valves opening and closing.

Ultrasound imaging detected abnormalities in fetal anatomy as well. With increasing familiarity with normal fetal anatomy, abnormal conditions became evident and diagnostic accuracy improved with experience. Ultrasonographers found anomalies long familiar to physicians and surgeons caring for newborn infants, but now specialists established the diagnoses before birth. Intestinal and urinary tract obstructions were clearly visible as dilated structures in the fetal abdomen. Viscera normally residing within the abdomen extruded out of the body cavity in fetuses later born with congenital defects of the abdominal wall, or entered the thorax in congenital diaphragmatic hernia. Tumours became visible. Ultrasound thus expanded the range of newborn conditions detectable before birth. It added to chromosomal defects found from analysis of cells sampled at the time of amniocentesis, and later from percutaneous blood sampling from the umbilical cord, and chorionic villus biopsy. Ultrasound and chromosomal analysis thus gave obstetricians and neonatologists important information about their future patients.

Today, continued improvements in fetal diagnosis allow physicians to consider therapeutic options (Table 7.1). The choice is clear for anomalies with an effective treatment and good prognosis; examples include abdominal wall defects, intestinal obstructions, unilateral urinary obstructions, and uncomplicated sacrococcygeal teratomas. The expectant parents sit with the physicians and surgeons who will care for their child. The situation is like any discussion with parents before a planned elective operation, with a

Table 7.1   Therapeutic decisions after prenatal diagnosis

To continue with the pregnancy
  Conditions with effective postnatal treatment and good prognosis
  Conditions detected late in pregnancy
  Delivery in maternity unit close to neonatal surgical unit

To terminate pregnancy
  Incompatible with life
  High risk of mental or physical handicap

To attempt prenatal treatment
  Catheterisation
  Open procedures

thorough description of what to expect the operation to achieve, recovery, and risks. The doctors try to answer the entire list of parents' questions, including those that arise later. The patient, however, has not yet been born. When discovery of a critical condition requiring emergency care occurs after birth, however, such reasoned discussions are impossible. Physicians separate the ill infant from the parents, and transfer to another hospital offering speciality services often becomes necessary. Should the baby require surgery, the anxious parents' first contact with their surgeon, a stranger, is by telephone (in the USA). Prenatal diagnosis changes the focus of these conditions from an unexpected postnatal event to one which parents and physicians can anticipate and make plans for.

A tragic and difficult choice arises in the many fetuses with major chromosomal defects, such as trisomy 13, 18 and 21, and those with anomalies incompatible with survival, such as anencephaly. Diagnosis early in gestation allows elective termination of pregnancy after genetic counselling and thorough discussion of medical and ethical issues. Alternatively, parents may choose to give birth to an affected baby for whom there is no cure. Their prenatal discussions focus upon realistic expectations of their child's capacities and disabilities.

A few cases fall between the two large groups described above. Surgical procedures have developed to deal with them, but by the time of diagnosis pathologic processes have advanced to an irreversible degree despite early and aggressive postnatal care. In such cases, intervention before birth offers a theoretical advantage. Surgery *in utero* would allow correction of an anatomical defect before irreparable damage takes place. Examples include obstructive uropathy, which leads to renal failure if urinary tract obstruction is unrelieved, and hydrocephalus, where cerebral atrophy progresses in the

Table 7.2   Diagnoses potentially treatable *in utero*

Obstructive uropathy
Congenital diaphragmatic hernia
Hydrocephalus
Sacrococcygeal teratoma
Cystic adenomatoid malformation
Fetal hydrothorax
Abdominal wall defects
Oligohydramnios

---

presence of unrelieved obstruction to cerebrospinal fluid circulation. In congenital diaphragmatic hernia, the fetal lung would recover in a protected environment following removal of abdominal viscera from the fetal thorax. The placenta would continue its normal function of gas exchange, while the unencumbered lung could resume its growth and development. An inadequate lung would not have to support the baby's respiratory function which is the central problem in babies born with the condition.

A justification for fetal intervention is possible for a short list of conditions (Table 7.2). Obstructive uropathy, congenital diaphragmatic hernia, and hydrocephalus are most common, and each occur at a rate of one in 5000–10 000 births. The remainder occur less frequently. The process of selection excludes cases detected late in gestation, associated with other, more severe anomalies, or appear to have the potential for a good outcome with optimal postnatal treatment. Thus, of the large number of ultrasound examinations, only a handful of cases come under consideration for fetal surgery.

JUSTIFICATION FOR FETAL SURGERY

The work of Michael Harrison of the University of California, San Francisco, defined the criteria whereby fetal surgery becomes justified (Harrison and Adzick, 1991). First, the condition has a poor prognosis on the basis of present-day postnatal management. Clinical studies show that the natural history and pathophysiology of the fetal condition lead to fatalities in the majority of cases. The 50 per cent mortality of congenital diaphragmatic hernia represents such an example (Adzick *et al.*, 1985a). Bilateral obstructive uropathy evident at the time of birth similarly has a 50 per cent mortality, with the survivors being at risk of chronic renal failure (Harrison *et al.*, 1981a; Nakayama *et al.*, 1986).

Secondly, accurate prenatal diagnosis identifies the condition; mistaking an unaffected fetus as having the anomaly is unacceptable. Diagnostic efforts exclude other anomalies which further limit the potential for recovery. Ultrasound or other diagnostic procedures must detect subtle features that identify fetuses with worse prognosis, and thus exclude those expected to do well with conventional therapy. Obstructive uropathy illustrates how other features on prenatal evaluations influence decisions (Glick *et al.*, 1985). Oligohydramnios early in gestation (16–20 weeks) portends a poor outcome. Finding hypotonic urine in a sample of fetal urine indicates recoverability of renal function in fetal obstructive uropathy and in such cases fetal surgery may allow the obstructed kidneys to recover. In contrast, isotonic urine in a similar patient identifies kidneys with irrecoverable compromises in function; fetal surgery often is avoided in such cases.

Thirdly, experimental studies support the rationale for correction *in utero*. Harrison's laboratories used fetal animal models to reproduce congenital diaphragmatic hernia (Harrison *et al.*, 1980a), obstructive uropathy (Harrison *et al.*, 1983), and hydrocephalus (Nakayama *et al.*, 1983). Animals with the reproduced condition then underwent surgical correction (Harrison *et al.*, 1980b, 1982a, 1984). The studies documented amelioration of the induced pathology in models of obstructive uropathy and congenital diaphragmatic hernia. However, although decompression of the cerebral ventricles improved survival in lambs with experimental hydrocephalus, the fetal intervention did not reverse histologic damage (Glick *et al.*, 1984). Critics protested that the models were inexact representations of human disease. Still the results indicated that intervention during gestation would be beneficial.

Finally, fetal intervention and surgery should pose an acceptably low risk to the mother. Experiments in non-human primates (Harrison *et al.*, 1982b; Nakayama *et al.*, 1984) demonstrated that cutting the uterus and exposing the fetus induced uterine contractions. General anesthesia and standard medications however inhibited the contractions, demonstrating that labour and loss of the fetus was not inevitable. Importantly, proper surgical repair of the uterus preserved reproductive capacity (Adzick *et al.*, 1986). Female monkeys could later conceive and deliver live babies vaginally despite having undergone, in a previous gestation, a fetal operation through a hysterotomy.

In the first half of the 1980s, Harrison and colleagues justified fetal surgery for a small number of conditions which were reliably detected by prenatal ultrasound. All carried a high risk of death and disability even with aggressive therapy after birth, on the basis of retrospective reviews of the literature and reviews of clinical cases. Experiments in fetal animal models indicated that fetal surgery might improve outcome in human patients.

By the latter part of the decade and in the early 1990s, however, much of the enthusiasm for fetal surgery diminished because interventions could not demonstrate a clear benefit. Closer examination showed that the prognoses of some anomalies were not as bad as once thought, whilst for other conditions improvements in postnatal therapy made fetal surgery a less prominent option.

APPLICATION OF FETAL SURGERY TO HUMAN PATIENTS

Hydrocephalus

Catheters, placed into the cerebral ventricles under ultrasound guidance, drained cerebrospinal fluid into the amniotic fluid in a number of fetuses with hydrocephalus. Their intended function was to decompress the dilated ventricles and thereby to allow normal brain growth. In 1986 the members of the International Fetal Medicine and Surgery Society reviewed their experience with the procedure (Manning *et al.*, 1986). Mortality among fetuses undergoing the procedure was no different from that reported for hydrocephalic newborns treated shortly after birth (about 15 per cent). Neurological development was impaired in both treated and untreated fetuses, with 34 per cent and 20 per cent respectively being neurologically normal. The results did not compare favourably with treated newborns undergoing conventional treatment postnatally (66 per cent being neurologically normal). The Society reported a distressingly high procedure-related mortality (10 per cent).

Their review pointed out the need for prospective controlled trials. The only comparisons possible were with other retrospective reviews of series of babies treated after birth. Still, fetal intervention for hydrocephalus could demonstrate no dramatic benefit over procedures done in affected infants after birth. A later report could not identify a subgroup of ventriculomegaly which could potentially benefit from fetal intervention (Hudgins *et al.*, 1988). In fact, it included two fetuses with progressive ventriculomegaly *in utero* with treatment deferred until term. Both infants survived and were normal neurologically. By the late 1980s investigators largely abandoned fetal interventions for hydrocephalus.

Hydronephrosis

Like hydrocephalus, the first interventions were catheter decompressions using ultrasound guidance. Harrison devised an ingenious catheter with a twist ('pigtail') at both ends. One twist held its end in the bladder; the other, in the amniotic fluid. The hope was that the catheter would relieve pressure on the obstructed urinary system and allow recovery of function. Urine, a major source of amniotic fluid, would drain into the amniotic space and also would relieve oligohydramnios. Return of normal volumes of amniotic fluid would relieve the compressive effects of an abnormally small uterine cavity upon thoracic and lung growth. In theory, this simple intervention would also correct pulmonary hypoplasia, a major cause of mortality in fetal renal anomalies.

The 1986 report of the International Fetal Medicine and Surgery Society included 73 procedures for fetal obstructive uropathy (Manning *et al.*, 1986). Fetuses undergoing catheterisation had a mortality of nearly 60 per cent and survival appeared to depend mostly upon diagnosis. Most of the survivors had posterior urethal valves or prune belly syndrome as a cause of their obstruction. Fetuses with urethral dysplasia did not survive despite intervention. Urinary drainage into the amniotic cavity did not affect lung growth sufficiently to affect survival, and pulmonary hypoplasia remained a major cause of death among both treated and untreated fetuses. The procedure-related mortality was 4.6 per cent but there were also many procedural mishaps; for example, catheter misplacements, dislodgements, and bowel perforation.

Again, the Society's review could only compare results with retrospective studies in the literature. Most specialists in paediatric urology remain sceptical of the benefit of fetal intervention for obstructive uropathy (Elder *et al.*, 1987). Mortality for bilateral obstructive uropathy is relatively low (20 per cent; half due to renal failure or pulmonary hypoplasia, half from associated anomalies) and dependent upon diagnosis (nearly all babies born with posterior urethral valves or prune belly survive when managed with conventional postnatal approaches, Arthur *et al.*, 1989). As with hydrocephalus, by the later 1980s investigators largely abandoned fetal interventions for obstructive uropathy.

Harrison and colleagues (1982) found that several features were predictive of outcome. A fetus with unilateral hydronephrosis clearly did not require intervention. Even though bilaterally dilated urinary tracts indicated distal obstruction, an adequate amniotic fluid volume indicated a good outcome without fetal intervention. Bilateral hydronephrosis associated with scant amniotic fluid, however, appeared to be an unsalvageable situation, even when an open fetal procedure was performed (Harrison *et al.*, 1982c). Sampling fetal urine and testing its osmolarity and electrolyte content helped to clarify recoverable function (Glick *et al.*, 1985). The appearance of the fetal kidneys on ultrasound had prognostic significance; cystic-appearing kidneys tended to result in a poor outcome.

Harrison argues that decompressing the fetal urinary tract requires a large opening possible only in a direct surgical procedure. He recommends open surgical repair for fetuses with normal appearance on ultrasound, normal urinary function reflected in fetal urine analysis and amniotic fluid volume, and immature lungs (Harrison and Adzick, 1991). Fetuses with mature lungs should undergo early delivery and decompression after birth. Based upon his group's evaluation of more than 200 patients, seven underwent fetal surgery. Three survived, of which two had renal failure. Two of the four deaths were due to pulmonary hypoplasia. Present criteria (persistent oligohydramnios) would have excluded them from fetal surgery. Further refinement of patient selection may improve results.

Congenital Diaphragmatic Hernia

Decompression of the fetal chest of herniated abdominal viscera requires open fetal surgery. Harrison *et al.* (1990a) developed the techniques through hard experience. The liver dislocated into the thoracic cavity ruptured during the manipulation to return it to its normal position, leading to death in three fetuses. By operating only on fetuses with livers which were only mildly herniated or normally positioned, he subsequently had two of four babies survive. Replacement of abdominal viscera may compress the um-bilical vein and may interfere with placental circulation (Harrison *et al.*, 1981b). An important technical consideration unique to fetal surgery is the possibility of enlargement of the abdominal cavity with a patch.

The selection of patients for fetal intervention depends upon the identifi-cation of groups with poor prognosis despite postnatal care, particularly polyhydramnios (Adzick *et al.*, 1985a). However experience has since grown in new therapeutic techniques, such as extracorporeal membrane oxygenation (ECMO). Although some major centres have not noted im-provements in overall mortality (Adzick *et al.*, 1989), others have shown improved survival with ECMO (Heiss *et al.*, 1989). Others recently advo-cated an intentional delay in the treatment of congenital diaphragmatic hernia, in direct contrast to the traditional surgical ethic of early operation and of which fetal surgery is the logical extension (Langer *et al.*, 1988). The delayed approach results in no improvements of survival, and some babies die without an attempt at operation. Those who survive the period of 'preoperative stabilisation', however, may be in better physiological shape to withstand surgery (Sakai *et al.*, 1987; Nakayama *et al.*, 1991a). Refine-ments in postnatal care also begin to select babies with previously poor prognosis who may begin to have an improved survival. They therefore may not require fetal intervention. Selection criteria for fetal surgery and postnatal care approaches must undergo continuing re-examination.

Fetal Tumours

In most cases effectively treated after birth, sacrococcygeal teratoma may cause death *in utero*. Circulation through the tumour may shunt flow away from the placenta, leading to high output cardiac failure. Hydrops and placentomegaly reflect fetal distress and thus identify fetuses at risk (Flake *et al.*, 1986). Interestingly, the fetal condition affects the mother, who may suffer pre-eclampsia and pulmonary edema, a syndrome called 'mirror syndrome'. The mother does not recover until delivery. Harrison removed a sacrococcygeal teratoma *in utero* in a 21-week hydropic fetus (Langer *et al.*, 1989). Fetal hydrops subsequently resolved, but the mother continued to suffer mirror syndrome. The mother recovered after caesarean delivery 12 days later, but the baby died from respiratory insufficiency associated with prematurity.

Cystic adenomatoid malformation, a congenital intrathoracic tumour, may cause fatal respiratory insufficiency after birth. Like sacroccygeal teratoma, hydrops and placentomegaly identify a fetus with a poor outcome (Adzick *et al.*, 1985b). Harrison removed such a tumour from a 27-week fetus, with hydrops (Harrison *et al.*, 1990b). However, the mother, suffering from mirror syndrome, continued to do poorly. She recovered after caesarean delivery six weeks later, but the baby died, again from prematurity.

Recent experience suggests that hydropic fetuses with fetal tumours do not uniformly have a fatal outcome. Two with hydrops and sacrococcygeal teratoma survived, with pulmonary and renal function improving dramatically after removal of the tumour (Nakayama *et al.*, 1991b). Delivery of the infants took place at 30 and 35 weeks, allowing lung maturation beyond that possible in Harrison's cases. Mirror syndrome, present in one mother, resolved after delivery. An alternative approach to fetal removal of a sacrococcygeal teratoma, therefore, may be to wait until lungs mature if the maternal condition will allow.

FUTURE OF FETAL SURGERY

Harrison and colleagues have developed most of our present day concepts of prenatal management of surgical conditions of the newborn. Their group is the only one consistently performing open procedures on the fetus. As noted by O'Neill, most centres would do better to refer their patients or do nothing at all (O'Neill, 1991).

Continuing refinements in patient selection have equal importance to the refinements in fetal surgical techniques. For a given condition, fetal surgery becomes a consideration for a selected few who would have a dismal prognosis with optimal postnatal management. Improvements in postnatal care may influence the application of prenatal interventions. The development of fetal surgery therefore depends upon the continued development of postnatal care.

References

Adzick, N. S., M. R. Harrison, P. L. Glick *et al.* (1985a) 'Diaphragmatic hernia in the fetus: prenatal diagnosis and outcome in 94 cases', *Journal of Pediatric Surgery*, vol. 20, pp. 357–61.
Adzick, N. S., M. R. Harrison, P. L. Glick *et al.* (1985b) 'Fetal cystic adenomatoid malformation: prenatal diagnosis and natural history', *Journal of Pediatric Surgery*, vol. 20, pp. 483–8.
Adzick, N. S., M. R. Harrison, M. Seron-Ferre *et al.* (1986) 'Fetal surgery in the primate. III. Maternal outcome after fetal surgery', *Journal of Pediatric Surgery*, vol. 21, pp. 477–80.
Adzick, N. S., J. P. Vacanti, C. W. Lillehei *et al.* (1989) 'Fetal diaphragmatic hernia: Ultrasound diagnosis and clinical outcome in 38 cases from a single medical center', *Journal of Pediatric Surgery*, vol. 24, pp. 654–8.
Arthur, R. J., H. C. Irving, D. F. M. Thomas *et al.* (1989) 'Bilateral fetal uropathy: What is the outlook?', *British Medical Journal*, vol. 298, pp. 1419–20.
Elder, J. S., J. W. Duckett and H. M. Snyder (1987) 'Intervention for fetal obstructive uropathy: has it been effective?', *Lancet*, vol. ii, p. 1007.
Flake, A. W., M. R. Harrison, N. S. Adzick *et al.* (1986) 'Fetal sacrococcygeal teratoma', *Journal of Pediatric Surgery*, vol. 21, pp. 563–6.
Glick, P. L., M. R. Harrison, M. Halks-Miller *et al.* (1984) 'Correction of congenital hydrocephalus *in utero*. II. Efficacy of *in utero* shunting', *Journal of Pediatric Surgery*, vol. 19, pp. 870–81.
Glick, P. L., M. R. Harrison, M. S. Golbus *et al.* (1985) 'Management of the fetus with congenital hydronephrosis. II. Prognostic criteria and selection for treatment', *Journal of Pediatric Surgery*, vol. 20, pp. 376–87.
Harrison, M. R., J. A. Jester and N. A. Ross (1980a) 'Correction of congenital diaphragmatic hernia *in utero*. I. The model: Intrathoracic balloon produces fatal pulmonary hypoplasia', *Surgery*, vol. 88, pp. 174–82.
Harrison, M. R., M. A. Bressack and A. M. Churg (1980b) 'Correction of congenital diaphragmatic hernia *in utero*. II. Simulated correction permits fetal lung growth with survival at birth', *Surgery*, vol. 88, pp. 260–8.
Harrison, M. R., R. A. Filly, J. R. T. Parer *et al.* (1981a) 'Management of the fetus with a urinary tract malformation', *Journal of the American Medical Association*, vol. 246, pp. 635–9.
Harrison, M. R., N. A. Ross and A. A. deLorimier (1981b) 'Correction of congenital diaphragmatic hernia *in utero*. III. Development of a successful surgical technique using abdominoplasty to avoid compromise of umbilical blood flow', *Journal of Pediatric Surgery*, vol. 16, pp. 934–42.

Harrison, M. R., D. K. Nakayama, R. Noall *et al.* (1982a) 'Correction of congenital hydronephrosis *in utero*. II. Decompression reverses the effects of obstruction on the fetal lung and urinary tract', *Journal of Pediatric Surgery*, vol. 17, pp. 965–74.

Harrison, M. R., J. Anderson, M. Rosen *et al.* (1982b) 'Fetal surgery in the primate. I. Anesthetic, surgical, and tocolytic management to maximize fetal-neonatal survival', *Journal of Pediatric Surgery*, vol. 17, pp. 115–22.

Harrison, M. R., M. S. Golbus, R. A. Filly *et al.* (1982c) 'Management of the fetus with congenital hydronephrosis', *Journal of Pediatric Surgery*, vol. 17, pp. 728–42.

Harrison, M. R., N. A. Ross, R. Noall *et al.* (1983) 'Correction of congenital hydronephrosis *in utero*. I. The model: fetal urethral obstruction produces hydronephrosis and pulmonary hypoplasia in fetal lambs', *Journal of Pediatric Surgery*, vol. 18, pp. 247–56.

Harrison, M. R., M. S. Golbus and R. A. Filly (1984) 'Congenital hydrocephalus', *The Unborn Patient* (Orlando, Fla.: Grune and Stratton) pp. 349–77.

Harrison, M. R., J. C. Langer, N. S. Adzick *et al.* (1990a) 'Correction of congenital diaphragmatic hernia *in utero*. V. Initial clinical experience', *Journal of Pediatric Surgery*, vol. 25, pp. 45–7.

Harrison, M. R., N. S. Adzick, R. W. Jennings *et al.* (1990b) 'Antenatal intervention for congenital cystic adenomatoid malformation', *Lancet*, vol. 336, pp. 965–7.

Harrison, M. R. and N. S. Adzick (1991) 'The fetus as a patient' (review), *Annals of Surgery*, vol. 213, pp. 279–91.

Heiss, K., P. Manning, K. T. Oldham *et al.* (1989) 'Reversal of mortality for congenital diaphragmatic hernia with ECMO', *Annals of Surgery*, vol. 209, pp. 225–30.

Hudgins, R. J., M. S. B. Edwards, R. Goldstein *et al.* (1988) 'Natural history of fetal ventriculomegaly', *Pediatrics*, vol. 82, pp. 692–7.

Langer, J. C., R. M. Filler, D. J. Bohn *et al.* (1988) 'Timing of surgery for congenital diaphragmatic hernia: Is emergency necessary?', *Journal of Pediatric Surgery*, vol. 23, pp. 731–4.

Langer, J. C., M. R. Harrison, K. G. Schmidt *et al.* (1989) 'Fetal hydrops and demise from sacrococcygeal teratoma. Rationale for fetal surgery', *American Journal of Obstetrics and Gyneology*, vol. 160, pp. 1145–50.

Manning, F. A., M. R. Harrison and C. Rodeck (1986) 'Catheter shunts for fetal hydronephrosis and hydrocephalus', *New England Journal of Medicine*, vol. 315, pp. 336–40.

Nakayama, D. K., M. R. Harrison, M. S. Berger *et al.* (1983) 'Correction of congenital hydrocephalus *in utero*. I. The model: Intracisternal kaolin produces hydrocephalus in fetal lambs and rhesus monkeys', *Journal of Pediatric Surgery*, vol. 18, pp. 347–53.

Nakayama, D. K., M. R. Harrison, M. Seron-Ferre *et al.* (1984) 'Fetal surgery in the primate. II. Uterine electromyographic response to operative procedures and pharmacologic agents', *Journal of Pediatric Surgery*, vol. 19, pp. 333–9.

Nakayama, D. K., M. R. Harrison and A. A. deLorimier (1986) 'Prognosis of posterior urethral valves presenting at birth', *Journal of Pediatric Surgery*, vol. 21, pp. 43–5.

Nakayama, D. K., E. K. Motoyama, R. Mutich *et al.* (1991a) 'Effect of preoperative stabilization on respiratory system compliance and outcome in newborn infants with congenital diaphragmatic hernia', *Journal of Pediatrics*, vol. 118, pp. 793–9.

Nakayama, D. K., A. Killian, L. M. Hill *et al.* (1991b) 'The newborn with hydrops and sacrococcygeal teratoma', *Journal of Pediatric Surgery*, vol. 26, pp. 1435–8.

O'Neill, J. A. Jr (1991) 'The fetus as a patient' (editorial), *Annals of Surgery*, vol. 213, pp. 277–8.

Sakai, H., M. Tamura, Y. Hosokawa *et al.* (1987) 'Effect of surgical repair on respiratory mechanics in congenital diaphragmatic hernia', *Journal of Pediatrics*, vol. 111, pp. 432–8.

8 Fetal Therapy

Martin J. Whittle

The development of different regimes for fetal therapy has spanned many years, and strategies have been modified as technology has advanced. The concept that intrauterine life could be influenced at all had a philosophical basis for only a few generations and indeed concerns for the fetus as a patient have only really developed as the risks of pregnancy and childbearing for the mother have lessened. Nevertheless it remains essential that the mother's health is not subjugated to that of the fetus and great care and sensitivity is required in advising and managing these difficult clinical problems.

One of the major challenges in devising methods of fetal treatment is the relative inaccessibility of the fetus. Ultrasound has made a major contribution in terms of our ability to see the fetus but nevertheless it still only provides a relatively limited view. The physiological barrier formed by the placenta may, in many ways, be even more formidable and certainly our understanding of the pharmacology of the materno-fetal blood barrier is limited.

The concept of the fetus as a patient in its own right demands the same precision in diagnosis as for the adult and indeed in many ways a similar approach is appropriate. Thus there is a need for a good history and a careful examination before any action ensues. As in all aspects of obstetrics the previous history can be extremely important since it is a basic rule that events do tend to repeat themselves and this applies not only to fetal abnormalities but also growth retardation and conditions such as rhesus isoimmunisation.

DIAGNOSIS

The developments in ultrasound technology over recent years have transformed our ability to visualise the fetus and to determine not only its structure but also its well-being. Features such as the volume of amniotic fluid, fetal activity and the placental appearances help to assess fetal condition and provide the ultrasonographer with considerable information about the baby.

In addition, it is now possible to collect tissue either from the developing placenta (chorionic villus sample), fetal blood or other fetal fluids (e.g.

urine or chest fluid) all of which may contribute to the accuracy of the eventual diagnosis. These invasive techniques have already been described (Walkinshaw, p. 73) and add another dimension to our diagnostic ability. They are not, however, without risk and they should be performed only by suitably trained individuals, ideally working in centres in which all the necessary back-up facilities are available. Their development has largely resulted from the advances in ultrasound, and also in fetoscopy which provided a vehicle for them but is not now generally used.

Although the issues of diagnosis and maternal safety are important, it is the prognosis of the condition about which the parents have most concern and upon which it is often most difficult to advise. Whilst it is usually easy to predict the short term risks for any particular procedure, long term follow-up is often limited and fragmented. How the treated children will be at five or ten years of age is usually unclear and the difficulties are exaggerated by the relatively small numbers which will contribute to any one unit's experience. Furthermore the natural history of many conditions remains uncertain, not only in infancy and childhood but particularly in the fetus.

This paper addresses those circumstances under which some treatment options exist and explores, where possible, their results.

MEDICAL TREATMENT

Correction of Functional Disorders

Fetal Lung Immaturity
The amelioration of fetal lung immaturity by giving the mother steroids, usually in the form of beta- or dexamethasone, was probably one of the first examples of intrauterine therapy. The initial observations were made by Liggins and Howie (1972) whose classic paper indicated that in those babies at less than 34 weeks gestation the maternal administration of steroids significantly reduced the incidence of respiratory distress syndrome and the death and morbidity associated with this condition. That paper was a milestone and although others questioned the role of steroids, subsequent studies confirmed their overall value (Crowley *et al.*, 1990). Interestingly this era saw the rapid improvement in neonatal care, particularly of the very pre-term infant, which seemed to reduce the need for this form of pretreatment, although most still consider it beneficial. One strong point in its favour is that the treatment appears to have few side effects and only under special circumstances may the mother be at risk.

Exactly how these steroids work is still unclear in spite of extensive research. More recent evidence has suggested that they are less likely to work before 28 weeks, at which time thyroxine given intra-amniotically or stimulated by the use of thyroid stimulating hormone, given to the mother, may be effective (Zegher *et al.*, 1992). Further studies are required to establish the efficacy of this approach.

Correction of Fetal Arrhythmias

Disorders of fetal cardiac rhythm, either bradycardias or tachycardias, are rare but can be severe enough to produce evidence of heart failure with the development of hydrops. Bradycardias are much more likely to be associated with structural cardiac abnormalities or occasionally the presence of maternal anti-cardiolipin antibodies; fetal cardiac output is usually maintained although occasionally failure intervenes.

The problems are different for the tachyarrhythmias of which supraventricular tachycardias are probably the commonest. Heart failure is a more frequent consequence but under these circumstances *in utero* treatment is an option (Allan *et al.*, 1991). Various drugs have been attempted included digoxin, procainamide and more recently flecainide. These drugs cross the placenta and will often control the arrhythmia. Unfortunately the drugs can also affect the mother and administration directly into the fetal vessels has been tried with some effect (Hansmann *et al.*, 1991).

Whether these drugs should be used in all cases of cardiac arrythmia, or only those complicated by hydrops remains uncertain since the number of cases in the literature is small. Often the presence of an arrhythmia itself is not an indication for *in utero* treatment and, in fact, delivery may be the better option if the pregnancy is close to term. However the immature hydropic baby may well not survive as a neonate and under these circumstances *in utero* treatment may be highly beneficial.

Metabolic Disorders

Phenylketonuria
Like many of the metabolic disorders, maternal phenylketonuria is relatively rare with an incidence of about 1 in 10 000 births. Nevertheless, when the mother is untreated, the condition is associated with a very high incidence of mental retardation and structural defects in the baby. The maintenance of a diet low in protein and supplemented by tyrosine will markedly reduce these complications. Nearly all babies with phenylketonuria are now identified soon after birth from Guthrie screening, or its equivalent, and these children should also be maintained on a suitable diet probably until about ten years of age to ensure normal mental development.

Congenital Adrenal Hyperplasia
Undiagnosed these conditions, of which there are several, can produce adrenal crises in early neonatal life which, if undiagnosed, can be fatal. *In utero* the female baby is at risk of masculinisation. The most common metabolic defect lies on the pathway which leads to the production of cortisol and when present causes an accumulation of predominantly andro-genic steroids. Early prenatal diagnosis is possible from chorionic villus material. The administration of dexamethasone to the mother suppresses the fetal ACTH levels, and reduces unwanted stimulation of the fetal adrenal gland. Unfortunately, masculinisation occurs early in pregnancy, so treat-ment must commence by about nine to ten weeks (Evans and Schulman, 1991).

Methylmalonic Aciduria
This is another rare metabolic disorder which in some cases can be modified by use of cyanocobalamin (Vitamin B12) given to the mother in large doses. This substance helps to overcome the metabolic block and so pre-vents the accumulation of methylmalonic acid. Several successful cases have been reported and long term treatment is by a protein-restricted diet (Evans and Schulman, 1991).

Multiple Carboxylase Deficiency
Biotin-responsive carboxylase deficiency provides a further example of an inborn error of metabolism resulting in severe metabolic acidosis. *In utero* treatment with large doses of biotin to the mother resulted in the delivery of babies in good condition; biotin treatment was continued postnatally allow-ing the baby to develop normally (Evans and Schulman, 1991).

Improvement in Fetal Condition

Aspirin
Some relatively small studies have suggested that conditions such as severe pre-eclampsia and intrauterine growth retardation can be modified by the use of low-dose aspirin given to the mother. It seems likely that the effect arises from the action of aspirin which interferes with the maternal produc-tion of thromboxane, a potent vasoconstrictor of both maternal and fetal vessels. A large study of the use of aspirin in pregnancy is currently under way, the CLASP study, which it is hoped will be completed in 1994.

Indomethacin
As a prostaglandin synthetase inhibitor this drug has been found to have two important actions; the first is the inhibition of uterine activity and the

second 'fetal effect' which is the reduction of fetal urine output and which hence helps to correct polyhydramnios. The latter effect can be construed as an example of fetal treatment but unfortunately it tends to be variable. There is also a possibility that one side effect may be to encourage premature closure of the ductus arteriosus with the subsequent development of pulmonary hypertension. In fact this seems more a theoretical than practical problem although the potential risk acts as a reminder that such treatment should not be used without good reason.

SURGICAL TREATMENT

Correction of Fetal Haematological Conditions

Anaemia

Rhesus disease has become a relatively uncommon pregnancy complication and nowadays is a small contributor to prenatal loss and morbidity. However cases still occur that are not caused solely by the anti-D antibody. Indeed in numerical terms other antibody systems of the rhesus type, especially anti-c̄ and anti-E, and also antibodies such as anti-Kell and anti-Kidd may be as important as producers of severe disease. The effect of these antibodies on the antigenically susceptible fetus is to produce progressive anaemia to the extent that the fetus eventually becomes hydropic, developing ascites, pleural effusions and skin edema. This is usually a fatal state for the fetus even if born at term. The baby is extremely sick, has both ventilatory problems and cardiovascular instability.

In the 1960s Liley realised that intraperitoneal transfusion given to the fetus could be lifesaving in some circumstances, and indeed Liley could be regarded as the 'father' of fetal medicine being the first to describe fetal treatment as such. Intraperitoneal transfusion became the standard method of care for these difficult cases and although many babies were saved as a result, it was apparent that it was of little use once the baby had hydrops.

The development of the technique of fetoscopy allowed the visualisation and needling of the fetal vessels in the cord. Blood could be transfused directly into the fetal circulation and although this was technically a difficult procedure it was successful in treating even the most severely anaemic babies. Hydropic changes usually resolve over a few weeks and although repeated transfusions are required, excellent results are usually achieved.

Thrombocytopaenia

Analogous to the development of fetal anaemia, due to the presence of maternal antibodies, is isoimmune thrombocytopaenia. The condition can reduce the fetal platelets to almost unrecordable levels, in some cases with the subsequent development of fetal bleeding, often in the form of intracerebral haemorrhages, which may occur at any time during the pregnancy. The haemorrhages themselves can be quite destructive, producing hydrocephalus and midbrain atrophy with serious effects on subsequent mental and physical development.

Treatment is possible for this condition both in the form of an intravascular transfusion of fresh platelets, which needs to be repeated weekly, and gammaglobulin and steroids given to the mother. The preferred management protocol has yet to be determined but the treatment plans are a daunting prospect for the mother even though the prospects without treatment are appalling.

Relief of Obstructive Conditions

Urinary Tract Obstruction

The possibility that outflow obstruction in the fetus, usually the result of urethral valves in the male, could be circumvented by the introduction of a vesico-amniotic shunt led to an aggressive policy for the management of this particular problem. However when the results from a world registry were analysed the benefits of the approach were less apparent (Manning *et al.*, 1986). One important message which emerged from this report was that the methods of evaluation used to assess renal function were inadequate and did not recognise the heterogeneity of the clinical problem. It was also apparent that the natural history of the disorders studied was uncertain or unclear.

Undoubtedly ultrasound has an important role in the accurate diagnosis and evaluation of fetal renal disorders. For example one study clearly showed that ultrasound helped to identify 15 per cent of babies with a lethal condition and a further group who had a renal problem which might have given rise to long term complications but which would otherwise have remained undetected at birth (Greig *et al.*, 1989).

Renal anomalies should be investigated systematically and this may include ultrasound and urinary biochemistry not only of the bladder fluid but also of the dilated renal pelvises. The most commonly used marker of fetal renal function is the sodium level in a sample of fetal urine collected under ultrasound control. Other analytes, such as calcium, may also be of value (Nicolaides *et al.*, 1992).

Once the diagnosis is clear and adequate renal function has been ascertained, the role of bladder shunt insertion needs to be assessed. The number of babies likely to benefit from the treatment is small but this remains unproven. However it should be noted that those babies with significant urethral valves who are successfully treated may still end up with chronic renal failure by the time they are teenagers, and it remains a possibility that *in utero* treatment may modify this adverse outcome.

Drainage of Body Cavities

Hydrothorax
The appearance of fluid in the fetal chest can occur in isolation or as a feature of generalised hydrops. When it occurs as a single event it is first necessary to exclude one of a number of conditions including infection, karyotypic abnormalities, anaemia, cardiac defects and occasionally diaphragmatic hernias, particularly of the right side.

Often these babies can be evaluated most efficiently not only by detailed ultrasound examination but also by fetal blood sampling, a single specimen being capable of diagnosing some of the above conditions. Aspiration of the chest fluid and its analysis can also be helpful since large amounts of protein may indicate an exudatic problem while the presence of many lymphocytes may point to a chylothorax.

Whether active drainage of the chest by thoraco-amniotic shunting is beneficial remains uncertain. It seems possible that in the most advanced cases the compressive effects of the fluid may lead to lung hypoplasia which would presumably be irreversible, whereas the less severe would probably survive in any case. Certainly the spontaneous resolution of a hydrothorax is well recognised. Once again the difficulties of developing a logical plan are complicated by an incomplete knowledge on natural history and inadequately accurate methods of diagnosis. A recent meta-analysis (Weber and Philipson, 1992) suggested that the best predictors of a poor outcome include a gestational age at delivery of <32 weeks and/or the presence of hydrops. Small numbers make it impossible to evaluate the role of drainage procedures.

Paracentesis
Although the presence of fetal ascites provides a temptation to drain there is, in fact, little purpose to such activity. The potential causes are similar to those for hydrothorax namely infection, aneuploidy or a major structural defect, and these demand that a careful ultrasound survey is made of the fetus. Of course conditions such as Rh disease should also be excluded but once all this is done treatment by paracentesis has little to offer. Aspiration of the ascitic fluid for diagnostic purposes, however, should be considered when appropriate.

MULTIPLE PREGNANCY

Perinatal mortality is consistently greater in multiple than singleton pregnancies, usually being between three to six times as high. The excess loss is
nearly always due to prematurity but other complications contribute. The
development of vascular disturbances between twins such as twin-to-twin
transfusion give rise to one plethoric and one anaemic twin, an event which
is often accompanied by polyhydramnios and indeed premature delivery.
When the condition develops early the results are usually poor, and if one
twin dies its co-twin may well suffer vascular collapse with the development of intracerebral problems such as porencephaly. Twin-to-twin transfusion occurs because the babies share an umbilical circulation which may
involve arterial/arterial, arterial/venous or venous/venous anastomoses. It is
the different combinations of vascular connections which give rise to the
clinical variety and to some extent explain why some cases do better than
others.

It seems possible that the development of the twin-twin transfusion
sequence can be modified by destruction of the anastomoses and attempts
have been made to achieve this both by clipping the vessels and by lasering
the vessels directly. Some early reports are encouraging.

A further complication of monozygotic twins is the so-called 'stuck
twin'. In this case one twin develops massive polyhydramnios whilst the
other appears to have no fluid at all around it and indeed a diagnosis of a
monoamniotic twin pregnancy is usually made. The situation will usually
result in premature labour and loss often between 22 and 26 weeks. For
reasons which are unclear, massive amniocentesis of the polyhydramniotic
sac can allow equalisation of fluid between the sacs and continuation of the
pregnancy. Again some early reports are optimistic (Saunders *et al.*, 1992).

DISCUSSION

The ability to investigate the fetus and its condition by ultrasound and by
sampling various fetal fluids has markedly enhanced not only our understanding of fetal disease but has indicated potential directions for both
indirect and direct treatment regimens with which to modify fetal problems.
However there have been, and still remain, serious barriers to the development of effective therapies and these include a rather poor understanding of
the natural history of many of the observed disorders. In addition, the
relative rarity of many of the disorders makes an assessment of the effec-

tiveness of various treatment regimes extremely difficult. Good communication between the different groups throughout the world engaged in this type of work is therefore essential and indeed already occurs.

The parents' role and views should never be forgotten and a vital part of treating the fetus is the careful and detailed counselling of the parents. The risks and potential value of a particular course of action must be explained and their wishes respected.

References

Allan, L. D., S. K. Chita, G. K. Sharland, D. Maxwell and K. Priestly (1991) 'Flecainide in the treatment of fetal tachycardias', *British Heart Journal*, vol. 65, pp. 46–8.

Crowley, P., I. Chalmers and M. J. N. C. Keirse (1990) 'The effects of corticosteroid administration before preterm delivery: an overview of the evidence from controlled trials', *British Journal of Obstetrics and Gynaecology*, vol. 97, pp. 11–25.

Evans, M. I. and J. D. Schulman (1991) '*In utero* treatment of fetal metabolic disorders', *Clinical Obstetrics and Gynecology*, vol. 34, pp. 268–76.

Greig, J. D., P. A. M. Raine, D. G. Young, A. F. Azmy, J. R. Mackenzie, F. Danskin, M. J. Whittle and M. B. MacNay (1989) 'Value of antenatal diagnosis of abnormalities of the renal tract', *British Medical Journal*, vol. 298, vol. 1417–8.

Hansmann, M., U. Gembruch, R. Bald, M. Manz and D. A. Redel (1991) 'Fetal tachyarrhythmias: transplacental and direct treatment of the fetus – a report of 60 cases', *Ultrasound in Obstetric Gynecology*, vol. 1, pp. 162–70.

Liggins, G. C. and R. N. Howie (1972) 'A controlled trial of antepartum corticosteroid treatment for the prevention of the respiratory distress syndrome in premature infants', *Pediatrics*, vol. 50, pp. 515–25.

Manning, F. A., M. R. Harrison and C. H. Rodeck (1986) 'Catheter shunts for fetal hydronephrosis and hydrocephalus', *New England Journal of Medicine*, vol. 315, pp. 336–40.

Nicolaides, K. P., H. H. Cheng, R. J. M. Snijders and C. F. Moniz (1992) 'Fetal urine biochemistry in the assessment of obstructive uropathy', *American Journal of Obstetrics and Gynecology*, vol. 166, pp. 932–7.

Saunders, N. J., R. J. M. Snijders and K. P. Nicolaides (1992) 'Therapeutic amniocentesis in the twin-twin transfusion syndrome appearing in the second trimester of pregnancy', *American Journal of Obstetrics and Gynecology*, vol. 166, pp. 820–5.

Weber, A. M. and E. H. Philipson (1992) 'Fetal pleural effusion: a review and meta-analysis for prognostic indicators', *Obstetrics and Gynecology*, vol. 79, pp. 281–6.

Zegher de F., B. Spitz and H. Devlieger (1992) 'Prenatal treatment with thyrotrophin releasing hormone to prevent neonatal respiratory distress', *Archives of Disease in Childhood*, vol. 67, pp. 450–4.

9 Gene Therapy and Fetal Medicine

M. Pembrey

INTRODUCTION

In the genetic clinic, once the couple have come to understand that their child's problems arise as a result of a particular change in the DNA sequence of a fully characterised gene, they sometimes ask whether it would be possible to correct the DNA mutation by genetic engineering. They may have seen articles in the press that refer to the recent successes in making mouse models of cystic fibrosis (CF) (see Wilson and Collins, 1992) and conclude, quite reasonably, that if the normal mouse equivalent of the human cystic fibrosis transmembrane conductance regulator (CFTR) gene can be deliberately changed to a mutant gene causing the mouse to have CF, then a naturally occurring CF mutation in a human could be changed back to normal. In terms of genetic engineering alone, their conclusion would be right. Combine the fact that generating CF mouse models involves genetic manipulation of the early embryo, with paragraph 1.1 of the Report of the Committee of Enquiry into Human Fertilisation and Embryology (Warnock, 1984) – 'It is now possible to observe the very earliest stages of human development and with these discoveries came the hope of remedying defects at this **very early stage**', and the couple can be forgiven for thinking that gene therapy for CF is likely to involve the human embryo. In this conclusion, they would be wrong.

Examination of the clinical needs and how best to meet them now and in the future, suggests that embryo *gene* therapy, at least, has relatively little to offer. That is not to say that other therapeutic procedures during embryonic life (i.e. between conception and eight weeks gestation) will not have a place, but broadly speaking the recent decision in Britain to outlaw the transfer of a genetically manipulated embryo to a woman does little to limit the clinical application of the new advances in genetics and embryology. The one area where this might not be so, namely in women with mitochondrial cytopathies, will be discussed later.

Why is there so much interest in embryo gene therapy? Why do so many commentators imply that there *would* be clinical benefit from embryo gene therapy (so-called germ-line gene therapy), even though it is currently outlawed on the grounds that, until the techniques are perfected, inadvertent genetic damage could be transmitted to subsequent generations?

Genetic Manipulation of Animal Embryos

I think there are two main reasons why the idea of embryo gene therapy has been promoted so strongly in the past. First, the creation of experimental transgenic animals, in which foreign DNA or transgene has been inserted into the fertilised egg or early embryo, is all too often justified to the public as understanding genetic disorders in the hope of finding a treatment. This gives the impression that the same approach is being planned as therapy for patients. These animal experiments are, in fact, designed simply to learn more about the genetic regulation of mammalian embryonic development and to create animal models of human genetic diseases suitable for thera-peutic research. Other experiments have discrete agricultural objectives or are related to the synthesis of a useful biological product.

When scientists first considered inserting a specific DNA sequence into experimental animals, they were faced with the problem of actually getting the new DNA into all or most of the relevant cells. Given that techniques existed to insert the new DNA into the host genome, so that this transgene thereafter was faithfully transmitted to progeny cells, the simplest solution was to insert the DNA into the fertilised egg or early embryo. Starting at this point meant that the transgene often ended up in all the tissues, includ-ing that special line of cells set aside early in development to become the eggs or sperm of the mature animal – the germ-line. Hence the term germ-line gene therapy does not mean a technique specifically aimed at the germ-line cells alone, but just the practice of gene insertion into the zygote or very early embryo. This technique of producing transgenic animals is now performed daily in many molecular genetics research establishments, and of course it is convenient for these laboratories if the transgene is passed on to the offspring. It allows experimental matings of various kinds and saves the time and trouble of repeated genetic manipulations of very early embryos. It is in no way intended as a trial run for human embryo gene therapy. Despite this, the well-publicised transgenic mouse experiment to test whether the Sry gene (sex-determining region of the Y chromosome) could alone direct male development in a chromosomally female mouse embryo (Koopman *et al.*, 1991) led to the usual crop of claims in the media that 'it will almost certainly provide an opportunity for human couples to decide the sex of a future offspring' (*Evening Standard*, 1991). In fact, in terms of the opportunities for human sex selection, it is absolutely no different from the knowledge that the Y chromosome determines maleness;

knowledge that has already been employed for clinically relevant sex selection for 25 years.

The second reason for the assumption that there will be a clinical need for embryo gene therapy stems simply from scientists failing to think through what would actually be the situation in clinical practice. The occasional flippant writing by protagonists of gene therapy hardly helps to reduce misunderstandings. A leader in *Nature* (Anonymous, 1988) questioned the consensus that genetic manipulation of the germ-line should be outlawed by arguing that 'Royal families with haemophilia would no doubt have jumped at the technique'. The author had completely overlooked the fact that a simpler and safer way of achieving the same end is preimplantation diagnosis and selective embryo transfer, which are described in an earlier chapter of this volume.

General education in these matters is now beginning to improve and some credit for this must go to documents like the Report of the Committee on the Ethics of Gene Therapy (Clothier, 1992), which is an excellent non-technical introduction to gene therapy in general as well as the ethical considerations that arise.

Therapeutic Approaches to Genetic Disease: Putting Gene Therapy into Perspective

It is important to appreciate that advances in our understanding of human genetics and the molecular pathogenesis of genetic diseases is likely to have a great impact on traditional approaches to treatment as well as allowing some forms of gene therapy to be attempted (Table 9.1). Most therapy will be applied postnatally, but there are one or two situations in which fetal therapy would be appropriate. Early surgical correction before irreversible damage occurs (e.g. vesico-amniotic shunt in urethral obstruction) is an obvious reason for fetal therapy and is discussed elsewhere in this volume. Another instructive example is hormone treatment given early enough to influence development favourably. It has to be remembered that hormones are usually proteins that when complexed with their receptor molecule in the cell nucleus, actually bind to specific DNA sequences to orchestrate the activity of other genes. Thus hormone treatment is akin to manipulation of gene activity and can have powerful and very specific effects on both development and metabolism.

A good example of hormone treatment of the embryo via the mother, is the case of the embryo at risk of the autosomal recessive disorder congenital adrenal hyperplasia (CAH) due to mutant or deleted 21 hydroxylase genes on the chromosome 6 pair. This example also provides some insight into

Table 9.1   Treatment of genetic disease

Approach	Example
Avoidance of risk factors	Avoidance of fava beans in glucose-6-phosphate dehydrogenase deficiency
Symptomatic treatment	Anticonvulsant therapy in tuberose sclerosis
Surgical correction before irreversible damage: postnatal : prenatal	Ramstedt's operation in infantile pyloric stenosis Vesico-amniotic shunt in urethral obstruction
Dietary restriction of a substrate that cannot be metabolised	Phenylalanine restriction in phenylketonuria
Replacement of a missing or inactive product	Factor VIII replacement in haemophilia A
Specific hormonal treatment of the embryo in the mother	Maternal dexamethasone for complicated adrenal hyperplasia in a female embryo
Removal of a toxic metabolite	Penicillamine treatment in Wilson's disease (hepatolenticular degeneration)
Pharmacological doses of co-factor	Pyridoxine treatment in homocystinuria
Pharmacological doses to overcome a specific malabsorption	Zinc treatment in acrodermatitis enteropathologica
Tissue transplants: to replace (? fetal cells) defective tissue : for enzyme augmentation	Bone marrow transplant in severe combined immunodeficiency Renal transplants in Fabry's disease
Somatic gene therapy	Immunodeficiency (ADA def): gene insertion into blood stem cells

how couples may weigh up new therapies, somatic gene therapy included, versus other options.

CAH occurs with a birth prevalence of about 1 in 10 000. The block in the synthetic pathway of cortisol and aldosterone leads not only to adrenal insufficiency requiring lifelong adrenocorticoid hormone replacement, but excess production of androgens. In the female embryo this causes variable virilisation of the external genitalia with enlargement of the clitoris, fusion of the labia and persistence of the urogenital sinus. As females in every other way, the clinical management after birth that is usually agreed with the parents includes corrective surgery to fashion acceptable female genitalia. This is relatively easy if just the clitoris is enlarged, predominantly the effect of androgens in the second and third trimester, or a difficult multi-stage operation if there is persistence of the urogenital sinus, predominantly an effect of androgens in the first trimester. There are now reports of several pregnancies where maternal dexamethasone therapy, from five or six weeks gestation onwards, has fully or partially suppressed virilisation in females who have inherited a double dose of the 21 hydroxylase mutation (Speiser *et al.*, 1990; Pang *et al.*, 1990). This creates an additional option for couples who know they face a 1-in-4 chance of a child with CAH, typically because they have had a previously affected child, although not necessarily a *female* with the additional complication of ambiguous genitalia.

General reproductive options include:

(a) forgoing further children,
(b) trusting to luck, and postnatal medical management if the child is affected,
(c) gamete donation to reduce the genetic risk,
(d) adoption.

Specific options include:

(i)   prenatal diagnosis by DNA analysis on a chorionic villus sample obtained at 9–10 weeks, followed by selective abortion of any affected fetus;
(ii) selective abortion of just an affected *female* fetus;
(iii) maternal dexamethasone medication from four weeks gestation if possible, to be discontinued except where the prenatal tests at 10 weeks gestation show the fetus is female and affected. In such a case maternal dexamethasone will be continued for as long as is judged to be safe for the mother;
(iv) alternatively, the maternal dexamethasone could be given only *after* the diagnosis of an affected female fetus at 10 weeks, but this is likely to be ineffective in preventing the most troublesome aspects of virilisation.

In the future, it may be technically possible to do some form of gene replacement or enhancement therapy for at least the ongoing enzyme defect and the ensuing cortisol deficiency, if not the genital virilisation, but this will have to be assessed alongside all the other management options, including prenatal diagnosis and selective abortion or preimplantation diagnosis and selective embryo transfer. **It cannot be emphasised strongly enough that gene therapy will complement, not replace, other approaches to achieving a healthy family.**

Putting Medical Treatment into Perspective

Whilst gene therapy will add significantly to the treatment options for a child unexpectedly affected with a serious genetic disease, it may not necessarily be regarded by parents as a solution to the anxieties related to the risk of *future* children being affected. From my somewhat limited experience of couples offered the option of the new prenatal treatment of embryos with CAH, they find the decision between treatment and selective abortion very difficult, with the alternatives finely balanced. One couple decided one way in one pregnancy and the opposite for the next pregnancy. I am fairly certain that if offered *preimplantation* diagnosis, for example, in the future, many couples would persist for some time in trying to establish a pregnancy with an unaffected embryo rather than rely on chance and then prenatal treatment of the virilisation if it transpired they were carrying an affected female.

As medical treatments go, the treatment of CAH in general is fairly effective and does not place too great a burden on the family or patient, but nevertheless some couples still opt for selective abortion. It is worth re-membering that the treating physician tends to have a very different per-spective from the parents wishing to complete their family. The physician tends to compare the patient kept alive and well by medical intervention with the untreated disease state, whilst the parent compares the treated child with a normal healthy child, who has no need to be dependent on doctors with endless visits to the hospital.

I was once party to assessing a paper that reported a study of the risk of a heart defect in children born to a parent who in infancy had surgically corrected congenital heart disease. In the discussion, the authors argued that despite a significantly increased offspring risk, prenatal diagnosis by ultra-sound examination of the fetal heart was unjustified because the heart defects were treatable. They appeared to have overlooked the fact that 30 per cent of the very same babies that constituted their study had died despite 'heart defects being treatable'. In addition to the different perspective that families at risk may have compared to physicians, a mother may have difficulty in telling the treating doctor what she really thinks:

> Thank you for treating my affected child, but actually I am none too impressed with what medical science can do, and although I do not generally believe in abortion (by which statement I mean to convey some respect for fetuses and that I do love my affected child), I would like to be offered prenatal diagnosis and selective abortion, although I can't necessarily expect you as a saver-of-life in general and my child's doctor

in particular, to understand why I still feel this way, despite promises of even better treatments in the future.

Physicians and medical scientists may well have misjudged the desire for treatment rather than selection, and therefore have over-stated the impact gene therapy is going to have. One example of this, to which I took exception at the time (Pembrey, 1984), comes from a 'News and Views on Gene Therapy' in *Nature* where Weatherall (1984) concluded his comments on gene transfection with the statement 'offers major encouragement to those who believe that the ultimate goal of clinical genetics is gene replacement therapy, rather than termination of pregnancy'. Many families I have met over the years would strongly disagree with this statement.

Bearing in mind these points, it is clear that even in weighing up *selective abortion* (let alone preimplantation diagnosis/selection) versus treatment, the medical profession may be over-estimating the degree of shift away from selection that will accompany the discovery of new treatments, somatic gene therapy included. As preimplantation diagnosis becomes more routine, the preference for selection rather than treatment is likely to be even stronger.

Highlighting this limited regard for therapeutic advance, is not to imply that families are increasingly seeking 'perfect babies', a term invented, as far as I can tell, by the media and people involved in the 'public debate' on the ethics of fetal medicine. In the 'private debate' of families at risk making real reproductive decisions, I have never heard the term 'perfect baby' and only rarely the phrase 'perfectly healthy'. Parents talk about their baby being 'all right' or 'normal' and in recent years sometimes specifically state that they are *not* seeking a perfect baby, as if to counter the implied criticism in the media and by some health professionals that parents have become too demanding and choosy.

I do not wish to overstate the case and imply that there is total disregard for therapeutic advance, only that parents may not be as impressed by medical miracles as the medical profession. There is, indeed, some evidence that the demand for prenatal diagnosis and selective abortion by couples is modified by effective treatment and good care for affected individuals, and influenced little by the availability of the test *per se*. The gene for phenylalanine hydroxylase and associated DNA polymorphisms suitable for first trimester prenatal diagnosis of phenylketonuria (PKU) was one of the first to be sequenced (Woo *et al.*, 1983). Since that time and particularly since 1985, prenatal diagnosis has been available to couples with an affected child and therefore facing a one in four risk. As one of two centres who agreed to provide a prenatal diagnostic service for Britain, we know of only three, possibly four, requests. Only two couples actually went ahead with the test. Over roughly the same time-scale this compares with about 40 British prenatal tests for CAH which has a similar birth prevalence and several hundred requests for cystic fibrosis which has four times the birth prevalence. One of the two couples who went ahead with prenatal diagnosis of PKU, did so partly because their children would have to spend much of their life in a country that had no provision for the special diet and regular monitoring. If, as now seems likely, a subset of adults with PKU run into neurological problems in middle age despite treatment, then the demand for prenatal diagnosis may well increase.

Obviously the factors influencing individual decisions are usually complex and cannot really be divined by crude comparisons of the rates of demand for tests, but there is nothing to suggest a tendency for these tests to be requested just because they are possible. To date, there is also nothing to indicate that the availability of a prenatal test *per se* induces a desire for selective abortion where previously a couple would not have wanted to avoid the birth of a child with that condition. Whatever the future developments bring, couples when deciding on future children are always going to be greatly influenced by their previous experience of the condition and the care and treatment their affected child received. It may be that gene therapy will become so effective in correcting any problems in their first affected child that they have the confidence to proceed with a further pregnancy regardless of the genetic risk. Only time will tell.

Somatic Gene Therapy – Strategies, Problems and Progress

There are a large number of reviews of the prospects for gene therapy, even a journal called 'Human Gene Therapy' that started in 1990 (see Murray, 1990); the more recent information in this article draws heavily on the review by Miller (1992).

At present the only kind of gene therapy being contemplated is somatic gene therapy and in the postnatal period rather than prenatally. It is possible that access to certain desirable target cells for gene therapy may turn out to be easier during fetal life, but for the moment gene therapy is unlikely to feature large in fetal medicine. The question of genetic manipulation of the early embryo, and with its alteration of the germ-line, is discussed later. Somatic gene therapy for a monogenic disease raises the same kinds of issues as the trial of any other novel treatment of a serious disease (for discussion, see Clothier, 1992). There eventually comes a time when no further animal experiments, or investigation of the genetic manipulation of the patient's cells in the laboratory, can provide additional information on

safety or the likelihood of therapeutic success. A carefully monitored therapeutic trial is the only way forward. Before this is attempted, certain criteria
must be met:

1. The gene involved must be identified and cloned, and the patient's
   particular mutation characterised.
2. The regulation of gene expression and the impact of different levels of
   expression must be understood. Ideally, until techniques improve, the
   gene involved should require neither very precise regulation nor very
   high levels of expression to correct the genetic deficiency. If there is a
   demand for tissue-specific gene expression, then the appropriate control elements must be characterised and incorporated into the new DNA
   that is inserted into the target cells.
3. There must be a suitable delivery system for the implantation of the
   genetically modified cells.
4. At least initially, the genetic disorder in which therapy is planned must
   be life threatening and have a predictable clinical course, with existing
   treatments being ineffective.

One general potential problem could be immune rejection of the new gene
product for, if the patient has produced absolutely none of the protein up
until the moment of gene therapy, it might be regarded as 'foreign'.

Getting new genes into cells
There are two types of methods for introducing cloned genes into cells,
namely, physical and viral. There are also two different general gene therapy
strategies under consideration. The ideal is probably true **gene replacement**, where the defective gene is removed and a normal functioning gene
inserted in its place by a process of homologous recombination. Although
elegant model systems have been developed, this method still has too low
an integration rate for clinical use at the present time. The other general
approach involves the introduction of an extra copy, or copies, by insertion
somewhere in the genome, or as extra-chromosomal DNA within the cell.
Such **gene augmentation** is suitable for those genetic disorders that are the
result of a functional deficiency of the gene product, and is the approach
that has now reached the clinical trials stage.

Physical methods of gene insertion include: co-precipitation of DNA
with calcium phosphate, the use of polycations or lipids to complex the
DNA, cell fusion techniques utilising liposomes, erythrocyte ghosts or
protoplasts, microinjection and electroporation techniques. Recent experiments have exploited receptors on the cell that specifically bind and inter-
nalise particular proteins. The new DNA is complexed with the particular

protein (e.g. transferrin) and is taken up by the appropriate receptor along with the protein. The main disadvantage of the physical methods is that the integration rate is still low and when integration does occur multiple copies of the DNA are often incorporated.

Viruses have often been used to introduce DNA into cells in culture, the first so-called expression vectors utilising the tumour viruses, SV40 and polyoma. More recently, work in this area has focused on the murine retroviruses, Moloney leukaemia virus and myeloproliferative sarcoma virus, and also on adenoviruses. Retroviruses have a number of features which make them suitable for use as vectors for gene therapy. It is possible to establish permanent, viral-producing cell lines suitable for efficient infection of target cells. The retroviral expression vector is constructed so that the new human DNA replaces the viral genes necessary to make infectious capsules, thereby making the expression vector unable to infect further cells once in the target cell. The *initial* infection of the target cell is achieved by using a cell line containing a mutant retrovirus that can only produce empty viral capsules components; when the expression vector is added to this cell, just a **single round** of infectious particles is produced (see Figure 9.1). This approach can infect up to 100 per cent of target cells and the DNA is usually integrated as a single copy. Once integrated into the host genome the new transgene acts as a cellular gene in that it is faithfully passed on to progeny cells.

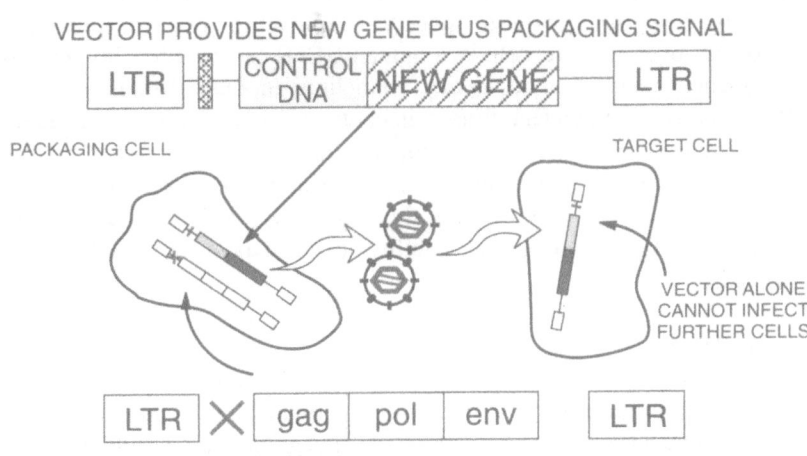

Figure 9.1   Use of expression vector.
Use of the combination of a packaging-defective mutant and the expression vector to give one round of infection of the target cell.

Whilst most is known about the use of retroviral vectors and these vectors are currently the only ones approved for human clinical trials, there are some problems. First, only about 7 kilobases of DNA can be incorporated into the retroviral vector; otherwise it will not function. Many genes, plus their necessary regulatory sequences, are much longer than 7 kb. Secondly, retroviruses appear not to infect non-dividing cells, so this poses constraints on what target tissues can be used. In particular, bone marrow stem cells do not readily divide in culture and yet these would be the preferred target cells for many types of gene therapy. Thirdly, there is a theoretical potential for production of replication-competent (helper) viruses during the production of the retroviral vector based on some form of recombination between the vector and the packaging-deficient mutant or some endogenous virus in the packaging cell. There are ways of minimising this potential and infective virus has not arisen so far in practice. If it did, it should be efficiently neutralised by complement present in the patient's own serum. Additional potential problems relate to the 'random' insertion of retroviral vectors into the genome. The insertion site may reduce expression of the gene in the vector for some reason or the retroviral vector may disrupt an endogenous gene. More worryingly, the insertion may activate a gene concerned with cell replication and cause a malignancy.

Recent work suggests that adenovirus vectors may be useful in gene therapy. Major advantages are their potential to carry large segments of DNA (possibly up to 36 kb) and their ability to infect non-replicating cells including lung tissue *in situ*. Indeed, a replication-deficient adenovirus vector has been used to deliver a human CFTR (cystic fibrosis) gene by intratracheal instillation to airway epithelium in rats (Rosenfeld *et al.*, 1992). Whilst natural adenoviruses, in contrast to retroviruses, are believed to integrate at one particular region of chromosome 19 rather than at random, the current adenovirus-based vectors do not integrate into chromosomal DNA at all. This avoids the potential problem of insertional mutagenesis, but may result in instability of gene expression as cell division proceeds.

Target Tissues

Getting genes into cells and then getting the gene to function properly is just the first step in gene therapy. If a long term treatment or a cure is the aim, then the gene has to be introduced into sufficient numbers of self-renewing stem cells or very long-lived cells of the right tissue.

Whilst considerable attention has been paid to targeting muscle tissue and a clinical trial has been approved for low density lipoprotein (LDL) receptor gene transfer into hepatocytes of patients suffering from LDL receptor deficiency, bone marrow is currently the main target for gene therapy. Haematopoietic stem cells occur at low frequency in bone marrow. Enrichment can be achieved using a system of stem cell 'capture' that exploits the cell surface marker CD34. As indicated earlier, efficient retroviral vector integration into stem cells is proving difficult, and the first clinical trial has used reinfusion of the patients T lymphocytes into which a retroviral vector expressing adenosine deaminase (ADA) had been introduced.

The First Patients
The first recipient of gene therapy was a four-year-old girl who inherited a lack of the enzyme ADA and therefore suffered from a severe combined immunodeficiency (M. Blaese, personal communication; see also Miller, 1992). This autosomal recessive disorder was a good choice for an initial trial of somatic gene therapy, because the ADA gene is a so-called 'house-keeping' gene, expressed in all cells and subject to no complicated tissue-specific regulation. It was known that even slight production of ADA could rescue the T lymphocytes that are particularly vulnerable to ADA deficiency. The girl received the first T cells carrying the ADA gene in late 1990. Now she and another girl of eleven years of age whose treatment began in early 1991 have much stronger immune systems, as indicated by their production of antibodies in response to vaccinations. Regular reinfusions of genetically modified lymphocytes were initially used, but interestingly a large number of corrected T cells have persisted in the first patient for over six months after cell infusions were stopped.

As mentioned earlier, it is difficult to predict whether or not there will be clinical indications to perform somatic gene therapy during fetal life. It is not too difficult to imagine that some tissues, such as the brain for example, will more readily accommodate genetically corrected cells, if these are injected during fetal life. If this sort of thing comes about, the couple may have to choose between gene therapy and mid-trimester abortion following prenatal diagnosis. The earlier in fetal life one goes, the easier gene therapy is likely to be, but the more selective abortion becomes an acceptable alternative to many parents. Taken to the extreme of the preimplantation embryo, the balance shifts strongly in favour of selection, especially as gene therapy at this stage almost inevitably involves the germ-line as well.

Gene Therapy in the Preimplantation Embryo Versus Embryo Selection

Preimplantation diagnosis of genetic disorders by embryo biopsy and DNA analysis has already been described in an earlier chapter. Despite the technical problems still to be overcome (not least the low success rate of IVF as a means of conceiving), preimplantation diagnosis is likely to be a realistic option in the future for most couples facing a known genetic risk. The great majority of couples facing a genetic risk for their offspring can produce a winning combination of their own genes. For autosomal dominant inheritance, where one parent carries the mutation, the offspring risk is 50 per cent. This means that with five preimplantation embryos there is a 97 per cent chance that *at least* one 'unaffected' embryo will be obtained. With autosomal recessive inheritance the risk of an affected embryo is 25 per cent, giving 98.5 per cent chance of getting *at least* one unaffected in a collection of three preimplantation embryos. Given the current widely accepted practice of generating several embryos *in vitro* simultaneously, the option of embryo selection by preimplantation genetic diagnosis is going to be feasible. Indeed, both preimplantation embryo sexing (Handyside *et al.*, 1990) and cystic fibrosis exclusion (Handyside *et al.*, 1992) have already been performed as part of clinical trials.

Imagine the clinical situation in which a couple are facing a one in four risk of their child being born with cystic fibrosis. A clinical embryologist contemplating gene therapy on the preimplantation embryo will first have to diagnose whether the embryo in question is homozygous for the cystic fibrosis mutation. If that were the case, the couple would have a stark choice; to be the first to have transferred a genetically manipulated embryo in the hope that the experiment will lead to the birth of a healthy baby, or select another embryo that has a winning combination of their own normal genes. For both practical and ethical reasons, I think the choice will always be selection.

Even if embryo gene therapy were planned, most practical situations I can think of would require several embryos to be generated in the first place, given the two-stage procedure of first finding an affected embryo and then successfully treating it. It has to be remembered that a second diagnostic biopsy would be necessary before implantation to check that the gene insertion had worked. Since the success rate of producing undamaged 'corrected' embryos would be (much) less than 100 per cent, I believe one would have to aim for the treatment of several affected embryos. The process of finding these affected embryos in the first place is very likely to reveal unaffected embryos. If it is desirable to transfer a 'corrected' embryo with less than certainty that the baby will escape cystic fibrosis, surely it is even more desirable to transfer the unaffected embryo that does not have the potential to produce a baby with cystic fibrosis? If there is a theoretical small risk of damaging the preimplantation embryo by biopsy of one of its cells, then it is clearly more risky to perform two such biopsies plus a gene insertion procedure. Thus, where the chance of a couple producing an unaffected embryo equals or is greater than that of producing an affected embryo, I have been unable to imagine any situation that would constitute a reasonable request for preimplantation gene therapy rather than embryo selection.

Couples Who Cannot Produce a Winning Combination of Genes

Having, on balance, supported the current ban on preimplantation embryo gene therapy, I am duty bound to draw attention to some unusual genetic circumstances in which *all* the offspring are at risk of genetic disease. What are the options for these families and are they likely to regard the current ban as closing the door on their dream of normal healthy children?

Profound hearing loss, present at birth and therefore interfering with the easy acquisition of speech, is usually inherited in an autosomal recessive manner. This means that a proportion of couples where both are profoundly deaf (but not all because different *gene loci* can be involved) will produce only deaf children. Whilst the same principle applies to all autosomal recessive disorders, the probability of similarly affected people marrying is usually extremely small. Profound hearing loss, and to a lesser extent blindness, tends to be an exception, being a disorder that draws similarly affected people together through special educational establishments. My guess is that with genetic information made available to them before their marriage, the demand in the distant future from deaf couples for a genetic correction of the gene defect by embryo therapy would be small, given that there are much improved cochlear implants to restore a form of hearing in the baby.

A second example comes as more of a 'bolt from the blue'. It concerns couples who, after their first baby is diagnosed as Down's Syndrome, are told that *all* future children of theirs would be so affected. The extra chromosome 21 that causes Down's Syndrome can sometimes be attached to another chromosome, and occasionally this is another chromosome 21. In a proportion of such families, it is found that one or other parent is carrying a balanced 21/21 translocation. This healthy parent has the usual two 21s, but they are attached to each other; this abnormality having arisen in the egg or sperm that led to their conception. As a consequence, that person can only produce gametes that either have two 21s (to give a baby with Down's Syndrome) or no 21, which leads to early miscarriage. It is possible to imagine techniques developing in the future to add a normal 21 from a donor cell to the zygote with only one, or destroy by highly focused ultrasound or laser beam one half of the 21/21 composite chromosome in

the zygote that has this abnormal chromosome. The former situation over-
laps somewhat with gamete donation which might well be an acceptable
option for many such couples, but one has to admit that, if legalised, there
could be 'takers' for ultrasonic or laser chromosome surgery (perfected, one
might imagine, for legitimate genetic research purposes in animals). Since
this technique could only ever remove excess chromosome material, it is
very difficult to see how it could be exploited for undesirable positive
eugenic purposes, which may therefore make it a more acceptable technical
development from the ethical point of view.

The final example poses more immediate ethical problems, and concerns
the options available for women who are suffering from (or carrying in an
asymptomatic fashion) mutant mitochondria. It is only in the last decade
that the role of mitochondrial mutations in human disease has begun to be
defined (reviewed by Hammans and Harding, 1991) and recent findings
suggest that they may contribute to a wide range of adult onset disorders
(Reardon *et al.*, 1992). Mitochondria are organelles in the cytoplasm of
cells concerned principally with energy production. In evolutionary terms,
they are believed to represent bacterial cells entrapped in a symbiotic
relationship within the cytoplasm of the cells of multicellular organisms. In
keeping with this, mitochondria have their own circular chromosome with
expressed genes that replicate independently of the 46 regular chromosomes making up the human nuclear genome. A mature ovum has about
2000 mitochondria, but during the passage from one generation to the next
the number of mitochondria in the germ cell lineage is thought to go
through a 'bottleneck' of less than 10 mitochondria. Whilst both eggs and
sperm have mitochondria, none is transferred with the sperm pronucleus at
fertilisation, so mitochondrial inheritance is exclusively maternal. What is
true of normal mitochondria is true of mutant mitochondria, and exclusive
maternal transmission characterises those diseases due to mutation in the
mitochondrial chromosome. The mitochondria accumulate mutations at a
relatively fast rate and, due to the 'bottleneck' effect, some offspring of a
woman carrying one or a few mutant mitochondria can end up with the
majority, even all, of their mitochondria of the mutant variety. There are
now several serious mitochondrial diseases described and at the severe end
of the spectrum they can result in progressive neurological deterioration,
stroke-like episodes, epilepsy, deafness, visual impairment, and a myopathy
affecting skeletal muscle as well as the heart (see Van Hellenberg *et al.*,
1991).

Genetic counselling can be very difficult. *All* the offspring of a mildly
affected or asymptomatic carrier woman are at risk of serious disease,
although only a proportion (perhaps 10 to 15 per cent) will in fact be

seriously affected. In general, these are likely to be the embryos that end up with a high proportion or all the mitochondria in their cells being the mutant ones. Preimplantation diagnosis followed by embryo selection will be problematic because the proportion of mutant mitochondria in the biopsied cell may not faithfully represent the proportion in the remaining seven or so cells and ultimately the baby.

One solution, worthy of at least careful consideration, arose out of discussions at the 2nd Philosophy and Ethics of Reproductive Medicine Conference (Pembrey, 1992). It is likely to be technically possible to transfer a cell nucleus from the couple's preimplantation embryo into an enucleated cell from a donor embryo of the same postconceptional age; in other words, to perform a 'cytoplasmic exchange'. The resulting embryo would have all its regular nuclear genes from the couple concerned (and in a real sense be their own baby), but not have the mutant mitochondria. My feeling is that there could well be a clinical demand for such a procedure, if it were permitted. However, the wording of the Human Fertilisation and Embryology Act (1990), although designed to outlaw 'cloning' of many genetically identical people from one embryo, does appear also to outlaw 'cytoplasmic exchange' therapy for embryos carrying mutant mitochondria if this were to be done by straight nuclear switching. The Act prohibits 'replacing a nucleus of a cell of an embryo with a nucleus taken from the cell of another person, another embryo or a subsequent development of an embryo' and 'altering the genetic structure of any cell while it forms part of an embryo'. There are, however, alternative ways of achieving a cytoplasmic exchange and Figure 9.2 illustrates one that is probably allowable under the Act. This would involve selective poisoning of the mitochondria in the couple's embryonic cell and then fusing it with an enucleated donor blastomere.

Knowledge is increasing of a number of mitochondrially inherited diseases, which put all descendants in the female line at risk. They are no longer just rare diseases; they include familial adult onset diabetes mellitus with or without deafness (Ballinger *et al.*, 1992, Van den Ouweland *et al.*, 1992, Reardon *et al.*, 1992). Unlike regular nuclear genes (normal or mutant) that can be re-assorted in descendants by the process of sexual reproduction, once most of the mitochondrial genomes in a matriarchal lineage accumulate one or more mutations, the descendants are stuck with it, unless there is a fortuitous distribution of the few normal mitochondria during early embryo cleavage, or a deliberate therapeutic 'cytoplasmic exchange' as I propose. Women who carry or suffer from mitochondrial mutations may feel acutely the burden of responsibility towards their descendants, and seek a way out that would enable them to have their own children, but not pass on their mitochondria. This situation could indeed become a clinical

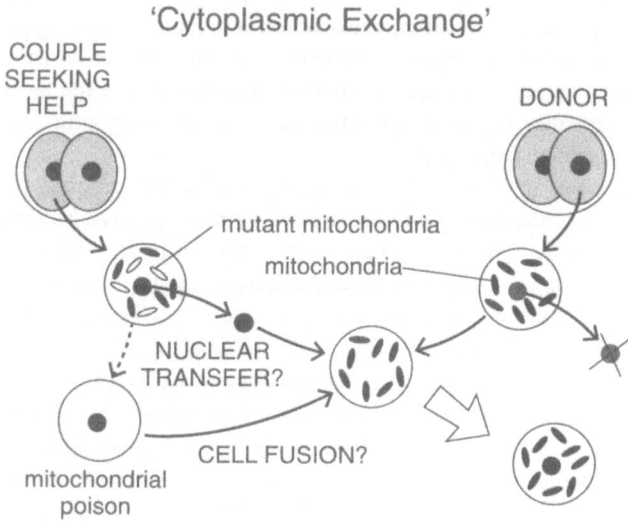

Figure 9.2 Cytoplasmic exchange

indication for genetic (albeit, mitochondrial) manipulation in the preimplantation embryo. Much research in animal models and then human embryos in the first few days after fertilisation will be needed to establish the efficacy and safety of the procedure, provided, of course, this approach to cytoplasmic exchange is allowed to be licenced under the new Act.

Conclusion

This contribution has been as much about the alternatives to gene therapy as gene therapy itself, but I make no apology for that. Whilst the dramatic advances in embryology, fetal medicine and molecular genetics have raised new therapeutic options that could be applied in fetal life if necessary, it is the families facing known genetic risks who will be the final arbitrator between therapy and selection; between trying to restore to health the embryo or fetus they have created, or discarding those with serious genetic problems and trying again. The clinicians and scientists involved have not only a responsibility to improve and validate the interventions they offer, but to provide the information that the couples need in order to reach a decision that is right for them. The burden of choice weighs heavy upon them and they need all the help and understanding they can get.

References

Anonymous (1988) 'Are germ-lines special?', *Nature*, vol. 381, p. 100.

Ballinger, S. W., J. M. Shoffner, E. V. Hedaya, I. Trounce, M. A. Polak, D. A. Koontz and D. C. Wallace (1992) 'Maternally transmitted diabetes and deafness associated with a 10.4 kb mitochondrial DNA deletion', *Nature Genetics*, vol. 1, pp. 11–15.

Clothier, C. M. (1992) *Report of the Committee on the Ethics of Gene Therapy*. Cm 1788 (London: HMSO).

Evening Standard (1991) 9 May.

Hammans, S. R. and A. E. Harding (1991) 'Mitochondrial disease and mitochondrial DNA', *British Journal of Hospital Medicine*, vol. 46, pp. 20–6.

Handyside, A. H., K. Kontogianni, E. Hardy and R. M. L. Winston (1990) 'Pregnancies from biopsied human preimplantation embryos sexed by Y-specific DNA amplification', *Nature*, vol. 344, pp. 768–70.

Handyside, A. H., J. G. Lesko, J. J. Tarin, R. M. L. Winston and M. R. Hughes (1992) 'Birth of a normal girl after *in vitro* fertilization and preimplantation diagnostic testing for cystic fibrosis', *New England Journal of Medicine*, vol. 317, pp. 907–9.

Koopman, P., J. Gubbay, N. Vivian, P. Goodfellow and R. Lovell-Badge (1991) 'Male development of chromosomally female mice transgenic for Sry', *Nature*, vol. 351, pp. 117–21.

Miller, A. D. (1992) 'Human gene therapy comes of age', *Nature*, vol. 357, pp. 455–60.

Murray, T. H. (1990) 'Human gene therapy, the public, and public policy', *Human Gene Therapy*, vol. 1, pp. 49–54.

Pang, S., M. S. Pollack, R. N. Marshall and L. Immken (1990) 'Prenatal treatment of congenital adrenal hyperplasia due to 21-hydroxylase deficiency', *New England Journal of Medicine*, vol. 322, pp. 111–5.

Pembrey, M. E. (1984) 'Do we need gene therapy?', *Nature*, vol. 311, p. 200.

Pembrey, M. E. (1992) 'Embryo therapy: Is there a clinical need?'. In Bromham, D. R., M. E. Dalton, J. C. Jackson and P. J. R. Millican, (eds) *Ethics in Reproductive Medicine* (London: Springer-Verlag) pp. 11–20.

Reardon, W., R. J. M. Ross, M. G. Sweeney, L. M. Luxon, M. E. Pembrey, A. E. Harding and R. C. Trembath (1992) 'Diabetes mellitus due to a pathogenic mitochondrial DNA point mutation', *Lancet*, vol. 304, pp. 1376–9.

Rosenfeld M. A., K. Yoshimura, B. C. Trapnell *et al.* (1992) '*In vivo* transfer of the human cystic fibrosis transmembrane conductance regulator gene to the airway epithelium', *Cell*, vol. 68, pp. 143–55.

Speiser, P. W., N. Laforgia, K. Kato, J. Pareira, R. Khan and Y. Y. Soo (1990) 'First trimester prenatal, treatment and molecular genetic diagnosis of congenital adrenal hyperplasia (21-hydroxylase deficiency)', *Journal of Clinical Endocrinology and Metabolism*, vol. 70, pp. 838–48.

Van Hellenberg, J. M. L. Hubar and F. J. M. Gabreels (1991) 'Melas syndrome. Report of two patients and comparison with data of 24 patients derived from the literature', *Neuroped*, vol. 22, pp. 10–14.

Van den Ouweland, J. M. W., H. H. P. J. Lemkes, W. Ruitenbeek, L. A. Sandkuijl, M. F. de Vijlder, P. A. A. Struyvenberg, J. J. P. van de Kemp and J. A. Massen (1992) 'Mutation in mitochondrial tRNA$^{Leu(UUR)}$ gene in a large pedigree with maternally transmitted type II diabetes mellitus and deafness', *Nature Genetics*, vol. 1, pp. 358–71.

Warnock, M. (1984) *Report of the Committee of Inquiry into Human Fertilisation and Embryology*. Cm 9314 (London: HMSO).

Weatherall, D. J. (1984) 'A step nearer gene therapy', *Nature*, vol. 310, p. 451.

Wilson, J. M. and F. S. Collins (1992) 'Cystic fibrosis – more from the modellers', *Nature*, vol. 359, p. 195.

Woo, S. L. C., A. S. Lidsky, F. Guttler, T. Chandra and K.J. Robson (1983) 'Cloned human phenylalanine hydroxylase gene allows prenatal diagnosis and carrier detection of classical phenylketonuria', *Nature*, vol. 306, pp. 151–5.

Part III
Ethical and Legal Issues

10 'Calming or Harming?' The Ethics of Screening for Fetal Defects

G. R. Dunstan

INTRODUCTION

In this chapter, only diagnostic screening for individual patients is considered; and that at any stage from the polar body onwards. Notice is taken of new diagnostic techniques which disclose function as well as genetic composition and structure. Screening is widely accepted, and provision for it is increasing, if slowly. Ethics implies choice: primarily choice by the patient based on the information which it is a clinical duty to provide. Choice is complicated by inherent uncertainty. It is not unlimited: it must be within the law and consistent with professional obligation.

'Autonomy', the now fashionable word for liberty to make responsible decisions, is inapplicable to the fetus. In its totally dependent state its protection stands on the concept of duty, parental and professional, to act in its best interest. The presumption in favour of its life is rebuttable only for grave reason. Choices are inevitable, and it is within the moral and legal competence of parents, professionally advised, to make them. Lack of consent by the fetus is no impediment, for the fetus is not capable of consenting. Decisions are rightly taken by proxy to those with responsibility for it.

Abnormality, while capable of anatomical and physiological description, is also a subjective experience not open to objective grading or definition. The experience of abnormality may well differ between the subject and the observer. Medical intervention, whether corrective or to terminate, is governed by clinical indication. It cannot be invoked to meet mere preference within normal variation: e.g. a preferred sex unrelated to genetic defect. The strength of society's commitment to the fostering of life will be measured by the quality of its service to the handicapped and those who care for them.

My instructions for this symposium were provocative and precise. I was to address the ethics of screening for fetal defects; the autonomy of the fetus; lack of consent; and what is abnormality? The rhetorical question, 'Calming or harming?' was put in, I suppose, to indicate the tension that must pervade all ethical discourse. If the analysis is done well, we need not stay to answer the question: it will be seen as what it is, merely rhetorical.

FETAL SCREENING

I have assumed that the 'fetal screening' which we are to discuss is that with a diagnostic purpose, undertaken in the interest of patients as individuals; not the screening of populations for epidemiological or other extra-clinical purposes. In recent years, screening has moved back from the fetus to the embryonic and pre-embryonic stages of development, even, within its limitations, to biopsy of the first polar body. To examine the fertilised ovum at the very beginning of fertilisation has been one of the major research tasks of the last decade, and its ethics have been vigorously debated. It has been made possible by advances in molecular biology and DNA technology. The other major new factor is the progress in methods of diagnostic fetal screening such as echo-cardiography, Doppler ultrasound and magnetic resonance imaging. These techniques are yielding clear pictures of the heart and of the brain and are virtually free of hazard. By these means accurate information can be gained, not only about structure, but also about function, like the flow of blood through the fetal heart. Fetal screening is therefore no longer confined to the narrow range of chorionic villus sampling, amniocentesis and the diagnostic X-ray, or to a calculation of statistical possibilities. It is now wider in the range of what it detects, wider in its allowance of critical time, and more accurate and precise in the information which it yields. Add to this the widening acceptance of screening by potential parents, advances in fetal and neonatal medicine, and the establishment (if still limited) of a pattern of clinical genetics services throughout the country, and we have an outline of the practice which we are asked to assess.

This last conjunction is important, of medical services with the provision of diagnostic and prognostic skills: ante-natal screening now does not offer a simple choice between retention and disposal of the fetus. Accurate diagnosis may lead to medical or dietetic management, or to therapeutic intervention on the fetus in the womb; it may prepare for designed neonatal care at birth. If we were, so early, to make a choice between the 'calming or harming' of my given title, the bias, in simple terms of medical possibilities, must surely lie on the side of calming.

ETHICS AND CHOICE

But I am not allowed to limit myself simply to medical possibilities. I am required to look at their ethical implications, that interplay of fact with obligation out of which doctor, counsellor and patient have to emerge with a decision, and to act upon it. The first duty of the diagnostician is clear, whether he be embryologist, geneticist or sonographer. It is to provide the patient with an accurate description of what is disclosed, of the implications of that disclosure for the potential child and the carrying mother, and the options open to her in her circumstances and with the medical and social services available in her community (Ferguson-Smith, 1989). The information may be entirely reassuring, which is great gain if it was a well-grounded anxiety which brought the mother for examination. Or it might disclose an anomaly of a seriousness calculable in broad terms, but not, yet, with precision. (The relation of the *degree* of handicap is not yet predictable between, for instance, trisomy 21 and Down's syndrome, or the Delta F508 mutation and cystic fibrosis, although a positive relation is now said to exist between severity in myotonic dystrophy and the length of the relevant fragment of DNA on chromosome 19 (Maddox, 1992)). The gene pattern might offer a prediction of a crippling and fatal disease developing later in life, or a susceptibility which might never be realised unless triggered by other endogenous or environmental factors. Within these certainties and uncertainties the mother has to choose – and always with the risk, however rare, of diagnostic error. She may abandon the compromised embryo and await another, uncompromised. She may ask for the termination of an established pregnancy. She may accept medical management for herself or surgical intervention for the fetus – the transplanting of haematopoietic cells, for instance, to combat a blood disorder. She may await delivery and accept neonatal paediatric care. She may choose to keep and cherish the child, however handicapped, into an uncertain future.

Her choice, within the law and our contemporary ethics, is not absolute. The doctor, too, has a conscience, personal and professional; and she may not oblige him to violate it. He could decline to terminate a pregnancy merely to relieve disappointment over some normal characteristic: a child of unwanted sex, for instance, where there is no sex-linked disorder. But, given an adverse prognosis, the presumption is in favour of her being free to choose; and the relevant duty is to help her, with information, clarification and responsive attention, to make that choice responsibly; and to support her after it.

'AUTONOMY' OF THE FETUS

All that looks like common sense, and there we would leave it, except for those who would claim absolute protection for unborn human life, from the beginning of fertilisation, inviolable for any cause or in any circumstances. But the slogan-ridden conscience of our day has thrust upon us a new impediment: the so-called 'autonomy' of the fetus. What is this 'autonomy'?

'Autonomy' is a word newly transplanted from politics into medical ethics; and so immuno-suppressed are our critical faculties that the host is slow to reject the graft. 'Autonomy' is a Greek word: it means 'living by one's own laws'. It is what the Greek city-states fought for so fiercely in their determination to remain independent of one another. It broke down, of course, when they had to unite to defend their common interest against invaders. And there is our first clue: autonomy, although claimed as a personal possession, must stand in tension with other claims in society. In medieval Europe we developed self-governing corporations within the state, kingdom or Empire, each recognising itself to some extent as against the state: chartered boroughs and cities; the Inns of Court; colleges and universities; the Church. The medieval Church over-reached itself, and when it went beyond self-government within the state to exalt its sovereignty over the state, it had to be slapped down. Autonomy stands always in tension with the society within which it is claimed. None of us is free to live by our own laws: we have to live within the laws of our society; and only when we do so can law discharge its proper function, which is to protect our liberties.

'Autonomy' in medical ethics is a dangerous myth, whether claimed for the patient or for the doctor. Restated in simple English, what we stand to defend is the liberty to make responsible decisions in matters of vital concern, personal and social. The decisions are necessarily taken in awareness of the liberties and duties of others. So we cannot allow the autonomy of the doctor to assert itself against the patient, or the autonomy of the patient against the doctor. We require that each shall make responsible decisions, in consultation and with consent. That is no xenograft; it is native to our constitution (Dunstan and Seller, 1983).

How, then, can we attribute this to the fetus? Clearly, we cannot. The freedom to choose, to make responsible decisions, rests on a neural and rational capacity which the fetus does not possess. This is why the fetus is not recognised as a person, a bearer of rights, in our jurisprudence. Any attempt, therefore, on this ground to protect the fetus against the combined wills of doctor and patient is bound to fail; the foundation simply is not there. For the true ground of protection we must go back again into our own tradition.

That ground is the concept and language of *duty*. We have a duty to protect the unborn child, even though it has no rights. To assert duties where there are no rights is not singular. We have a duty not to inflict cruelty on animals, even though they have no rights; or to conserve works of art, or scenes of natural beauty, all without rights. The whole profession of medicine stands on a duty to serve the interest of patients in health and in a good and timely death. So there! We take no refuge in autonomy; we assert a joint duty of parent and doctor to serve the best interest of the fetus. That duty of care and protection is old in our civilisation. In our narrow, western sector of it, we can trace it back in literary evidences for 4000 years (Dunstan and Seller, 1988). The duty of protection has always been held to grow stronger with growth towards maturity: moral status advanced with morphological development, step by step. That principle underlies our ethics; it is at the basis of the latest of our relevant laws, the Human Fertilisation and Embryology Act 1990.

Our question turns, then, on what are the interests of the fetus, and how are they to be served? There is a *prima facie* or presumptive interest in life, and so a presumptive duty to protect that interest from conception to birth. Fetal medicine stands on that presumption, and witnesses to its strength. The duty of protection cannot be absolute, because regard must be had to other, rare, contingent interests and, above all, to related interests in the fetus itself. There are rare, and decreasing, indications for which fetal life may need to be terminated in order to save the life of the mother, no less drastic option being available. There are those who would maintain that the fetal interest in life is paramount: no consideration of the quality of life may be allowed to lessen the duty to preserve that life and bring it to birth. This would appear to be the formal position of the Vatican. Its Instruction on *Respect for Human Life and its Origin and on the Dignity of Procreation*, issued on 22 February 1987, declares that a woman 'would be committing a gravely illicit act if she were to request a pre-natal diagnosis with the deliberate intention of having an abortion should the results confirm the evidence of a malformation or abnormality.' Whatever the status of this judgment as a domestic rule of the Roman Catholic Church, it does not govern medical practice in liberal societies, precisely because their concept of human dignity includes freedom to make responsible decisions within the law and limits already described. It is therefore licit in those societies to consider whether it is in the best interest of a fetus to enable it to come to birth with a reasonable certainty of such grave handicap that the child's life would be one of predictable and severe suffering for which there might be a measure of palliation, at the cost, perhaps, of more and more invasive treatment, but no cure. If this consideration were strong enough to overthrow the presumption in favour of fetal life, the law and professional ethics would allow termination to be licit. But it must be a free parental choice, without coercion, even social coercion; every effort must be made to secure that it were free.

LACK OF CONSENT

But we have ignored yet another ideological hurdle. By what authority can you do such things to a fetus – expose it to the hazards of fetal surgery, or of cellular implants or of total blood transfusion: how can you even terminate its life without its consent? The question can be asked only by those who have already invested the fetus – or the embryo, or the pre-embryonic cells – with that right to consent which is proper only to competent human beings, those sufficiently developed and mature to be capable of choosing for themselves, and whose liberty to do so is protected by ethics and by law. We may escape absurdity if we ask: What do these objectors seek to protect and have we better language with which to protect it? If they seek to protect the interest of the fetus, we have the language of duty with which to protect it. It is an established parental duty to serve the interest of the fetus, and so to consent by proxy to what is responsibly held to be for its good, and to refuse consent to what is not. It is an indication of how far the necessary protective principle of informed consent is degenerating into a slogan, a fetish, when it is the objection is that parental and medical decisions are unethical because of lack of consent by the fetus.

The ethically serious question of consent refers, of course, to the mother (Kennedy, 1991). Except under strict conditions set out in the Mental Health Act 1983, a woman's body is inviolable without her consent: no medical or surgical intervention may take place without it. May an exception be made if intervention is required in the interest of her unborn child? May she be forced to abstain from tobacco, alcohol or drugs toxic to the fetus? May she have a transfusion, or fetal surgery, or a Caesarian section, imposed upon her without consent? May her unborn child be made a Ward of Court in order that a court may overrule her refusal of consent? Despite case law and ideological persuasions from North America, the answers to all these questions in English statute and common law is No: there may be no violation of her bodily integrity or of her freedom of action without her consent, even though the fetus should suffer handicap or even death in consequence.

Professor Ian Kennedy has analysed well the moral calculus between these conflicting interests, and given due weight to the moral claims of the fetus, claims which grow stronger as it develops. In terms of law his only tenable remedy would be statute empowering judges to determine, by reasoned argument, an extreme case where a serious fetal interest was imperilled by, for instance, persistent and flagrant harmful conduct by the mother. There is no alternative, meanwhile, to the ethical task of general education and personal antenatal persuasion when conflicts of interest arise.

That is not quite a digression. I have discussed the proper issue of consent by the mother; not lack of consent by the fetus.

WHAT IS ABNORMALITY?

One last serious question awaits us. What is abnormality? What degree of abnormality can justify the sort of interventions we have been considering, either in corrective therapy or for termination of the pregnancy?

Here it must be admitted at the outset that the goal of objectivity, of established criteria, standards of measurement universally accepted, which medical scientists seek in their descriptive and diagnostic pursuits, are unattainable in any description of abnormality influencing parental decision in the context of antenatal diagnosis. It is true that there is a technical language to describe a chromosomal abnormality or a genetic mutation; there is another to denote a cardiac abnormality like a septal defect or transposition of arteries; yet another to describe lesions of the brain; and so on. Those descriptions are clinically relevant to the question which a potential mother is asking; they do not answer the question itself. Her question is: What degree of abnormality justifies the risk and strain of fetal surgery? What justifies a request for termination? What does abnormality mean when translated into capacity for living in human relationship, in which all available care will be mounted to offset disadvantage, with physical and emotional pain if that be so, for however long that life lasts? Judgements here are essentially subjective. The observer may project feelings upon the handicapped which that person may not share. Yet there must be some external point of reference, some testing against professional and social norms.

It is a commonplace in the discussion of gene therapy to exclude any attempt to manipulate genes to enhance 'normal' human traits; gene therapy may be attempted only to alleviate disease in individual patients. 'Designer babies' are *not* on offer. Similarly, sex is held to be relevant in embryonic biopsy, or at later cell sampling, only when attended by a sex-linked disorder. Preference is not a criterion for normality or abnormality. But when abnormality is going to express in severe disease or crippling handicap, the subjective element cannot be excluded. If a vital element in life is its relational capacity, the capacity of parents or of surrogate parents to care for the child is a fact, material to its interest, to be considered. A true community, a just society, should not leave them to care alone: it would give them all necessary support, social and economic, as well as the generous encouragement of friends. Support is not only a practical necessity; it is also a necessary expression of a common commitment to the presumption in favour of life which is basic to human relations. Without it, words are hollow: neither law, nor ethics, nor parental will, can maintain for long what we do not effectively believe in. It is within this context that lawful decisions require to be taken. Is the abnormality, in this child, grave enough to overthrow the presumption in favour of its life? Granted that nature itself has not rejected this fetus, as it rejects some – and those by no means all the most abnormal; granted that fetal medicine can yet do little to correct or to palliate the abnormality – if it cannot; what does the fetal interest require or permit?

That, it seems to me, is the state of the question. It calls to be answered sometimes because, within our humanity, our rational nature obliges us to exercise some measure of control over our biological nature, that which we share with other orders of creation. And rationality, in association with humanity, both enables and calls for moral decision. Instinct prompts some other animals to expel the abnormal from the herd, or to push it out of the nest to die. We have to work it out, and to decide; and to take responsibility for our decision.

References

Dunstan, G. R. and M. J. Seller (1983) (eds) *Consent in Medicine: Convergence and Divergence in Tradition* (London: King Edward's Hospital Fund for London) 128 pp.

Dunstan, G. R. and M. J. Seller (1988) (eds) *The Status of the Human Embryo: Perspectives from moral tradition* (London: King Edward's Hospital Fund for London) 119 pp.

Ferguson-Smith, M. A. and E. M. Ferguson-Smith (1989) 'Relationships between patient, clinician, and scientist in prenatal diagnosis', in G. R. Dunstan and E. A. Shinebourne (eds) *Doctors' Decisions: Ethical Conflicts in Medical Practice* (Oxford, New York, Tokyo: Oxford University Press) pp. 18–34.

Kennedy, I. (1991) 'A woman and her unborn child', in *Treat Me Right: Essays in Medical Law and Ethics* (2nd edn) (Oxford: Clarendon Press) pp. 364–84.

Maddox, J. (1992) 'Melodrama in research publication', *Nature*, vol. 355, p. 767.

11 The Legal Status of the Embryo and the Fetus

Derek Morgan

The question of control over genetic products and the limits to be imposed creates problems in terms of both application of existing legislation and principles of law, and respect for the fundamental principles and values of our society, in particular individual freedoms and human dignity. (Council of Europe, 1989)

EARLY ATTITUDES TO THE FETUS

Legal attitudes to fetuses and newborns have varied over time, some cultures proscribing abortion and infanticide, some early codes giving the fetus indirect protection by prohibiting the striking of a woman so as to cause the death of her unborn child (Codes). In other cultures, abortion and infanticides were seen as acceptable resolutions of dilemmas posed by scarce resources, birth defects or sexual balance. Neither ancient Greek nor early Roman law forbade abortion, the latter not regarding the unborn child as a living human being. The common law has long drawn a fundamental distinction between the fetus and the child following birth. Recent developments in common law jurisprudence have, however, seen the recognition of interests – notice the importance of that term, interests, not rights – against harm to the child before its birth.

It is perhaps important to distinguish at this early stage between law, philosophy and public policy. The distinguished American jurisprudent Oliver Wendell Holmes wrote that 'The life of the law is not logic but experience' (Holmes, 1881). Put another way, law is not so much the handmaiden of philosophy as the servant of public policy. There is, indeed, a tension between the analytic demands of philosophy, the pressures of public policy and the service which law provides. The pragmatism, so often remarked, of English common law, lends more to the requirements of public policy than to dissection by philosophy. Thus Andrew Grubb, in one of the few domestic attempts to grapple with this question has suggested that:

When a court is seized of a case . . . [it] would have no choice but to treat an extra-corporeal embryo as either a person or a chattel. The likely outcome is that it would be held to be a chattel. Such law as exists points in this direction and the pragmatism of the common law would see that to treat an extra-corporeal embryo as a chattel is more consistent with common sense than for it to be given the rights of a person. (Grubb, 1991)

Unfortunately, the notion of common sense to which Grubb appeals is not here made explicit. The general point, however, is that the pragmatist of the common law will often want to know, in advance of her answer, who is asking the question and for what purposes. Thus, if asked 'what is the legal status of the embryo and the fetus?' the usual reply of the English common lawyer will be in the form of a question, rather than a direct reply. What is remarkable about this pragmatism is that it is often prepared to endure philosophical, and indeed sociological obloquy, hostility and approbation, in order to avoid answering directly a question posed, or to avoid answering it in a way which would seem to provoke hostility from the prevailing currents of political values.

The main questions with which a lawyer, confronted with determining the status of the embryo, will be concerned are: Who has control over the frozen embryo? In what way, if at all, is that control restricted? And what limits apply to the way in which gametes and embryos can be used? The Human Fertilisation and Embryology Act 1990, although not commonly seen in this way, was a major piece of restrictive legislation. It imposed limits on the use and control of embryos where none had effectively operated before. The limitations on the research use of the embryo, the restrictions on their use in the provision of treatment services and the protection given to children subsequently born alive who can show that they have suffered injury as a result of the negligent handling of gametes or embryonic material, are all major steps forward in the legal recognition given to the embryo.

That this is not always apparent, may be gauged from some of the responses to the recommendations of the Warnock Committee (DHSS, 1984). Recall that the Committee had concluded that the embryo of the human species was entitled to special consideration and yet recommended that the couple who have stored an embryo should have rights to use and dispose of it (para. 10.11 and 12); that there be rights of sale of gametes and embryos where licensed (para. 13.13); and limited circumstances where drug testing may be carried out on embryos created specifically for that purpose (para. 12.5). This led Ian Kennedy and Andrew Grubb pointedly to ask:

> What special status does an embryo have if it may be the object of research during the first fourteen days of gestation and thereafter destroyed? What is ownership if it is not the right to control, including to dispose of by sale, or otherwise? (Kennedy and Grubb, 1989)

First I shall briefly identify some legal conundrums to which the embryo has given rise and introduce a short philosophical excursus. Secondly, I shall set out what may be thought of as the 'classical' view of the fetus and the embryo. This is followed by a survey of recent jurisprudence. Turning first to the provisions of the Human Fertilisation and Embryology Act 1990; I examine the limitations on research which the Act introduced, the 'consent' requirements established under Schedule 3 for the use of embryos and gametes and finally the additional legal protections for any child injured in the course of the provision of infertility treatment services.

LEGAL CONUNDRUMS AND PHILOSOPHICAL EXCURSUS

Before the 1990 Act there were a number of cases which might have arisen where the status of the embryo would be critical in determining its fate; some of these conundrums may have survived the legislation. First, suppose that a clinician deliberately destroys an embryo, created from A and B's gametes, in a fire at an IVF clinic:

(i)   Does s/he kill the embryos?
(ii) Does s/he convert them?
(iii) Is the claim on any insurance policy for damage to goods or loss of life?
(iv) Can A and B claim for post traumatic stress disorder caused by the loss of the embryos?

The point of this example is that the clinician's act operates against the genitors but especially the woman's interests; thus recognising the embryo as a 'person' would hardly interfere with any interest which she has, on the contrary it would serve to protect or preserve it. Additionally, the clinic would be likely to carry insurance against the loss.

These two remarkable features – that allowing the claim would not interfere with any interest of the woman and liability insurance would cover any general damages recoverable – are the salient features of the single exception to general maternal immunity to suit from a fetus and 'furnishes a rare instance of a legal duty owed directly to the unborn infant' (Brazier, 1988 at p. 21 n. 14). In this hitherto unique case, a child born with congenital disabilities as a result of injuries incurred as a result of its mother's negligent driving has a direct cause of action against her; in reality, of course, against the company with which she has placed the risk against which she must by law insure. While we may conclude that even in our hypothetical case the law would not recognise the embryo as a 'person' this is merely symptomatic of the blindness of English law to the need to make supportable distinctions based on the sort of interest which requires protection (Wells and Morgan, 1991).

Secondly, suppose that a clinic storing a couple's gametes or embryos is faced with an eventuality which had not previously been contemplated. For example, suppose that the clinic receives a demand from one of them that stored embryos be allowed to perish, either because the relationship has ended in divorce or death of one of the parties, or because the genitors now disagree about proceeding with the treatment services (Davis, 1989, 1990). A variant would be that on the death of one of the parties, the clinic is faced with a demand from the survivor to release to them their partner's stored gametes or embryos for use (Parpalaix, 1984). Or on the death of both parties? (Rios, 1985). Finally, imagine a dispute between the clinic and the couple about release of stored embryos for the couple's continued use against the clinical judgement of those in charge of the clinic (York, 1989). What in each case should be the response of the clinic?

Happily, the Human Fertilisation and Embryology Act 1990 provides that these questions must at least be addressed. There is then some temporary legal finality to some questions of the status of the human embryo. But there will hardly be ethical agreement. I do not want to rehearse the debates about embryo research or the different philosophical traditions upon which they rest; I have attempted that task elsewhere (Morgan and Lee, 1990). For the present it is sufficient to recall one example from each wing of the philosophical plane to illustrate the general tenor of the debate and the flights of fancy sometimes involved. On the linguistic turn complained of in the invention of the term pre-embryo Jonathan Glover has, in my view quite rightly, observed that 'any right a pre-embryo may have is not diminished by calling it a pre-embryo rather than an embryo,' (Glover, 1989). More contentiously, he then goes on to argue that:

> no-one denies that [the pre-embryo] is alive, and that it is surely a member of our species rather than any other. But the problem with this argument is that it applies equally to the unfertilized egg or to the human

sperm cell. This argument easily enough proves that the embryo or fetus is a human being, but it is not clear that the status 'human being' in this minimal sense brings with it any moral rights. It is widely assumed that qualifying as a human being is sufficient to guarantee the possession of a right to life. But this assumption is questionable, and perhaps derives much of its plausibility from our thinking of 'human beings' in terms of our friends and neighbours. An embryo is not the kind of human being you can share a joke with or have as a friend. (Ibid., p. 96)

The essential fallacy with this sort of argument is that there may be many of one's friends or colleagues about whom one might say the same thing; in short this objection shows us nothing of any moral substance. And notice what the argument entails; it is clear that we have a human being, but it is not clear that the status "human being" brings with it any moral rights'. That may be thought by many to be offensive and morally outrageous in itself. It is indeed widely assumed that qualifying as a human being is sufficient to guarantee the possession of a right to life. The history of the centuries shows us that it is when we begin to think of the status human being as being insufficient to guarantee a certain moral respect that many of our troubles and ills have begun. As current world events in the Balkans, the former Soviet Union and countries in Africa disclose, it is precisely when we begin to regard one another only as human beings of a particular sort that our woes begin to multiply.

The argument that an embryo is a person is based upon the proposition that life begins at conception when a genetically unique entity with the potential for development comes into existence. Of course, there are those for whom the prospect of research upon, as they see it, living human beings in their embryonic form, is of the highest moral repugnance and that in sanctioning non-therapeutic research Parliament, in the 1990s, took a step across a Rubicon for which there is no return ticket. For example, Lord Rawlinson posed this question in a House of Lords debate on the Human Fertilisation and Embryology Bill which proposed to allow research until the appearance of the 'primitive streak' fourteen days after the onset of the process of conception:

The question is asked: 'when does life commence?' Surely, if it has commenced the killing is not acceptable. To those who reply 'after fourteen days' I say 'fourteen days after what?' (Rawlinson, 1990)

This position has been upheld by the Tennessee Circuit Court in *Davis v. Davis* (1989), at least two US states' legislatures (Missouri, 1986; Louisiana, 1986) and has been ruled to be a constitutional declaration of State policy in the Supreme Court's decision in *Webster v. Reproductive Health Services* (1989) and formed the basis of the Danish legislation of 1987 establishing its Council of Ethics which was charged by the legislation to proceed on the basis that human life begins at the time of conception (Morgan and Nielsen, 1992).

In *Davis v. Davis*, Judge Dale W. Young at first instance awarded 'custody' of seven cryopreserved fertilised ova to a now divorced woman in a divorce suit and declared that she should be 'permitted the opportunity to bring these children to term through implantation.' He held that the embryos were in law persons because life began at conception such that 'the manifest best interest of the children, *in vitro*, [is] that they be made available for implantation to assure their opportunity for live birth.' Among the reasons for his ruling were that '7) Human life begins at conception. 8) Mr and Mrs Davis have produced human beings, *in vitro*, to be known as their child or children.'

On appeal, the Court remanded the case to the Circuit Court to enter judgment vesting joint control in the former husband and wife (both now remarried) and giving them equal voice over their disposition. The Appeals Court held that awarding sole custody to Mary Sue Davis, such that she could attempt implantation without her former husband's consent, was impermissible state action. Judge Franks, writing the leading opinion, held that such an award infringed Junior Davis's constitutionally protected rights concerning procreation; in particular, that it might force him to become a parent against his will. The Appeals Court could find no compelling state interest to justify ordering implantation against the will of either party. To this extent, the lower court's action usurped the exercise by Junior of 'the decision whether to bear or beget a child [which is] a constitutionally protected choice.' However nascent, this seems to recognise an emergent sphere of mens' rights to control their fertility and conception, which will lead to a direct clash with women's rights (as in this case) and any emergent notion of fetal rights.

Grubb commenting on Judge Young's initial ruling writes:

the biological reality added to the philosophical imperative gave rise to a legal determination that the embryos were persons ... there is no silliness in the question 'what should be the fate of the frozen embryos?' Nor necessarily is there any foolishness in the answer that their custody should be awarded to [the woman who wanted the implantation to proceed]. Instead, the defect in the judgment lies in the reasoning process which equates biological life with legal personhood and, as a consequence, treats embryos and children alike. That transition is a non sequitur. (Grubb, 1991)

It may be that Grubb dislikes the conclusions which flow from Young's ruling, but it hardly correct to object that the reasoning discloses a non sequitur. Indeed the transition from equating biological life with legal personhood, to treating embryos and children alike is – on one view at least – a smooth, defensible progression and not a non sequitur at all. On this view of legal personhood it does indeed follow that embryos and children should be treated alike. Grubb's objection, then, should be directed towards the premises or assumptions which Young makes and not the relationship between the variables. Of course it would be possible to hold a third view, one close to that which I hold myself, which is that even though there is a close relationship between biological life and personhood, it does not follow from that that research on human embryos should be legally proscribed or indeed is morally impermissible (which again may be two very different things).

But it is indeed the potential consequences of Judge Young's ruling to which Grubb really takes objection. Although the judge's conclusion was set aside by the Tennessee Court of Appeals (awarding joint custody) the 'person analysis' leads to the conclusion that the party seeking custody for the purposes for implantation should be awarded it. Grubb again 'There is no room for flexibility and there is no room for manoeuvre' (Grubb, 1991, p. 74). In a definitional sense this is probably correct, but in terms of what one may lawfully do with the embryos, that is another matter:

> . . . the knock-on consequences of the trial judge's reasoning make his position very unattractive for the normal pragmatism of the common law judge. Some of these consequences would be as follows: – embryo research leading to death could be murder; – embryos could not be harmed in any way; hence research of all kinds (except the purely observational) would be unlawful; – inheritance rights would seem to exist even before implantation. (Ibid., p. 74)

This kind of objection is shared by the distinguished jurists who composed the now sadly defunct Law Reform Commission of Canada. In their commentary on the trial judge's ruling they wrote 'The ruling of the trial judge in the Davis case illustrates the dangers of absolutism.' (LRCC, 1992) Unfortunately, the LRCC here falls into the familiar trap of equating 'dangers' with 'consequences which personally I don't like.' The absolutism is 'dangerous' only if you want to try to produce some other result; if those are the consequences which flow from the 'absolutist' position, then, arguably, those are the consequences. For myself, I do not accept that those are the consequences which necessarily and inexorably flow from that position, but I do not want to be detained longer on this excursus than I have already.

THE CLASSICAL COMMON LAW POSITION

Whatever the philosophical proposition that life begins at conception, it is not a position adopted by the English common law. The classical position is quite clear: a fetus, still less an embryo, is not a person. This is not the same, of course, as saying that it enjoys no legal protection whatsoever. The embryo, or at least the child **en ventre sa mere** as the common law would have it, has some protected interests, such as the right to inherit (Administration of Estates Act 1925 s. 55(2)) and to be classified as a dependant for the purposes of the Fatal Accidents Act (The George and the Richard, 1871). But in both cases, these interests crystalise only on the fetuses' live birth and are at best contingent rights. And, as I shall later show, further protected interests have been recognised by statute and latterly common law which have implications not only for this abstract analysis in which I am now engaged, but also for the practice of fetal medicine and infertility treatment services.

The Classical view was restated by the Warnock Committee in their Report (DHSS, 1984) para. 11.16–17):

> We examined the current position of the *in vivo* embryo in law. The human embryo *per se* has no legal status. It is not, under law in the United Kingdom, accorded the same status as a child or an adult, and the law does not treat the human embryo as having a right to life. However, there are certain statutory provisions that give some level of protection in various respects.

They then cited the Offences Against the Person Act 1861, the Abortion Act 1967 (abortion is a criminal offence save in some cases provided for in the legislation); the Infant Life (Preservation) Act 1929 (the protection of the life of a child 'capable of being born alive' on which see Rance 1991) and the Congenital Disabilities (Civil Liability) Act 1976, which allows in limited circumstances an action for damages where an embryo or fetus has been injured *in utero* (I return to discuss this statute below). Each of these provisions might be thought of as extending some forms of indirect benefit or protection under the law. None of this, of course, related to the *in vitro*

embryo; the Offences Against the Person Act which contains the still extant
abortion provisions in England and Wales, does not apply to the extra-
corporeal embryo because it speaks of the 'procurement of a miscarriage'.
An embryo *in vitro* is never carried by a woman and hence it falls outside
the law's ambit in this regard. As Margaret Brazier wrote of the embryo
before the passage of the 1990 Act 'it exists and dies in a legal limbo'
(Brazier, 1988).

No such limbo attended the fetus outwith these limited, but exceptionally
important statutory enactments. That a fetus is not a person has been
reiterated on a number of occasions when the issue has arisen in a variety of
ways in common law courts. Some examples will illustrate this point:

(i)   in *Paton v. BPAS* (Paton, 1979; husband's attempt to prevent his wife
      seeking an abortion) Sir George Baker said 'A fetus cannot, in English
      law, in my view, have any right of its own at least until it is born and
      has a separate existence from the mother.'

(ii) in *Re F (in utero)* (*Re F* [1988]: attempt to make a fetus a ward of court
      to guard its health against feared harm from its mother's behaviour)
      the Court of Appeal held that an unborn child lacks legal personality
      to be made a ward of court because it would be incompatible with the
      rights of the mother. It has been suggested by John Keown that that
      case establishes nothing about forms of protection which could have
      been made available to the *in vitro* embryo before the 1990 Act. In
      particular he suggested that because it was *in vitro*, no question of
      conflict with the mother's rights arose, and hence it could be possible
      to make such an embryo a ward of court (Keown, 1989). This view is
      strongly challenged by Andrew Grubb, according to whom:

        it would be quite wrong to see the cases as only failing to recognise
        the legal status of the unborn child because to do so would lead to
        a certain conflict with the pregnant mother's interests . . . if an
        unborn child is not a legal person, it cannot seriously be argued that
        a frozen two-, four- or eight-cell embryo is a legal person with all
        the legal consequences stemming from such recognition by the law.
        (Grubb, 1991 p. 75)

      Although I suspect that Grubb is right, it is again on the level of
      pragmatism more than principle. Of course, to recognise the wardship
      jurisdiction over an embryo would interfere with the genitor/parents'
      interests, and that may be sufficient reason to deny it legal status.

(iii) in *C v. S* [1988] (putative father attempts as next friend of the fetus to prevent his former girlfriend from having an abortion) Mrs Justice Heilbron in holding that a child injured while in the womb may be the subject of a legal action by the child once it is born; 'the claim crystalises on the birth, at which date, but not before, the child attains the status of a legal **persona**; and thereupon can then exercise that legal right.'

(iv) A variant view has recently been suggested by Lord Prosser in *Hamilton v. Fife*, challenging not the view that the fetus is not a person but the view that any rights which are nascent, crystalise on the child's subsequent live birth (Hamilton, 1992). Lord Prosser said that for the purposes of section 1(1) of the Damages (Scotland) Act 1976, personal injuries had to be seen as sustained at the time when they first came into existence. If that time was before birth and only injuries sustained by a person were within the scope of the section, then the pursuer's claim would fail. Here, the child had died as a consequence of injuries sustained when he was a fetus; thus he was not a 'person dying in consequence of personal injuries sustained by him.' Although Scottish law has long adopted the fiction of the civil law that in all matters affecting its interests, the unborn child *in utero* should be deemed to be already born (Elliot, 1935), the defenders submitted that while the child might have invoked the fiction so as to have himself deemed to be already born at times prior to his birth, that fiction could not be invoked in the interests of third parties such as the pursuer (his parents). Lord Prosser thus held that the words used in section 1 of the Damages (Scotland) Act 1976 did not cover the situation where injury was sustained by a fetus rather than a person.

Lord Prosser's judgment is under appeal, and has recently been rejected by Lord Morton (McWilliams, 1992) who held on similar facts that injury sustained in the womb could give rise to a relevant claim. This position has now been supported by recent Court of Appeal authority in England in the following.

(v) *Burton v. Islington Health Authority* and *de Martell v. Merton and Sutton HA* (Burton, 1992). Both cases involved damage done to a fetus in the womb prior to 1976 when parliament passed the Congenital Disabilities (Civil Liability) Act; both cases involved a claim against hospital authorities for negligence in the performance of an operation (in the first case a D&C and in the latter while the plaintiff's mother was in labour). At first instance in de Martell, Mr Justice Phillips observed that:

> The human being does not exist as a legal person until after birth. The fetus enjoys no independent legal personality. . . . An unborn child lacks the status to be the subject of a legal duty. If injury is done to an unborn child, no duty is broken. If injury is negligently caused to a newly-born babe, liability in negligence arises. . . . In law and logic no damage can have been caused to the plaintiff before the plaintiff existed. The damage was suffered by the plaintiff at the moment that, in law, the plaintiff achieved personality and inherited the damaged body for which the defendants (on the assumed facts) were responsible. The events prior to the birth were mere links in the chain of causation between the defendant's assumed lack of: 'skill and care and the consequential damage to the plaintiff. . . . The lack of legal status of the unborn child poses a peculiar problem in the law of negligence.' (de Martell, 1992)

On appeal, in a case joined with *Burton v. Islington Health Authority* [1992], Lord Justice Dillon said that the civil law maxim that an unborn child shall be deemed to be born whenever its interests require it could have been applied directly to these two cases, such that the two plaintiffs were treated as lives in being at the times of the events which injured them as they were later born alive.' (Burton, 1992 at 839) However, Dillon LJ held that it was not necessary to do this. Citing and approving the main Commonwealth authority of *Watt v. Rama* (Watt, 1972) and the reasoning of Winneke CJ and Pape J., Lord Justice Dillon held that on birth:

> . . . the relationship crystalised and out of it arose a duty on the defendant in relation to the child. . . . as the child could not in the very nature of things acquire rights correlative to a duty until it became by birth a living person, and as it was not until then that it could sustain injuries as a living person, it was, we think, at that stage that the duty arising out of the relationship was attached to the defendant . . . (*Watt v. Rama* [1972])

The injury whilst **en ventre sa mere** was but an evidentary incident in the causation of damage suffered at birth by the fault of the defendant. (Burton, 1992, per Dillon LJ at p. 841 citing Gillard J. (Watt, 1972 at pp. 374–5).

What the court was not prepared to do in this case was to go as far as some American states and hold that this theory of contingent rights can apply to the case of a child who is stillborn. 'The effect of the post-1945 decisions is that the courts of every American state have now held, as a development of the common law and despite previous decisions to the contrary, that a child can recover damages for a pre-natal injury, and even that damages can be recovered by the estate of a stillborn child. It is wholly unnecessary to go that far in the present case . . .' (Burton, 1992 at pp. 839–40).

One final point is worthy of note in the context of the development of theories of fetal rights or legal interests. One objection which had been put in argument by Counsel for the defendant health authorities, if the fetus on live birth acquired standing to sue for injuries negligently inflicted while in the womb, was the danger to which this could give rise of potential conflict between mother and child. Without here commenting at length on the desirability or otherwise of this – I think in fact it is highly undesirable – Dillon LJ observed in response that if this opened the way to a flood of claims Parliament could intervene, although he doubted whether there would be many cases now outstanding which are not statute-barred, in respect of children stillborn before 22 July 1976 (when the Congenital Disabilities (Civil Liability) Act 1976 came into force) or any children born before that date, 'who are locked in litigation with their mothers over whether the mother tasted alcohol or followed a diet other than that recommended by the current phase of medical opinion during pregnancy' (Burton, 1992 at pp. 843–44).

THE HUMAN FERTILISATION AND EMBRYOLOGY ACT 1990

Finally, I can turn to look at the statutory provisions of the Human Fertilisation and Embryology Act 1990. Although the embryo is nowhere given a status as either a chattel or as a person, the Act introduces through the licensing scheme, to be overseen by the Human Fertilisation and Embryology Authority, the most comprehensive statements as to how embryos are to be treated. Recall that Warnock had observed that:

Until now the law has never had to consider the existence of embryos outside the mother's uterus. The existence of such embryos raises potentially difficult problems as to ownership. The concept of ownership of human embryos seems to us to be undesirable. We recommend that legislation be enacted to ensure that there is no right of ownership in a human embryo. (DHSS 1984, para. 10.11)

The ensuing legislation does not take such an opportunity, although in debates on the Human Fertilisation and Embryology Bill, Lord Kennet moved Amendment 9A in the House of Lords Committee consideration of the Bill. That amendment provided that 'For the avoidance of doubt it is hereby declared that an embryo shall have the legal status of a person.' The opening words of the amendment are salutary; they do not suggest that we have forgotten that the embryo is a person, they remind us that the legal status of an embryo (and the amendment did not differentiate between extra-corporeal embryos and those *in vivo*) is a doubtful and difficult concept with which lawyers and others have to struggle.

The ensuing debate brought this intervention from the former Lord Chancellor, Lord Hailsham:

> An embryo is not a chattel, and to destroy it if it were would be a trespass to someone else's property. A human entity which is living is not a chattel and neither is it a person in any ordinary sense. Most extraordinary results would follow if it were. . . . It would be able to bring an action for personal injury if it were damaged. I suppose the loss of expectation of life might be among the general effects for which general damages could be awarded. . . . It is wrong to try to define a human embryo in terms of establishing legal definitions which are plainly inapplicable to human embryos. Why must an embryo be one or the other? Why cannot it be just an embryo? (Hailsham, 1990)

It may be that developments in the future will render the question of excess embryos irrelevant, in that technologies or practices will advance to such an extent that superovulation will be unnecessary or that cryopreservation of ova will achieve all that the production of surplus embryos now achieves in terms of treatment without the on-cost of questions about embryo research.

General Prohibitions

Section 3 defines activities which are beyond the power of the HFEA to licence. The Authority may not authorise the use or retention of a live human embryo after the appearance of the 'primitive streak' (s. 3(3)(a)). Unless the embryo is stored by way of freezing this is taken to be 'not later than the end of the period of fourteen days beginning with the day when the gametes are mixed' (s. 3(4)). This much criticised pragmatic solution was adopted by the Warnock Committee as the point when human life begins to matter morally (DHSS, 1984, para. 11.2–9).

Similarly, the Authority may not authorise the placing of a human embryo in any animal, keeping or use of an embryo where regulations prohibit this or nucleus substitution, (sometimes referred to as cloning). This is where the nucleus of the cell of an embryo (which contains the hereditary genetic material) is removed and replaced with the nucleus taken from a cell of another person, embryo or later developed embryo (s. 3(3)(b), (c) and (d)). This latter technique has been claimed to hold important prospects for work with genetically inherited disease and the production of immunologically identical organs for transplantation purposes. But, it raises the spectre of the production of genetically identical humans, clones, or humans with specific characteristics. The Authority will not presently be able to licence such work. Section 3(3)(b) prohibits 'placing an embryo in any animal'.

Schedule 2 'treatment licences' may authorise a variety of practices designed 'to secure that embryos are in a suitable condition to be placed in a woman or to determine whether embryos are suitable for that purpose' (para. 1(1)(d), which may in practice look uncommonly like research.

Section 4 provides more contentious reading. Sections 4(1)(a) and (c) provide for offences in respect of storing gametes (ova or sperm) and cross species fertilisation using live human gametes without an HFEA licence.

Human Embryo Research

To June 1990 the ILA had approved 38 IVF centres in the UK of which 17 are engaged in licensed *in vitro* fertilisation research. This work involves the use of either 'surplus' fertilised eggs following a woman's superovulation as part of her fertility treatment or unfertilised eggs donated and subsequently fertilised *in vitro*.

And again, to June 1990 the ILA had licensed 66 research projects; 13 new projects in 1989–90 having started with 22 in 1985–86. The HFEA first Annual Report discloses that of 109 Treatment and Research Centres operating under the transitional arrangements, 68 provide licensed IVF treatment, 98 donor insemination, and 17 centres are responsible for 34 approved projects of research; only 2 centres are research-only facilities (HFEA Annual Report 1992 Annex 1).

Originally, there was nothing in the Bill which would have prevented unlicensed 'research' up to the point of syngamy. Section 1 was amended to deal with this point; it adopts a scientific understanding as its definition of an embryo; in s. 1(1) it provides that references to an embryo are to a live human embryo 'where fertilisation is complete' but that references to an embryo 'include an egg in the process of fertilisation' (ss. 1(1)(a) and (b). Fertilisation is not complete 'until the appearance of a two-cell zygote' (s. 1(a)(b)).

A licence authorising specific research under the 1990 Act may be granted by the HFEA for a maximum period of three years (Sch. 2

para. 3(8)). Any research licence may be made subject to conditions imposed by HFEA and specified in the licence (Sch. 2 para 3(6)).

Each research protocol must be shown to relate, broadly, to one of the existing categories of research aim (Sch. 2 para. 3(2)), and then again only if the Authority is satisfied that the research is 'necessary for the purposes of the research' (Sch. 2 para. 3(5)). These aims are:

– promoting advances in the treatment of infertility (para. 3(2)(a))
– increasing knowledge about the causes of congenital disease (para. 3(2)(b); an amendment seeking to limit this to life-threatening or severely disabling conditions was withdrawn)
– increasing knowledge about the causes of miscarriage (para. 3(2)(c))
– developing more effective techniques of contraception (para. 3(2)(d); an amendment condemning this as 'frivolous' was defeated
– developing methods for detecting the presence of gene or chromosome abnormalities in embryos before implantation (para. 3(2)(e))
– more generally for the purpose of increasing knowledge about the creation and development of embryos and enabling such knowledge to be applied (para. 3(2)).

The Consent Requirements of the Act: Schedule 3

The consent requirements which are elaborated in Schedule 3, play an important part in the determination of some substantive points of principle and practice which arise. Failure to observe the provisions of Schedule 3 by proceeding (for example) without an effective consent, is one ground for revocation of the licence under s. 17(1)(c).

The consents provisions of schedule 3 are not just limited to the formal process of protecting the providers of treatment services. All consents must be in writing, and before consents to use or storage of gametes or embryos are given, a person must be given a 'suitable' opportunity to receive 'proper' counselling about the implications of such a step and 'such relevant information as is proper.' Paragraph 4(1) provides that the terms of any consent in the third schedule may be varied or withdrawn at any time, unless the embryo has already been used in providing treatment services or for research purposes. Consents for the use of any embryo must specify to what use(s) it may be put and specify any associated conditions to that consent (Sch. 3 para. 2(1)). An example might be whether gametes or embryo may be used only for the consent giver, or for any other people requiring treatment services or for the purposes of research.

In respect of gamete or embryo storage the maximum period of storage must be specified in the consent. In addition, and importantly, the consent must address the question of what is to happen to stored gametes or embryos if the consent-giver dies or becomes incapacitated and is therefore unable to revoke or vary their consent. The Act does not provide for what should happen, it requires only that the consent-giver(s) address the issue. This provision is inserted to obviate difficulties exemplified by requests for use of the embryos or gametes after the death of one consent-giver (the Parpalaix case) and also in the 'Rios embryos' case. In the Rios case, the Rios were Californian citizens and parents of frozen embryos held in store in Melbourne when they were killed in a plane crash. They died intestate and the Californian intestate succession laws appeared to apply, giving a share of the estate to Mr Rios's son by a previous marriage and to Mrs Rios's mother. In December 1987, the Californian Superior Court declared Mrs Rios's mother to be the sole heir. The Medical Center in Melbourne then declared that the embryos would be thawed and allowed to perish. This led to an outcry, culminating in the intervention of the State Minister of Health, who had to make special provision for them. In the event, the embryos were to be held in storage until a suitable recipient could be found, although the chances of survival were put at less than 5 per cent.

It seems desirable that the powers granted to the Authority under para. 3(3) of Schedule 3, to provide for other matters which must be dealt with in the consents, include that specific questions should be answered. For example, in the event of death, does the surviving partner have the right of access to the gametes or embryos? While s. 27(4)(b) provides that a man whose sperm, or an embryo derived in part from his sperm, is used after his death is not to be treated as the father of any resulting child, this is not directly relevant to the point here. Similarly, should the gametes or embryos be allowed to perish, or may they be used by the Authority?

An important point of difference arises in respect of consent when dealing with embryos created *in vitro* and those obtained from a woman following lavage (recovering the embryo by flushing the uterus) or laparoscopy (a micro surgical technique which permits the recovery of the embryo instrumentally). The continued storage of embryos will depend on how the embryos were 'brought into being'. With an embryo created *in vitro* following gamete donation, the embryo may not be kept in storage without the effective consent (written consent which has not been withdrawn) of both gamete donors (Sch. 3 para. 8(2)). Withdrawal of the consent of either donor to the embryo's creation appears to mean that it must be allowed to perish.

Where the embryo has come into being in the uterus and is subsequently extracted, not only may it not be used for any purpose unless the woman alone gives consent for that use (para. 7(1)), it may not be stored unless there is an effective consent by her, and her alone (para. 8(3)). This appears to be the Government's chosen way of avoiding the litigation spawned over cryopreserved embryos in the divorce proceedings of *Davis v. Davis.*

The lessons from mistakes made in that case have clearly been learnt. For example, there was no discussion between the Davises and the Center about the consequences of separation or divorce occurring while the ova remained frozen, nor were the Davises required to sign any agreement about the terms of storage or disposition at the time the fertilised ova were cryopreserved. The 1990 Act attempts to address these questions. In the first case, where the the embryo is brought about outside the body, the woman's partner can, by withdrawing his consent, effectively require that the embryo perish. In the second case of an embryo recovered by lavage, he cannot. In both cases the woman can achieve this result.

Posthumous Treatments

The effect of reading together clauses 14(1)(b) and 4(1)(b) is that where a clinic decides, or the treatment services contract or agreement provides, that the death of one of the partners is to terminate the provision of treatment services, the other partner will have no right to insist on the clinic making available to them any stored gametes or embryos. If the clinic decides that it will, for example, honour the wishes which the now deceased partner was required to express as to use of stored gametes or embryos following their death (Sch. 3 para. 2(b)(b), written consent '. . . must . . . state what is to be done with the gametes or embryo if the person who gave the consent dies . . .') that appears to be a matter for the exercise of clinical judgement and discretion. Otherwise, an embryo created *in vitro* may only lawfully be kept 'in storage' with effective consent of both partners, whereas an embryo which was formed within the woman's body and subsequently recovered surgically, (by lavage or laprascopy), may only be stored with the consent of the woman from whom it was obtained (Sch. 3 para. 8(2) and (3) respectively).

CIVIL LIABILITY: CONGENITAL DISABILITY

The Congenital Disability (Civil Liability) Act 1976, which replaced any previous common law, provides for civil liability in the case of children born disabled in consequence of the intentional act, negligence, or breach of statutory duty of some person prior to the birth of the child. The Act covers liability for children born alive; 'born' here meaning reaching the point at which the child has life separate from its mother and surviving for 48 hours

(s. 4(2) 1976 Act, and see Rance 1991). The defendant is answerable to the child if that defendant was liable, in tort, to one or both of the parents in respect of the matters which gave rise to the disability at birth. Such matters could arise either before conception, or during the pregnancy of the mother or the process of childbirth. In relation to matters arising before conception, this would clearly cover an injury to the parent which, at the time of conception, was transmitted to the child. Note that under the 1976 Act, liability on the part of the mother to her own child is excluded, but the liability of the father is not. Such preconception or preimplantation liability is now additionally provided for in HFEA section 44.

The 1990 Act, by s. 44(1) introduces a new s. 1A to the 1976 Act specifically to provide for actions which might arise in the course of providing assisted conception. It follows the scheme of the 1976 Act, and introduces for children born as a result of assisted conception the same sort of regime in respect of statutory conditions for liability as that Act did for natural conception. It applies to any case where:

(i)   a child has been born disabled following the placing in a woman of an embryo, or sperm and eggs, or following her artificial insemination;

(ii) the disability results from an act or omission in the course of the selection of the embryo or the gametes used to bring about the embryo or;

(iii) the disability results from some act or omission in the keeping or use of the embryo or gametes outside the body;

(iv) the defendant is (or would if sued in time have been) liable for negligence or breach of statutory duty to one or both of the parents, irrespective of whether they suffered actionable injury as long as there was a breach of duty which if injury had occurred would have given rise to liability.

This section clearly covers damage caused by the keeping or storage of the embryos or gametes, whether they have been frozen or not. It also applies to the procedure of selection of the embryos for implantation, although so little is known about this process that it is more of a morphological check than a scientific screening procedure. There are on the face of it some difficulties. For example it is not clear that it applies to an act or omission which causes damage to an embryo being recovered from a woman by lavage for subsequent implantation in another woman who gestates the child subsequently born injured. It is arguable that the recovery of the embryo could be regarded as a 'selection', but it is probable that that wording would be more strictly confined to the selection of one rather than another embryo for transfer to the woman's uterus.

The 1976 Act provides a number of defences to an action. A significant one is that if the parents, or either of them, knew the risk of the child being born disabled and accepted that risk, then the creator of the occurrence carrying that risk is excused liability. Clearly, this applies only to matters which precede conception (s. 1(4)). This defence is not available to the father acting as defendant, where he but not the mother had no knowledge of the risk. For present purposes, however, s. 1(5) also provides a significant defence. Section 1(5) states that:

> The defendant is not answerable to the child, for anything he did or omitted to do when responsible in a professional capacity for treating or advising the parent, if he took reasonable care having due regard to then received professional opinion applicable to the particular class of case; but this does not mean that he is answerable only because he departed from received opinion.

Section 44(1)(1A(3)) provides a defence to an action by a child where at the time of the treatment either or both of the parents knew the risk created by the particular act or omission of their child being born disabled. The other defences available under the 1976 act are also available in this extended action (s. 44(1)(1A(4)).

Section 44(1)(1A(3)) provides the same defence in respect of parental knowledge as in the 1976 Act. Thus, where at the time the embryo, or sperm and eggs were placed in the woman, or at the time she was inseminated, either or both of the parents knew the particular risk created by the act or omission of their child being born disabled, then the defendant (a 'person answerable to the child') under s. 44(1)(1A)(2)) is not answerable to the child. It will be interesting to monitor the way in which infertility clinics attempt to discharge their liability under this section. It has been suggested by some clinicians that a blanket warning as to risks of handicap as a result of infertility treatment would be sufficient to exculpate from liability. It will probably develop as practice to include some provision in the consents form which the woman or the couple will sign at the outset of the treatment.

Where a surrogacy arrangement within the provisions of s. 30 (parental orders section) has taken place and the genetic parent(s) apply for an order, the provisions of the Congenital Disabilities section will still apply for the benefit of the child.

It is clear that, in a number of instances, for the purpose of instituting proceedings under section 1 of the 1976 Act, it would be necessary to identify the genetic father or mother of the child. Suppose, for example, a complete failure of genetic screening at a treatment centre resulted in the birth of a child disabled within the meaning of the 1976 Act. If a mother were then to make a claim that the failure of genetic screening at the centre 'affected . . . her ability to have a normal, healthy child' since she was introduced to a donor whose sperm was always likely to give rise to a disabled child, it might be necessary for evidential purposes to trace that donor. Similarly the donor himself might be liable where, knowing that he was HIV positive, he none the less allowed his sperm to be used for infertility treatment. As the act places liability upon 'a person (other than the child's own mother)', it is clear that there is nothing in the 1976 act itself which would exempt the donor, even if considered as father, from liability. Again, however, the problem would be identifying the donor. Finally, the state of the father's knowledge may be relevant to the s. 1(4) defence considered above. But who is the 'father' for these purposes?

A new section 4(4) of the Congenital Disabilities Act is included to allow that where as the result of assisted conception a child carried by a woman is born disabled, then references within the 1976 Act to a 'parent' will include a reference to a person who would be a parent but for ss. 27–29 of the 1990 Act. Also, in an attempt to resolve some of the difficulties of identifying parents, s. 35(1) states that where for the purposes of initiating proceedings under the 1976 Act, it is necessary to identify a person who would or might be the parent of a child (cf. the wording in s. 30(4)) but for sections 27–29 of this Act, then the court may on the application of the child, make an order requiring HFEA to disclose registered information under s. 30 of the Act such that the person could be identified. Most importantly, this will include sections such as 27(1) and 28(6) which provide that donors who from other than the couple receiving treatment are not to be treated ordinarily as either the mother or the father of the child in question. Note that this is only available on a court order which requires the Authority to disclose such information.

References

Brazier, M. (1988) 'Embryos' "Rights": Abortion and Research', in M. Freeman (ed.), *Medicine, Ethics and the Law* (London: Stevens) pp. 9–22.
Burton v. Islington Health Authority [1992] 3 All ER 833.
C v. S [1988] 1 QB 135.
Codes, of Sumerian 2000 BC, Assyrian 1500 BC, Hittite 1300 BC and Persian 600 BC.
Council of Europe (1989) *Human Artificial Procreation*, Strasbourg, The Council, 1989, p. 11.
Davis v. Davis [1989] 15 FLR 2097 (on appeal [1990] WL 130807 (Tenn CA)).

de Martell v. Merton and Sutton HA [1992] 3 All ER 820 and, on appeal [1992] 3 All ER 833.

DHSS (1984) *Report of the Committee of Inquiry into Human Fertilisation and Embryology.* Cm 9314 (London: HMSO).

Elliot v. Joicey 1935 SC (HL) 57.

Glover, J. (1989) *Fertility and the Family: The Glover Report on Reproductive Technologies to the European Commission* (London: Fourth Estate) p. 94.

Grubb, A. (1991) 'The legal status of the frozen human embryo', in A. Grubb (ed.), *Challenges in Medical Care* (Chichester: John Wiley) pp. 69–90.

Hailsham, Lord (1990) House of Lords, *Hansard* vol. 515 col. 750–1.

Hamilton v. Fife Health Board (1992) The Times January 28, 1992 (Outer House of the Court of Session) now under appeal.

Holmes, O. W. (1881) *The Common Law* (Cambridge, Mass.: Harvard University Press) p. 1.

Kennedy, I. and A. Grubb (1989) *Medical Law: Text and Materials* (London: Butterworths) p. 682.

Keown, J. (1989) 'Creative Criminals', paper presented at 'Assisted Conception and the Law: A Medical/Legal Forum' Royal Society of Medicine, London.

Louisiana (1986) Louisiana Revised Statutes 9, ss. 121–33.

LRCC (1992) Law Reform Commission of Canada, Medically Assisted Procreation, Working Paper no. 64, pp. 139–40.

McWilliams v. Ministry of Defence (1992) Lord Morton, Court of Session.

Missouri (1986) Missouri Revised Statutes ss. 1.205(1).

Morgan, D. M. and R. G. Lee (1990) *Blackstone's Guide to the Human Fertilisation and Embryology Act 1990* (London: Blackstones) pp. 63–88.

Morgan, D. M. and L. Nielsen (1992) 'Dangerous Liaisons: Law, technology and European ethics – an Anglo-Danish comparison', in S. McVeigh and S. Wheeler (eds), *Medicine, Law and Regulation* (London: Dartmouth Press) pp. 64–87.

Parpalaix v. CECOS, Trib. gr. inst. Creteil, 1 August 1984, Gaz. Pal., 1984.II.560.

Paton v. Trustees of the BPAS [1979] 1 QB 276.

Rance v. Mid Downs Health Authority [1991] 1 All ER 801.

Rawlinson, Lord (1990) House of Lords, *Hansard*, 8 February 1990, col. 953.

Re F (in utero) [1988] 2 All ER 193.

Rios [1985] 'The Rios' Embryo case'. See G. F. Smith (1985–6) 'Australia's frozen 'orphan' embryos: a medical, legal and ethical dilemma', *Journal of Family Law*, vol. 24, pp. 27–45.

The George and the Richard [1871] LR 3 A & E 466.

Watt v. Rama [1972] VR 353, pp. 360–1.

Webster v. Reproductive Health Services [1989] 492 US 490.

Wells, C. K. and D. M. Morgan (1991) 'Whose fetus is it?', *Journal of Law and Society*, vol. 18, pp. 431–47.

York v. Jones [1989] 717 F Supp 42.

12 Fetal Medicine: Legal and Ethical Implications

Alexander McCall Smith

The whole point of having genies in bottles, is that one lets them out. The genie may be released by mistake – as where one doesn't know that the bottle contains a genie at all – or it may be let out after full discussion as to the ethical implications of release. To a great extent, advances in human reproduction fall into the latter category. For decades now, there have been warnings about the implications of our new knowledge of human reproduction and our ability to manipulate it. Yet, the voicings of these concerns have made comparatively little difference in the extent to which science has been free to pursue its goals, given the transnational nature of modern scientific research. And this leads one to the conclusion that genies out of bottles are indeed very difficult to put back in (as conventional wisdom warns us), and, in such circumstances, all that remains to be done is to attempt to limit the damage.

While advances in other areas (such as embryo research) have given rise to problems of the most profound nature, touching upon the very nature of human life, the problems to which advances in fetal medicine give rise are, to a great extent, problems of right. Not only is there the question of the status of the fetus, which is often couched in terms of fetal rights, but there is also the issue of the rights of parents. Do developments in fetal medicine threaten in any significant way the rights of the mother? If fetal medicine in the future is to offer considerably improved diagnostic and therapeutic options, then will these compromise the autonomy of the mother?

It is a fundamental principle of our legal system – and indeed of most legal systems – that the human body is protected against any intervention which is not wanted, or non-consensual. In the medical context, the ramifications of this principle have been spelled out in numerous decisions in which the courts have stressed that medical intervention without the consent of the patient is an actionable wrong (Brazier, 1992; Giesen, 1988; McLean, 1989). This is so even in fairly extreme circumstances, as in the Canadian case of *Malette v. Shulman* (1988) where a Jehovah's Witness succeeded in her claim for damages against a doctor who had given her a blood transfusion in the clear knowledge that she objected to this particular form of treatment. A therapeutic goal, then, is not enough to justify non-consensual treatment, and paternalistic motives on the part of a doctor will not justify proceeding against the will of a patient. It may be, of course, as was the case in the recent blood transfusion litigation in this country (*T* case, 1992) that the court will hold that the patient's views could not be adequately determined (given unconsciousness or confusion) and that compulsory treatment will therefore be legitimate, but this does not detract from the court's general endorsement of the principle of bodily autonomy.

This firm legal principle would seem to exclude the legitimacy of any treatment of a pregnant woman without her full consent, and indeed this is the current state of the law in the United Kingdom. And yet such a conclusion rests on an assumption that it is only one set of interests which is at stake here – the woman's interest in the preservation of her autonomy – and there are those who would not let this assumption go unchallenged. In the light of advances in fetal medicine, more prominence is given to the view that the pregnant woman is not one patient, but two, and that the mother has no right to engage in conduct which threatens an interest of the fetus. Any veto of treatment by the mother infringes, in this view, a legally-recognisable interest of the fetus.

There are two categories of case here. First, there is the case where a mother's self-harming conduct has the effect of harming the fetus. Secondly, there is the case where the mother refuses to allow a procedure on the fetus she is carrying. In the latter case, the mother, in one view at least, is not the patient, it is the fetus.

An example of the first sort of case would be where the mother engages in a course of risky conduct. The mother, for example, drinks heavily during pregnancy, or abuses drugs, or possibly even engages in sexual conduct which threatens to expose the fetus to infection. Or, at a possibly more innocuous level, the mother merely adopts a peripatetic lifestyle, sleeping rough, not eating properly, and avoiding medical attention. In these cases, should the law be able to prevent the mother from engaging in the harmful conduct in question?

From the ethical standpoint, the mother does indeed have a duty to act in such a way as to prevent harm to the fetus. This duty is merely part of the duty which all of us have not to harm others, a duty which is fundamental to any system of moral rules. It is a duty which is usually postulated in relation to positive acts and does not necessarily render omissions culpable, but where those who are harmed by our omissions stand in a relationship of close proximity to us, then even failures to act may be morally culpable.

Yet any duty of the mother not to harm her fetus is a qualified one. It is clear that she has an absolute obligation not to engage in harmful conduct where that conduct is directed solely towards the harming of the fetus: but fetal harm usually results from the mother's choice of conduct which has some evident utility to her. For example, if the fetus is exposed to unacceptably high levels of alcohol, this is likely to be because the mother gets pleasure from drinking; similarly, if the fetus is damaged by the mother's smoking, or is exposed to the effects of other drugs of abuse, this happens because the mother is doing something that gives her gratification. If the mother is to be stopped from doing this, this means that her freedom to engage in the harmful behaviour is deemed to be secondary to the fetal interest in not being harmed by this behaviour. In this view, the interest of the fetus in a healthy future is a more substantial interest than the interest of the mother in pursuing pleasure. There may be cases, of course, where the interest of the mother is preferred. In a straightforward conflict between the health of the fetus and the health of the mother, the mother's interest may be deemed to be weightier, on the grounds that the mother stands to lose more, or even on simple utilitarian grounds that any deterioration in the mother's health would cause more pain and suffering to interest-bearing persons than any comparable deterioration in the health of the fetus.

This comparative ranking of interests, which places fetal interests generally higher than any non-health related interest of the mother, may not be universally acceptable. The argument may be made out that the interest of the mother in freedom of action is the stronger interest – on the grounds that the interests of the community of persons are more worthy of recognition than the interests of the unborn or of future persons. There is also a sheer intelligibility argument to be considered. The interests of the mother, it may be argued, are more capable of being ascertained (and therefore more worthy of recognition) than the interest of a fetus who is not in a position to express any preferences.

Another tactic altogether is to deny that fetal interests exist at all. In this view, the fetus is incapable of having interests, because it lacks awareness of the interest. Such a view holds that the fetus is nothing but part of the body of the women, totally subservient to the interests of the mother. Not surprisingly, this assessment of the fetus appeals to those who argue for a woman's untrammelled right to abortion; in the words of one exponent of this position, ridding oneself of a fetus is no more significant than having a haircut.

Whatever moral stance is preferred, the current legal position, in English law at least, is that as long as she does not attempt to end the pregnancy through unapproved abortion, the mother is perfectly entitled to act in a way which compromises the fetus if that is her desire. There have been moves to test this. In the case of *Re F (in utero)* (1988), an attempt was made to make a fetus a ward of court, in order to enable social work authorities to control maternal behaviour which, in their view, threatened the well-being of the fetus (Sutherland, 1990). The court rejected this, taking the view that the maternal interest in freedom was stronger than any interest the authorities may have had in securing a safer fetal environment. By contrast, in a number of American decisions, there have been successful attempts at restricting the freedom of the pregnant woman in favour of the fetus. These decisions repay examination, because they demonstrate the extent to which a public health ethic may become something of a moral crusade and may result in a diminution of the protection otherwise afforded individual autonomy. They also raise very substantial issues of women's rights, and assume therefore a political dimension of some significance.

The issue is most starkly demonstrated in those cases where the pregnant woman herself is in need of treatment which, if not administered, will result in damage to the fetus or even its loss. In a case decided in 1964, *Raleigh-Fitkin Paul Memorial Hospital v. Anderson*, the court authorised a compulsory blood transfusion to be administered to a woman in the eighth month of her pregnancy who had refused blood on religious grounds. Even greater interventions have been approved, most remarkably in those cases where courts have allowed compulsory caesarian sections in attempts to ensure the safe delivery of the baby. Maternal opposition to caesarian section has been overriden in a number of cases on the grounds that the balancing of maternal and fetal interests here leads to the conclusion that the fetal interest in safe delivery outweighs the mother's claims to autonomy. Sometimes these cases are extremely harrowing: in the case of *Re A. C.* a terminally ill woman, in her twenty-sixth week of pregnancy, was subjected to a court-ordered caesarian section. She had not indicated prior disapproval of a caesarian, but was none the less not in a position to authorise it. What the court had to do then, was to consider whether it was permissible to authorise an operation which would have the effect of shortening the woman's life in order to save the child she was carrying. The decision was taken in favour of the child, and indeed this is a decision which many might support. The case demonstrates, though, an extreme in the process of balancing of interests which may occur in such cases. There will be few cases where the choice is so starkly one between the life of the mother or the life of the child.

These American decisions have been strongly criticised. A very high proportion of the cases – over 80 per cent in one survey (Kolder *et al.*, 1987) – involved women from disadvantaged sections of the community – poor women, inarticulate women, vulnerable women – who were clearly not in a position to fight the procedures in the same way as a better educated, more solvent person might be in a position to do. The hearings tended to be conducted speedily, sometimes without the woman being represented, and in such circumstances it was obviously much easier for the medical side to put a convincing case. Another criticism turns on the allocation of resources involved and on the questionable sense of priorities which this sort of action demonstrates. It has been pointed out, for example, that a great deal of energy has been devoted to establishing the right of the State to intervene against the mother in favour of the fetus even when there is comparatively little political commitment to ensuring the provision of maternity services to the many who are unable to pay for them (Purdy, 1990).

The American experience is different from ours in very important respects. First, there is a crucial difference in what one might term the medico-political cultures of the two countries. Many American child neglect and infant non-treatment cases take place against a backdrop of concern over abortion and are attempts to make a pro-life point. This may give rise to vigorous attempts to protect the fetus in such areas, as this can be done in jurisprudence where the law of abortion is, in the earlier stages of pregnancy, relatively liberal. Then there is a difference in the way in which issues are resolved. In this country, there is possibly a higher degree of moral consensus than in the highly pluralistic culture of the United States. Issues here are frequently resolved through persuasion and compromise (or inaction in some cases) rather than through litigation: the rapid reference of any tricky issue to legal resolution is not a feature of British society.

As already alluded to, the only British court to consider the question of wardship of the fetus decided against it in favour of maternal liberty. Similarly, in the case of *Paton v. British Pregnancy Advisory Service Trustees* (1978) the court held that a father of a fetus had no right to prevent a woman from having an abortion, a decision which was upheld on appeal to the European Court of Human Rights (1980). The same view was expressed in the later case of *C. v. S.* (1987) and has been followed, although sometimes on different grounds, in New Zealand and Australia. In the United States, the father's interest in abortion issues has been recognised by some courts, but has been held to be outweighed by the mother's right to make reproductive decisions (Mason and McCall Smith, 1991).

The fact that British courts have been unwilling to restrict the liberties of the pregnant woman indicates a generally non-interventionist stance, but would this necessarily apply in a case where what is required of the woman is not a substantial sacrifice (for example, submitting to a requirement that she live in an institution or report to a hospital regularly, or, indeed, that she allow her pregnancy to go to term) but where what is required is, say, a relatively safe medical procedure? No British court has addressed this issue yet, but the likely outcome would be that the woman's right of autonomy would outrank fetal interests and that compulsory treatment would not be authorised.

The arguments against such an attitude are compelling. The fetus may not enjoy full legal personality, but it is beyond contest that it has legal rights of some sort. Not only is it protected against prenatal injury in the civil sense, it is also protected by the criminal law against acts of violence (other than those authorised by the law on abortion). The fetus therefore has personality of some sort, with some but not all of the rights which are vested in the full member of the human community. It has the right to life, even if this right may in some cases be subjugated to a maternal right to decide on an abortion: it is a *prima facie* right to life none the less. It also has a right to a life of a certain quality, that is, it has a right to fulfil itself to the maximum extent which will be open to it in its particular human circumstances. To deprive a fetus of some potential which it would otherwise have is therefore a wrong to that fetus and, in due course, to the child it becomes. The fact that the wrong is committed some time before its effects will be felt in no sense detracts from the fact that it is a wrong. There may be good grounds, of course, for depriving an entity of an interest which it will have at some time in the future, and this is not to do it a wrong. For example, opting to have an abortion deprives that fetus of life in the future, but this may not be a wrong if the decision is reached on grounds considered to be adequate. What these grounds are, of course, is a matter of intense debate.

The right of a fetus to subsequent human fulfilment suggests that there is a right to healthy existence as opposed to an impaired one. We must be careful about a proliferation of alleged rights, but this right is surely a justifiable one in that it does no more than to claim that the position of the fetus should not be worsened in any appreciable way. This may involve a demand that others should take steps to prevent a worsening of its position, but, provided that this demand is not an unreasonable one, this should be acceptable. For example, is it unreasonable to expect a drug-abusing mother to refrain from drugs during pregnancy in order to prevent harm to the fetus she is carrying? Given the relative values of the alternatives, such an expectation does not seem unreasonable. The fact that an expectation is reasonable does not, however, necessarily resolve the issue. There are reasonable claims which may be unenforceable on the grounds that the coercion required in their enforcement is unjustified. And this leads to the real crux of the issue – the question as to whether the interference with the autonomy of the individual which is inevitably involved in compulsory treatment constitutes such an infringement of an important social value that it does greater harm than good. Compulsory treatment is generally an anathema to the medical profession in this country and is only undertaken in very limited circumstances, namely, where the patient is too young to decide for himself, or where rationality is affected by mental disorder. (Public health powers exist to allow the compulsory treatment of contagious diseases, but these are rarely invoked). In the case of mental disorders, the justification for compulsory treatment is paternalistic – the treatment can be seen as enhancing the autonomy of the patient rather than diminishing it. Compulsory treatment of a woman for the sake of a fetus could not be justified on paternalistic grounds, the motive in such a case being the good of the fetus rather than the eventual good of the woman. An analogy with the non-consensual treatment of mental disorder is therefore inappropriate.

On balance, it is preferable to protect the value of maternal autonomy even if in doing so the interests of a fetus are compromised. The reason for this is that the making of an exception in this case could seriously weaken the protection which the law affords human liberty. If the principle is admitted that rational persons can have treatment forced upon them, even for the admitted good of another, then the way is open to a range of interventions which could well prove unacceptable. Compulsory drug testing for employment purposes is one such example, which has ceased to be a fanciful notion in the United States (Draper, 1991).

There is another argument too, that of the implications for parental rights. The rights of parents in relation to their children have been steadily eroded over recent decades, and it could be argued that there is now very little left of paternal rights (McCall Smith, 1990). If the right of a pregnant woman to flout medical advice is to be denied, then a further erosion of parental discretion occurs. A woman's rejection of medical advice may be based on personal belief or religious conviction; it may be based, then, on firmer grounds than mere fecklessness. To deny the right to be misguided according to the medical criteria is to deny an important right of decision to the woman. It can be pointed out, of course, that this denial is already conceded in respect of children and their medical treatment. A child may be given a blood transfusion over the objections of a patient; what is the difference between this and imposing treatment on a woman in order to save a fetus from destruction? The difference probably lies in the question of intervention in autonomy. In each case, parental rights are overriden, but only in one of the cases is there an intervention in the integrity of the person for non-paternalistic motives. Where a child is given a blood transfusion against the wishes of the parent, there is no intervention in the parent's bodily integrity. It is significant that the courts will not hesitate to take protective measures once a child is born. In *Re P (a minor)* (1987) a place of safety order was granted on the day of the birth of a child into a family with a past history of sexual abuse.

Even if it is agreed that there is no justification for the use of coercion or compulsion to ensure compliance with medical objectives, there may still be strong pressures on a woman to submit to procedures which are directed towards the benefit of the fetus. These pressures may turn out to be coercive in all but name; the creation of a strong social expectation that a particular course of action be followed may be subtly coercive. For this reason, it may prove difficult for women to resist intrusive procedures if these are presented as being beneficial for the fetus. The withholding of consent may be portrayed as unreasonable conduct and if this is so, the reality of a woman's consent may be questionable. The principle of individual autonomy may therefore continue to be protected by the law but may be considerably undermined in practice.

Finally, a moment might be spent on another possible way in which the autonomy of the woman may be affected by the emergence of the fetus as both a legal entity and a patient. The possibility that a child may have legal claims against its mother in respect of her conduct during pregnancy strikes many as an appalling prospect, striking at the very nature of the maternal relationship. The Congenital Disabilities (Civil Liability) Act 1976 precludes such claims in English law, with the exception of driving negligence claims, and so the issue is currently academic in England. Yet blame may still be attributed for misconduct in pregnancy, or even for the conception of an unhealthy or handicapped child. This may be a concomitant of the development of ideas of the fetus with an identity which is distinct from that of the mother; in the chilling words of one commentator on this issue, the pregnant woman becomes little more than a 'fetal container', whose duty it is to consider the fetus as something 'entrusted' to her rather than as part of her. This depressingly mechanistic vision is alien to the human, one flesh, notion of motherhood which has traditionally informed moral thinking in this area. In assessing possible conflicts of rights, it is important that the law should bear in mind the broader consequences of any change in the existing notions of personal autonomy and its importance. The state, and the law, have no place in the most private realms of human behaviour, and the integrity of these areas of experience must be jealously guarded. This may sound like an argument for a right to behave wrongly – a bizarre notion at first blush – but one which, in some circumstances at least, requires to be defended.

References

Brazier, M. (1992) *Medicine, Patients and the Law* (London: Penguin) pp. 94–111.
C. v. S. [1987] 1 All ER 1230.

Draper, E. (1991) *Risky Business* (Cambridge: Cambridge University Press) p. 115.
Giesen, D. (1988) *International Medical Malpractice Law* (Tubingen: Mohr) p. 252.
Kolder, V. E., J. Gallagher and M. T. Parsons (1987) 'Court-ordered obstetrical interventions', *New England Journal of Medicine*, vol. 316, pp. 1192–6.
Malette v. Shulman [1988] 63 OR (2d) 243.
Mason J. K. and R. A. McCall Smith (1991) *Law and Medical Ethics* (London: Butterworths) p. 122.
McCall Smith, A. (1990) 'Is there anything left of parental rights?', in E. Sutherland and A. McCall Smith (eds), *Family Rights* (Edinburgh: Edinburgh University Press).
McLean, S. A. M. (1989) *The Patient's Right to Know* (Aldershot: Dartmouth).
Palton v. British Pregnancy Advisory Service Trustees [1978] 2 All ER 987 and (1980) 3 EHRR 408.
Purdy, L. M. (1990) 'Are pregnant women fetal containers?', *Bioethics*, vol. 4, pp. 273ff.
Raleigh-Fitkin Paul Memorial Hospital v. Anderson [1964] 201 A 2d 537 (NJ).
Re A. C. 539 A 2d 203 (DC).
Re F (in utero) [1988] 2 All ER 193.
Re P (a minor) [1987] 2 FLR 467 CA.
Sutherland, E. (1990) 'Regulating pregnancy: should we and can we?', in E. Sutherland and A. McCall Smith (eds), *Family Rights* (Edinburgh: Edinburgh University Press).
T case Court of Appeal (1992) unrepted.

Index